Golden

Poppies

Golden

Poppies

**California History and Contemporary Life
in Books and Other Media
for Young Readers**

AN ANNOTATED BIBLIOGRAPHY

Faye Brown Morrison and Kathryn Cusick

LIBRARY PROFESSIONAL PUBLICATIONS

1987

First published as a Library Professional Publication,
an imprint of The Shoe String Press, Inc.,
Hamden, Connecticut 06514

Printed in the United States of America

Library of Congress Cataloging-in-Publication Data

Morrison, Faye Brown.
  Golden poppies.

  Rev. ed. of: Golden poppies / Dorothy Pritchard
Wright. 1979.
  Includes indexes.
  1. California—History—Juvenile literature—
Bibliography. 2. California—History—Fiction—
Bibliography. 3. California—History—Juvenile fiction—
Bibliography. 4. California—History—Bibliography.
I. Cusick, Kathryn, 1929–   . II. Wright, Dorothy
Pritchard. Golden poppies. III. Title.
Z1261.M67   1987 [F861]   016.9794   86-19993
ISBN 0-208-02139-6

Contents

Preface

California has such a dramatic and interesting history! Even the name of our state came from a romantic novel—and certainly many of the actual happenings here have served as subjects for fascinating history and fiction. There's a wealth of such material for young readers as well as adults.

This completely revised edition of *Golden Poppies* contains fiction and nonfiction books, and a nonprint or nonbook media section as well. The nonbook media section includes filmstrips—with and without accompanying cassette tapes—coloring books, kits, study guides, plays, and more. What all the material has in common is that it deals with California history, political or natural—but the emphasis is on political. There is an author index, a book-title index, an index for nonbook media, and an integrated print/nonprint subject index with seventeen subheadings. If you are particularly interested in "Early Explorers," the index subheading so named will lead you to pertinent materials; if you need, instead, only "Gold Rush" books and media, use that index, and so on. To help you locate the material not available in your own schools and libraries, there is a partial listing of the book and media distributors and suppliers referred to in the annotations.

For the purpose of this book, we have made some arbitrary decisions which you should know about in order to make good use of the contents. We have listed as historical anything pertaining to the years through World War II. Materials dealing with 1945 and on are deemed contemporary. In general only books published since 1955 have been included, although sometimes an overriding value—literary or historical—would induce us to keep an older entry.

For reading level, we have noted *primary* (grades 1–3), *intermediate* (grades 4–6), *junior high* (grades 7–8), and *senior high* (grades 9–12). Of course, there is great leeway in any designation, but the noted levels can serve as a rough guide. The majority of entries are geared to the intermediate and junior-high reader; some are noted as suitable for all ages, or from a particular level to adult.

Out–of–print books are included when they seem reasonably easy to locate in libraries or schools. Every entry listed we have either previewed from current publishers' listings or found in our county schools or libraries. We did note the books as "OP"—out-of-print—when we were certain that they were.

In addition to our own comments on the book entries, we included, when such information was available, the opinion of the Association of Children's Librarians (ACL), a northern California group, who circulate their "nugget" and "fool's gold" reviews.

Our greatest debt of appreciation goes to the late Dorothy Pritchard Wright of San Jose State University who initiated this project and was senior author of the first edition of *Golden Poppies*. (Cupertino, Calif.: California History Center, De Anza College, 1979). She dreamed of bringing children's literature dealing with California history into more general usage in classrooms, libraries and homes. She and her students started reading and annotating appropriate books. And the project grew—and grew—and grew. Because of her vision, we had a nucleus to start with this time.

As we worked, we have grown to be ever more appreciative of the gracious helpfulness of librarians. What a wonderful group of people! We especially thank Katy Obringer and her staff at the Palo Alto Children's Library and Marian Eldridge, children's librarian at the Mountain View Library.

Faye Morrison and Kathryn Cusick

1
Historical Fiction and Nonfiction

Adler, Jack. **EXPLORING HISTORICAL CALIFORNIA.** Los Angeles: Ward Ritchie Press, 1974. 110 p. B/w photos.

Content: Profiles of personalities who have affected California history, among them Sam Brannan, Lola Montez, Agoston Haraszthy, Bret Harte, Joaquin Miller, Jedediah Smith, Captain Jack (of Modoc War), Leland Stanford, John Sutter, Luther Burbank, Mariano Vallejo, Thomas Larkin, and Nicolai Rezanov. Most of these people had their heyday in the nineteenth century and the beginning of the twentieth. Each profile contains little-known facts, many of them ignored in deifying biographies. At the close of each chapter are sightseeing leads to sites within California, such as museums, parks, and buildings relating to the profiled person. Most of the photos are from the California Historical Society.
Comment: This title has been used in high school history classes. The tone is informative and somewhat irreverent but not at the expense of accuracy. It is a combination history and travel book.
Nonfiction: senior high

ALL 21 CALIFORNIA MISSIONS. Hubert A. Lowman: Arroyo Grande, Calif.: n.d. 24 p. Color photos, map.

Content: All the missions are represented by at least one photo, some with several; the brief information on each mission varies in amount as well. Includes a list of missions with the founding dates and a sketched map showing locations.
Comment: This booklet would be useful mainly as an additional source of pictorial information on the missions. It is not known if it is still in print.
Nonfiction: intermediate–adult

3

Andrist, Ralph K., and Archibald Hanna, eds. **THE CALIFORNIA GOLD RUSH.** New York: American Heritage, 1961. 155 p. Illus. Maps and photos, bibliog., index.

Content: The chapters deal with Sutter, his building of Sutter's Fort, Sutter's and Marshall's sad fates as others grew rich, the routes goldseekers took to California, the types of mining, life in a mining camp, and the discovery of agriculture as the true source of wealth in California.

Comment: The book has many prints, paintings, drawings, maps, and photographs. The wide variety of visual aids makes it an easy-reading text. The reader becomes acquainted with characters such as "Dame Shirley" and Lotta Crabtree.

Nonfiction: junior high–adult

Atkins, Elizabeth Howard. **TREASURES OF THE MEDRANOS.** Eau Claire, Wis.: E. M. Hale, 1962. 112 p. Illus. by Peggie Bach, glossary.

Content: A story of a young girl and her beautiful doll—the only wax doll in California—who lived on a rancho near Santa Barbara Mission when California still belonged to Spain. A family wedding fiesta, a dashing bandit, and valuable Spanish heirloom treasures figure in a rather contrived story.

Comment: Although some realistic details of rancho life are given, including transportation, food, and the traditional love of fancy clothes and fiestas, the overall tone of the story creates the unrealistic impression that California was settled by high-born Spaniards continuing an aristocratic tradition in the New World. There are other stories that give a truer picture of California mission days.

Fiction: upper primary–lower intermediate

Ault, Philip H. **THIS IS THE DESERT.** New York: Dodd, Mead, 1959. 175 p. Drawings by Leonard Fisher.

Content: The drama of the American desert comes alive in this exciting book as the author weaves a story from the many intriguing aspects of a unique setting and describes its future potential. Few people realize that the United States does indeed have its own desert, not a Sahara with endless sand dunes, but, nonetheless, vast.

Comment: This is the author's first book for young people. He has a dramatic storytelling ability and great familiarity with the desert.

Nonfiction: intermediate–junior high

Ault, Philip H. **WIRES WEST.** New York: Dodd, Mead, 1974. 169 p. B/w photos, sketches, maps, bibliog., index.

Content: Fourteen lively chapters stress the importance of communications and transportation and describe the establishment of the telegraph, the railroad, and the telephone lines that linked the eastern United States and the rest of the country with the new state of California. The tremendous difficulties encountered and overcome are dramatized through tales of the Pony Express, train wrecks, and a train robbery. Information is provided about personalities seldom discussed in other accounts through such devices as excerpts from the diary of a man who is working on the building of the telegraph. The attempt to link America and Russia with a telegraph line in the 1860s is recounted. The maps are helpful additions.

Comment: Though there is much information here not directly tied to California, this book would be very useful and interesting to those studying California history. The vocabulary is rich in intriguing words to look up (harquebus—an early portable gun.)

Nonfiction: intermediate–junior high

Austin, Mary. **THE LAND OF LITTLE RAIN.** 1903. Reprint. Albuquerque: University of New Mexico Press, 1974. 171 p. Ink and wash drawings by E. Boyd Smith.

Content: Fourteen essays written by a poetic and imaginative naturalist during the time she was living in Independence, California, about the land of little rain, midway between the great range of the Sierra Nevada and Death Valley. Here are the coyotes, the buzzards, the burros, the roadrunners, and other creatures of the region, and also the prospectors, the Indian basket makers, the medicine men, and the people living in the frontier towns. Several different stories help us appreciate the sparse water resources, as well as the special human resources, which enable a few to live a satisfying life in this region.

Comment: This is a special book to be read by those who *really* appreciate nature and good descriptive writing.

Nonfiction: senior high–adult

Bailey, Bernardine. **PICTURE BOOK OF CALIFORNIA.** The United States Books Series. 1966. Reprint. Chicago: Whitman, 1968. 32 p. Color and b/w illus. by Kurt Wiese, map, index.

Content: Strictly a fact book containing a thumbnail history, descriptions of agriculture, industry, natural resources, scenic attractions, and very brief notations of several cities and their "claims to fame."

Comment: Information is presented in one continuous narrative in easily understood language. Although this book is quite out of date, it is one of the very few fact books written for younger or less able students, which explains why many libraries still keep the series.

Nonfiction: upper primary–intermediate

Baker, Laura Nelson. **GROUND AFIRE: THE STORY OF DEATH VALLEY NATIONAL MONUMENT.** New York: Atheneum, 1971. 166 p. Map, color photos.

Content: The first of fourteen chapters starts with the Smith-Bennett, Manly-Hunt wagon train party of 1849. It moves on to the breakup of the wagon train and disaster at Death Valley. The book goes on to tell of the Indians of Death Valley, the first white residents, surveying expeditions, and mining. There are chapters on Death Valley legends and characters, the first school and hotels, designation as a national monument, and Death Valley today.

Comment: Baker writes simply and directly about Death Valley, from the curiously named Bugmashers, an 1849 crossing party, to the publicized Scotty's Castle, and supplies detailed facts about the role of this hostile environment in California history.

Nonfiction: junior high

Baker, Laura Nelson. **A TREE CALLED MOSES.** New York: Atheneum, 1966. 69 p. Drawings by Penelope Naylor.

Content: This is a story about the *Sequoiadendron giganteum,* the big tree of northern California, of its great age and beauty and particularly of the Moses Tree, and of the white man who scoured many areas near the tree in his greedy search for valuable lumber logs.

Comment: This could have been written in a more entertaining style. The author's note says that the material included is mostly factual but that the "growth" of the tree is fictionalized. A list of pamphlets and books which tell about the Sequoias and the flowers, animals, insects, birds, and other trees that live in their environment is included.

Nonfiction: intermediate–junior high

Baker, Laura Nelson. **WILD PENINSULA: THE STORY OF POINT REYES NATIONAL SEASHORE.** New York: Atheneum, 1969. 118 p. Drawings by Earl Thollander. Introduction by Stewart L. Udall, former Secretary of the Interior.

Content: Beginning with Cermeno's arrival at Drake's Bay in 1595, this is an interesting, if somewhat staccato, history of the evolution of the Point Reyes area from the site of Indian villages and Spanish exploration to its present day status as a well-used national seashore. Information about the Miwok Indians, the building of a lighthouse, the effects of the 1906 earthquake, and the discovery of Drake's brass plate are interesting highlights.

Comment: The book suffers from the lack of a map. Because of its leaps in time, with lack of transitional passages, it might be more effective as a read-aloud to middle graders.

Nonfiction: intermediate

Barras, Judy. **THEIR PLACES SHALL KNOW THEM NO MORE.** Tehachapi, Calif.: Judy and Budd Barras, 1984. 86 p. B/w photos. Illus. by Helen Green, bibliog.

Content: This softcover book is filled with lore and legends of the Tehachapi area Indians (The People) and poetry and philosophy about Indian ways. The sections of most interest to students might include: the report of an 1872 great feast, Indian superstitions, information on basketweaving, acorn gathering, an intertribal antelope hunt, and gathering of plants and materials. The last chapters chronicle the sad fate of the Indians in their dealings with white men.

Comment: The informal, loosely structured format of the book is probably more suitable for sophisticated readers than for others. There's lots of interesting information here but no index. As the book is published by the author, it would be easiest to obtain it by writing to her at P.O. Box 869, North Fork, CA 93643.

Nonfiction: upper intermediate–adult

Bauer, Helen. **CALIFORNIA GOLD DAYS.** New York: Doubleday, 1954. 128 p. B/w pen and ink sketches, photos, charts, maps, glossary, index.

Content: This is a well-organized history of the gold-country region of California from the earliest explorations to the restoration of abandoned gold towns. It tells of Sutter, the discovery of gold, the gold-seekers, and mining—as well as the decline of the industry and the abandonment of many towns. A ten page supplement entitled "Gold Trail Today" lists thirty-three towns associated with the gold rush and tells how the names were acquired, what happened there, and what you can see today.

Comment: Bauer's books are basic tools in teaching California history. This one meets the information needs of most students though children might prefer color photos and illustrations.

Nonfiction: intermediate

Bauer, Helen. **CALIFORNIA INDIAN DAYS.** New York: Doubleday, 1963. 192 p. B/w illus. by Don Freeman, maps, charts, index.

Content: A presentation of various groups of California Indians, their geographic locations, their food and how they gathered it, the types of housing used, art and artifacts, clothing, weapons, tools, and other necessities. It includes their social organizations, games, customs and religion, as well as material about reservations, tribes, recipes for dyes, and other information about forty-two tribes.

Comment: An excellent source of information written in a pleasing manner with good maps, photos, and illustrations. This is an invaluable handbook which children can use with little direction. Bauer's pronunciation guide, the various charts, and information in the addenda add to its worth for those in a hurry to find "all they want to know."

Nonfiction: intermediate

Bauer, Helen. **CALIFORNIA MISSION DAYS.** New York: Doubleday, 1951; California State Dept. of Education, 1957. 126 p. B/w photos and drawings.

Content: Beginning with Spanish explorers seeking a California harbor, the book goes on to tell of the dreams of Father Junipero Serra and the coming of the padres to start the missions. A chapter devoted to each of the twenty-one missions relates a local story of each mission or includes information about mission life in general.

Comment: A reading of the entire book would give a student a fairly comprehensive notion of mission days. The book suffers from the lack of an index. A glossary tells how to pronounce Spanish names and words.

Nonfiction: intermediate

Bauer, Helen. **CALIFORNIA RANCHO DAYS.** New York: Doubleday, 1956, California State Dept. of Education, 1957. 128 p. Photos and diagrams.

Content: Beginning with the development of the ranchos and general descriptions of them, the author then gives information about specific southern ranchos: Juan Domingues Rancho in the San Pedro area, Jose Maria Verdugo Rancho in the Verdugo area, Bernardo Yorba Rancho in Santa Ana Valley, Antonio Lugo Rancho in Los Angeles County, Don Ygnacio Palomares Rancho in Pomona Valley. The author tells the story of Santa Barbara, then turns to ranchos in the north and tells about

Monterey, San Francisco, and Mariano Vallejo. Also included is a guide to adobes and landmarks of rancho days.

Comment: This is more text than literature and should have an index. Though pedantic in style, the book includes much information about life in early California. Includes a pronunciation guide.

Nonfiction: intermediate

Baxter, Don J. **GATEWAYS TO CALIFORNIA.** San Francisco: Pacific Gas and Electric Co., 1968. 47 p. Photos.

Content: Brief articles give historical information on the major mountain passes into and within California. The amount of use each pass has had, with reasons, including terrain or weather, is explained in fairly simple language. These articles emphasize, more than other manuscripts on California history, the hostility of the Indians in the early days and the fierceness of their attacks.

Comment: Teachers, students, and others will find here much interesting California history. However, the print is not good and the photos are hard to decipher.

This stapled, unbound photocopy is available, free, in limited quantities from P. G. & E., although the original softcover booklet is out of print.

Nonfiction: intermediate-adult

Baxter, Don J. **LAKES OF CALIFORNIA.** San Francisco: Pacific Gas and Electric Co., 1972. 47 p. Maps and photos.

Content: A collection of twenty-seven short articles about natural and man-made lakes in the state, which gives information on history, natural history, water management, and the development of hydroelectric power. It's interesting to read about the accidental creation of Salton Sea, about Tule Lake being nine-tenths drained by order of the Bureau of Reclamation, about Lake Elsinore being an "on again, off again" lake until regulated by the government.

Comment: This booklet, compiled from a series of articles in *P.G. & E. Progress,* has much to interest a student of California. Although the original softcover booklet is now out of print,

this stapled, unbound photocopy is available, free, in limited quantities from P.G. & E.
Nonfiction: intermediate–adult

Baxter, Don J. **MISSIONS OF CALIFORNIA.** San Francisco: Pacific Gas and Electric Co., 1970. 40 p. B/w illus.

Content: Short articles explain the history of each of the twenty-one missions. Vignettes are included as well.
Comment: Informative and fairly easy to read, these articles would be useful to students of any age studying the California missions. The illustrations do not reproduce well in the reprint; their effectiveness is lost. Compiled from a series of articles in *P.G. & E. Progress,* this booklet is out of print in its original softcover edition; it is available free, stapled and unbound, in limited quantities from P.G. & E.
Nonfiction: intermediate–adult

Beatty, Patricia. **THE BAD BELL OF SAN SALVADOR.** New York: William Morrow, 1973. 245 p. Frontispiece by Ben F. Stahl.

Content: This historical tale takes place in southern California in the 1840s. A thirteen-year-old Comanche Indian boy who had been kidnapped as a child is sold for a barrel of whiskey, and brought to the Santa Ana River area by a band of Mexicans who settle there. Called Jacinto, the boy refuses to accept Mexican ways and lives for the day he can steal a horse and go back to his people, but he is watched with ever-increasing suspicion. He redeems himself by helping to cast the bell of San Salvador and then sounds an alarm on it which saves the villagers.
Comment: This fascinating tale builds to a rousing climax.
Fiction: upper intermediate–junior high

Beatty, Patricia. **BLUE STARS WATCHING.** New York: William Morrow, 1969. 191 p.

Content: Beginning in Delaware with slave runaways, the underground railroad, and the murder of a hired hand who works for a farmer, the story continues with the adventures of the

farmer's two children sent to California to escape the Civil War. They become involved in spying and plotting. The San Francisco wharves, Chinatown—even the U.S. Secret Service—become involved in the plot.
Comment: This is an exciting adventure tale.
Fiction: intermediate

Beatty, Patricia. **EIGHT MULES FROM MONTEREY.** New York: William Morrow, 1982. 192 p.

Content: In 1916 a lady librarian, her two children, a mule skinner, and eight mules headed out from Monterey to take books to the mountain people living in the Santa Lucias. How they accomplished their mission and their adventures along the way are loosely based on what a librarian really did at this time and place.
Comment: An irresistible mix of a librarian, mountain folks with their own culture (a la Appalachia), spunky, likeable kids, a helper with a mysterious background, sprinkled throughout with details of the era. A look at an interesting area and subculture that has modern-day echoes.
Fiction: intermediate–junior high

Beatty, Patricia. **LACY MAKES A MATCH.** New York: William Morrow, 1979. 222 p.

Content: Thirteen-year-old Lacy Bingham turns matchmaker for her two older brothers in a California mining town of the 1890s. She also discovers who her real family may have been. An author's note explains some of the historical elements used in the story.
Comment: Although this is set in a California town the story is not especially Californian. However, details of daily life, mining methods (dynamiting in tunnels under the town), landmarks and sights of San Francisco highlight the California connection, and bring to life a particular era in the state's history. A possible read-aloud.
Fiction: intermediate–junior high

Beatty, Patricia. **ME, CALIFORNIA PERKINS.** New York: William Morrow, 1968. 253 p. B/w illus.

Content: California Perkins's Pa had an itchy foot which brought Callie and her family to a mining town on a ledge of the mountains in the Mojave Desert. How the town acquired a school—and wives for some of the town's bachelors—and how Callie's Ma managed to persuade Pa to move makes for a lively and entertaining story with many historically accurate details.

Comment: Readers will enjoy reading this story while learning what it was like to live in a desert mining town. Callie and her family are real people coping with situations the way pioneers have usually done—with common sense, imagination, and humor. A good read-aloud.

Fiction: intermediate–junior high

Beatty, Patricia. **THE QUEEN'S OWN GROVE.** New York: William Morrow, 1966. 221 p. Illus. by Liz Dauber.

Content: Amelia, the thirteen-year-old narrator, tells the story of her family's relocation to Riverside, California. The Thorups left a comfortable home and successful business in England to buy a pest-infected orange orchard, and resettle in a climate recommended for the father's health. Through Amelia's eyes, we relive the experiences of an alien family in a small community of the early 1900s, becoming a happy, successful, and contributing group in a "new world."

Comment: This is an interesting, easy-to-read story which can entertain and inform children and adults.

Fiction: intermediate–junior high

THE BEAUTIFUL CALIFORNIA MISSIONS. Text by Lee Foster. Beaverton, Oregon: Beautiful America Publishing, 1977. 72 p. Color photos.

Content: The introduction briefly notes the reasons for the founding of the missions, and their lasting influences on California place names, agriculture, and architecture. From south to north, each mission is described and a short history given along with other interesting facts of California life and history. The photos show some interiors as well as various exterior views of all the missions.

Comment: An interesting overall thumbnail history and description, this would be helpful to sightseers and not too overwhelming for younger readers. Excellent photos. Although out-of-print now (August 1985), the publisher plans a reprint in the near future.

Nonfiction: intermediate–adult

Beck, Warren A., and Ynez D. Haase. **HISTORICAL ATLAS OF CALIFORNIA.** Norman, Okla.: University of Oklahoma Press, 1974. 101 p. Maps, index.

Content: This collection of maps covers a broad span in the history of California—from the first map drawn in 1625, to regional maps showing Mexican land grants, and to maps of current political districts.

Comment: This atlas gives important, interesting, and often little-known information about California. It should be on everyone's shelf.

Nonfiction: upper intermediate–adult

Behrens, June, and Pauline Brower. **DEATH VALLEY.** Chicago: Childrens Press, 1980. 31 p. Color photos by Pauline Brower.

Content: In story form, this soft-cover booklet details the visit of two children to their grandfather who lives in Death Valley. He takes the children to a celebration of forty-niner days at Furnace Creek and recalls stories about the forty-niners and how their need for a shorter route to the gold led many to attempt a shortcut through Death Valley. The discovery and mining of borax in the 1870s and the problems of getting it to market led to the use of mule teams. Gold mining and ghost towns all figure in the old-timer's stories, and he takes the children to the ruins of the Harmony Borax Works, the Wildrose charcoal kilns, and the Keane Wonder Mine.

Comment: This could be a good read-aloud for younger children learning about Death Valley.

Fiction: primary–lower intermediate

Benezra, Barbara. **FIRE DRAGON.** New York: Criterion Books, 1970. 223 p. Illus. by Franc and Constance Roggeri. Map.

Content: San Francisco, April 1906—and Sam Watkins delivering milk on his new job is hurled about as *the* earthquake begins. He observes the wreckage and on his way to inform his boss that the milk wagon horse has been killed becomes aware of the fires starting, fires which are to engulf his home and separate him from his family for months. In the midst of the disaster Sam meets and helps the Lee family from Chinatown. It is their friendship that sustains him in the hard and lonely times ahead. The adventures of Sam and Charlie Lee give a vivid picture of the San Francisco earthquake and fire and dramatize the ignorance and prejudice of San Franciscans of the period concerning their Chinese-American citizens.
Comment: The book would benefit from a more detailed map of the city.
Fiction: intermediate

Benezra, Barbara. **GOLD DUST AND PETTICOATS.** New York: Bobbs-Merrill, 1964. 179 p.

Content: Thirteen-year-old Marcy Miller arrives in San Francisco with her family during the rainy season after almost a year on the road from New Orleans. Her subsequent escapades include separation from her parents during the 1850 fire, rescue by a famous outlaw, capture and imprisonment, and ingenious escape.
Comment: Girls with an adventurous spirit could easily identify with Marcy, but boys might not be interested in this story.
Fiction: intermediate

Benezra, Barbara. **NUGGETS IN MY POCKET.** New York: Bobbs-Merrill, 1966. 176 p.

Content: The author followed her first story, *Gold Dust and Petticoats* by writing of Jeb Miller's exciting adventures in the gold fields. Jeb is Marcy's sixteen-year-old brother, whose slight physical handicap, a limp, does not deter him from leaving a note for his parents and taking off to the gold country.

He encounters many dangerous situations: his horse is stolen, coyotes attack at night, a gold mine caves in on him, but it all leads to his character development. The reader will enjoy noting the changes in how he thinks and feels about his life and future. He never seems to lose sight of his ultimate goal—to save enough gold to start raising horses.
Comment: This book should be appealing to both sexes.
Fiction: intermediate

Bernstein, Margery. **COYOTE GOES HUNTING FOR FIRE: A CALIFORNIA INDIAN MYTH.** New York: Charles Scribner's Sons, 1974. 40 p. Illus.

Content: A short, breezy account of how the animals went looking for fire and almost brought it back from the Wind People.
Comment: However this folktale was originally told, this retelling, in its style and unresolved ending, doesn't have much zip. The illustrations are cartoon-like line drawings and are fun. *Earth Namer* by the same author is a better story.
Fiction: primary

Bernstein, Margery, and Jane Kobrin. **EARTH NAMER: A CALIFORNIA INDIAN MYTH.** New York: Charles Scribner's Sons, 1974. 40 p. Illus. by Ed Heffernan.

Content: In the beginning of the world, there were no living things except Turtle. There was water everywhere and no dry land. One day Earth Namer appeared on Turtle's raft. Because Earth Namer had come from the sky, Turtle knew that Earth Namer must be magic. He asked him for a favor. "Can you make dry land?" Turtle asked. "I would like to rest." And that begins this wonderful story about how Earth Namer made the world, including the sun, the moon, and the animals.
Comment: This story was first told long ago by the Maidu Indians who wondered how the world began and thought this was the way it could have happened.
Fiction: primary

Bidwell, John. "To California 1841" in **FIRST THREE WAGON TRAINS,** by John Bidwell, Hubert Howe Bancroft, and James Longmire. Portland, Ore.: Binford & Mort, 1956, 104 p.

Content: This is reprinted from a personal account by Bidwell in *Century Magazine,* November 1890, of the Bidwell-Bartleson party's journey west—the first to cross the Sierra into California—with enough details to recreate vividly the people and places.

Comment: This brief account doesn't present the difficulties a longer, more detailed or scholarly account might for junior high students. Could be read aloud to younger students. The Remington prints are well chosen to illustrate the story.

Nonfiction: junior high–adult

Blackburn, Edith H. **ONE BIT OF LAND: A STORY OF IMPERIAL VALLEY.** New York: Aladdin Books, 1955. 192 p. Illus. by Frank Nicholas.

Content: For years the Gomez family had followed the crops up and down California without a home of their own. When Mamacita inherits the old family homesite near El Centro, she sets out with her family to "buy back" the title from the land company that had taken it over. Because the family has a year to pay the taxes, everyone pitches in. Cousin Carlos takes in the family while Senor Gomez goes to work on the All-American Canal being built near Yuma. Mamacita takes care of the children and the house and does odd jobs for the neighbors. Paco, the teenage son, works after school and on weekends, dreaming about the day he can become an engineer like his friend Mark Holmes.

Comment: How this family with determination, hard work, and much love acquired its "one bit of land" is a heart-warming story. Set in the 1930s.

Fiction: intermediate

Blassingame, Wyatt, and Richard Glendinning. **MEN WHO**

OPENED THE WEST. New York: G. P. Putnam's Sons, 1969. 159 p. Illus. by Frank Aloise, index.

2 m

Content: The authors deal with some of the first white men in the West—John Ledyard, Jedediah Smith, General Stephen Kearney, Brigham Young, and John Sutter. Railroads in the West and cattlemen also each rate a chapter.

Comment: The book suffers from a lack of illustrations, both in number and quality. There is a simple pen and ink sketch (one-third of a page) at the beginning of each chapter.

The writing lacks a sense of style. Most of the individuals written about seem stereotyped.

Nonfiction: intermediate

979.4 B Bleeker, Sonia. **THE MISSION INDIANS OF CALIFORNIA.** New York: William Morrow, 1956. 137 p. Illus. by Althea Karr.

4 m (J)
I m (A)

Content: Initiation ceremonies—girls', boys', and new moon— are explained, as is acorn preparation, food prohibitions, and medical practices. Coastal Indian life is depicted and the legend of the creation of earth is told. The book ends with Indian history, the submersion of the Indian culture to the Spanish and a summary of the post-Mexican period to the 1950s. The author tells much about the values and customs of early southern California Indians through the eyes of Little Singer, a Cahuille Indian boy; the chapter, "Mission Days," gives a most matter of fact account of mission-Indian relationships from the Indians' point of view.

Comment: In very easy wording and a rather primary format, there's much to be learned from this book; it would be interesting to compare it with other sources.

Nonfiction: intermediate

921 Serr Bolton, Ivy. **FATHER JUNIPERO SERRA.** New York: Julian
UCG Messner, 1952. 160 p. B/w illus. by Robert Burns, bibliog., index.

I m
OP

Content: The story of the founder of the California mission chain, using Father Francisco Palou's biography of his friend and Father Serra's own diary of the trek to San Diego as well as secondary sources. Father Serra's great desire to serve in the missionary field, his determination to establish the California mission system, and his love for the Indians he served and taught is stressed.

Comment: In this clearly written biography, the author's use of primary material takes a straight narrative form making the book easier for younger students to read.

Nonfiction: intermediate–junior high

Bonham, Frank. **HONOR BOUND.** New York: Thomas Y. Crowell, 1963. 243 p.

Content: Young Cullen Cooke becomes involved in slavery and antislavery factions in California. He is carrying a message from President Buchanan to a California senator which could cause California to become one of the proslave states. Cullen's personal code of honor is threatened, but can he become disloyal to his country? The resolution is certainly exciting.

Comment: A nice look at personal honor which might cause some young readers to examine their own values. The Association of Children's Librarians reviewed it and liked it, too.

Fiction: junior high

Booth, Edwin. **JOHN SUTTER: CALIFORNIAN.** New York: Bobbs-Merrill, 1963. 191 p. Illus. by Gerald McCaun.

Content: Starting with Sutter's early life in Germany, the story tells of his early experiences in America and his efforts to reach California—which he eventually does via Vancouver, Hawaii, and Alaska. Then Sutter obtains a land grant and applies for Mexican citizenship. After beginning the building of Sutter's Fort, he runs into trouble with General Vallejo, with local Indians, and, later, with John C. Fremont. Sutter's Fort survives and prospers, but Sutter becomes embroiled in the political upheaval and lands in jail. After release, he sees increasing tension between Mexico and the United States. The Bear Flag Revolt adds to the turbulence. Sutter comes to the rescue of the Donner Party and offers shelter to the survivors. The discovery of gold at Sutter's Mill proves to be a disaster for him. The book ends with the granting of statehood to California.

Comment: This book gives much information about Sutter, Sutter's Fort, and early American maneuverings in California. It also presents Vallejo in a most unfavorable light: "The general was a clever and calculating man, always on the lookout for an opportunity to better himself financially or politically, and certain in his own mind that everybody else was doing the same thing." (p. 68)

It would be interesting for a student to compare this characterization with another one of Vallejo. Fremont, too, is presented as a blackguard. A student reading of him here, and then in *Jessie Benton Fremont* by Marguerite Higgins would have trouble recognizing him as the same man.

Nonfiction: junior high

Breen, Patrick. **DIARY OF PATRICK BREEN: ONE OF THE DONNER PARTY.** Edited by Frederick J. Teggart. Reno, Nevada: Outbooks, 1979. 16 p. B/w illus.

Content: This is a reproduction of the diary Breen kept during the months camped at Donner Lake, and is the only on-the-spot account made. Other participant accounts were written after the fact (see Virginia Reed Murphy). Breen's terse comments on the weather and the names of sick, dying, and dead bring home the tragedy. Even the two remarks on cannibalism are matter-of-factly stated although Breen calls it "distressing". Breen's entire family survived.

Comment: Because the notations are abbreviated, younger students might find it difficult to read, but this could be a read-aloud.

Nonfiction: intermediate–adult

Bristow, Gwen. **CALICO PALACE.** New York: Thomas Y. Crowell, 1970. 589 p. Map.

Content: Kendra Logan, an unwelcomed daughter, comes to San Francisco in 1847 to live with her mother and stepfather, an army officer. She has completed her boarding school education and now becomes involved in the social life of this small community. After a whirlwind courtship with a reluctant suitor, she marries and accompanies her husband to the goldfields where she establishes herself as the cook for a group of friends. At this point, her husband admits to bigamy and leaves.

Kendra and friends return to San Francisco and set up various businesses, the most interesting of which is Calico Palace, a gambling casino. Through the lives of those involved with the casino we glimpse the growth of the city with its discomforts, casualties, violence, and frequent fires from 1848 to 1851. A street map of San Francisco in 1851 is included.

Comment: Though not written as a novel for young readers, this is a good story which depicts the hardship, confusion, fires, and especially the lawlessness of early days in San Francisco.
Fiction: senior high

Bronson, William. **THE EARTH SHOOK, THE SKY BURNED.** New York: Pocket Books, 1971. 192 p. Photos, index.

Content: A very readable day-by-day account of the four days of the 1906 San Francisco earthquake, fire, and aftermath. The author interviewed survivors and families of survivors as well as consulting contemporary news stories and other printed accounts.
Comment: Written for adults, this is interesting and comprehensible to many younger readers as well because of the many pictures and the high-interest subject matter. The endpaper maps showing the extent and the progress of the fire are very good.
Nonfiction: upper intermediate–adult

Brown, Vinson, and David Hoover. **THE CALIFORNIA WILDLIFE MAP BOOK.** Revised from **THE CALIFORNIA WILDLIFE MAP.** Healdsburg, Calif.: Naturegraph Publishers, 1967. 134 p. Illus. B/w sketches, index, map keys to habitats.

Content: This natural-wildlife guide shows almost all the common mammals, birds, reptiles, amphibians, and fish, plus most of the common plants of the state. There are brief descriptions of each and a key to determine the habitat and location where each species lives.
Comment: This natural-history guide could augment the study of the political history of an area in the state. Of the many flora

and fauna guides published by Naturegraph, this title seems of the most general interest, and thus, the one most useful to younger readers.

Nonfiction: intermediate–adult

Brown, Vinson, and Douglas Andrews. **THE POMO INDIANS OF CALIFORNIA AND THEIR NEIGHBORS.** Happy Camp, Calif.: Naturegraph Publishers, 1969. 64 p. Map, photos, and drawings, appendix, index.

Content: This is one of a series of book-map combinations on the major Indian tribes of America and their neighbors. It ties description and pictures of the social culture of the Indians to a large map that shows their native country as it was before the white man came. The old villages, trails, and tribal divisions are shown. The Pomos were not actually a tribe but a group of tribelets speaking similar languages and dialects. As with most California Indians, their culture, little understood by white people, had some quite complex elements including an elaborate money and counting system, also fine basketwork, and complicated dance costumes.

Comment: Although not written especially for young readers, this book and its large color map of old trails and villages are organized so as to lend themselves to clarity and understanding. The numerous drawings are clear and explicit, and the photographs excellent. In addition, the book contains an appendix of "Place Names and Their Meanings" and a page of suggested references. Young readers would do well to consult this book for an unromanticized, accurate portrayal of one group of tribelets in California.

Nonfiction: intermediate–adult

Brusa, Betty War. **SALINAN INDIANS OF CALIFORNIA AND THEIR NEIGHBORS.** Happy Camp, Calif.: Naturegraph Publishers, 1975. 77 p. B/w illus. by Eugenia Bonnot, maps, appendix, bibliog., index.

Content: Division One contains four chapters on the Salinan Indians detailing their boundaries, economic and social life, and aesthetic pursuits. Division Two tells in less detail about other tribes: the Esselen, Chumash, Costanoans, and Yokuts.

Comment: A student could use this title to find specific information about one of the tribes included.

Nonfiction: upper intermediate–senior high

Bryant, Will. **KIT CARSON AND THE MOUNTAIN MEN.** New York: Grosset and Dunlap, 1960. 60 p. Illus. by the author.

Content: This title contains stories of some of the more important mountain men who crossed back and forth over the Rockies and the Sierra Nevada seeking furs, blazing trails, and later leading explorers and pioneers across the treacherous passes. The author says, "In a few short years, the mountain men were gone altogether, along with the grizzly bear and beaver and gray, winking wolves and the Indian as he was in his glory. In all history, the mountain man was a unique breed, and the world will never see his like again. This (book) is a part of his story." The emphasis is mainly on Kit Carson, but stories of others—Jim Bridger, Ewing Young, Jedediah Smith, Jim Clyman, Tom Fitzpatrick, Joe Meek, Bill Mitchell—are included.

Comment: This romanticized look at the doughty mountain men is full of adventure and sure to appeal to a young reader. The author's illustrations add greatly to his stories.

Fiction: intermediate

BUF   Buff, Mary, and Conrad Buff. **KEMI, AN INDIAN BOY BEFORE THE WHITE MAN CAME.** Pasadena, Calif.: Ward Ritchie Press, 1966. 100 p.

2m   **Content:** Kemi, a young Indian, breaks his mother's precious soapstone pot. With the help of his father, he goes with the other men of the tribe to trade with Indians on the coast where he is able to get another pot.

Comment: Although a particular tribe is not named, the setting is the southern California coast where the Gabrielino Indians lived more than 500 years ago. The story offers some insight into Indian culture.

Fiction: intermediate

RvL   Bulla, Clyde Robert. **GHOST TOWN TREASURE.** New York: Thomas Y. Crowell, 1957. 86 p. B/w illus. by Don Freeman.

Im
Ib

Content: Twelve year-old Ty Jackson loves living in the ghost town of Gold Rock, but his parents need to move to the city where their grocery store will have more customers. They do agree to stay in Gold Rock, however, until after Ty's pen pals come for their visit. Paul and Nora are especially interested in the area because their great grandfather had been there during the gold rush, and they were fascinated with the diary he had left.

Paul, Nora, and Ty search for the cave described in the diary, certain they'll find gold. They finally *do* find the cave but no treasure. Disappointed, Paul and Nora go home, and Ty prepares to leave his beloved ghost town. But wait! Word has spread about the cave. Tourists start coming, and the grocery business becomes profitable enough for Ty's family to stay.

Comment: A modern reenactment of the disappointment most gold miners felt ties this story of modern day to the gold rush of '49. And the unexpected "treasure" of promoting tourism could be tied to the unexpected riches many gold miners found in providing services to others, even in the nineteenth century.

Fiction: upper primary

RvL   Bulla, Clyde Robert. **THE SECRET VALLEY.** New York: Thomas Y. Crowell, 1949. 100 p.

Im

Content: The Davis family members were unhappy in Missouri and hoped that if they found gold out West each of them could have what she or he wanted most. So off they went in 1849 across deserts and mountains with a group of other pioneers taking all their possessions and Nugget, the kitten. After many an adventure on the way, they reached California and lived for a time in a tent city with hundreds of others who had come looking for gold. They worked hard and kept hoping riches would be theirs. Sometimes the floods and rains made them despair of fulfilling their dreams, but eventually they do. Songs about gold, the prairie, going west are included.

Comment: Although this title is out-of-print, many libraries still

have it, and it continues to circulate. It's a well-told story of an exciting time in the history of our state and an honest presentation of values which even the very young reader will comprehend and appreciate.
Fiction: intermediate

Burt, Olive W. **GHOST TOWNS OF THE WEST.** New York: Simon and Schuster, 1976. 96 p. Illus. by Paul Frame. B/w photos.

Content: One chapter of the book is devoted to California. It includes the story of Allensworth, California built by Lt. Colonel Allensworth, a former slave, who joined the Union Army during the Civil War and retired as the highest-ranking black officer in the army. He was also a minister who dreamed of building his own town. With the money he had saved he started his all-black community in southwestern Tulare County in 1908. The city grew until 1914 when the Colonel died. It became a ghost town but has now been restored by the state as a living museum of black history and culture.
Comment: Ghost towns in Montana, Utah, Oregon, Nevada, and California are described. The author has a lively style; the illustrations and photographs add greatly to the stories.
Nonfiction: intermediate

Burt, Olive. **JEDEDIAH SMITH—FUR TRAPPER OF THE OLD WEST.** New York: Julian Messner, 1951. 187 p. B/w illus. by Robert Doremus, bibliog., index.

Content: This book covers Smith's life from the time he first joined a trapping expedition at age twenty-three, until he was killed by Indians in May 1831 at age thirty-two. Smith was a well known mountain man who led the first American trapping expedition across the Sierra Nevada into California in 1827. Burt stresses Smith's leadership, mountaineering skills, and his sense of fairness in dealing with Indians. The story moves well as it details the hardships of mountain men in their explorations into America's unknown wildernesses.
Comment: Jed Smith is made to look almost too good to be true, but that goes with the territory in juvenile biographies. The

dialogue is sometimes contrived in the attempts at duplicating mountain men's speech.
Nonfiction: intermediate–junior high

92| F872 Burt, Olive. **JOHN CHARLES FREMONT, TRAIL MARKER OF THE OLD WEST.** New York: Julian Messner, 1955. 192 p. B/w illus. by Albert Orbaan, bibliog., index.

I m   **Content:** The entire career of John Charles "Charley" Fremont from his days as a poor boy in Charleston to the clouded days of military leadership and disappointment in his later years is covered in Burt's book. The emphasis, however, is on the years Fremont spent surveying the West, exploring passes to California, and through his reports and maps, opening the way for Western migration. Fremont's political ambition and skill, his dedication to winning the West for the United States, and his leadership and charm are well documented. The teamwork he and Kit Carson enjoyed is stressed more than the benefits he reaped from the considerable help of his wife, Jessie Benton Fremont.
Comment: Students will respond to the adventure-filled biography. The attitudes of Fremont and Kit Carson toward Indians reflect the feelings of the times. The attack on the California Indian village from Fremont's point of view could be compared with the same attack described in Meyer's *ISHI* or Kroeber's *ISHI, Last of His Tribe.*
Nonfiction: intermediate–junior high

978 13   Burt, Olive W. **NEGROES IN THE EARLY WEST.** New York: Julian Messner, 1969. 90 p. Illus. by F. Bjorklund, bibliog., index.

I m   **Content:** The chapters include information on blacks as explorers, mountain men, founders of cities, businessmen, soldiers, and cowboys. There is one chapter on black women—Mamie Pleasant, Biddy Mason, and Mary Fields. Among the men described are: Jacob Dodson, an aide to Captain John Fremont; James Beckwourth, a mountain man who discovered Beckwourth Pass; Polite (or Paulette) Haboss, a trusted aide of Jedediah Smith.

Comment: This is a lively, historical treatment of eighteen black men and women who played both major and minor roles in the exploration and settling of the West, but who are given sketchy (if any) coverage in routine history books. The author brings them to life in these biographical sketches.
Nonfiction: intermediate

Calder-Marshall, Arthur. **LONE WOLF, THE STORY OF JACK LONDON.** New York: Duell, Sloan and Pearce, 1961. 165 p. B/w illus. by Biro, bibliog.

Content: The story begins with London's early life in and around the San Francisco Bay area from his birth in 1876 to age fifteen when he was living as an oyster pirate in Benicia. After almost drowning, London decided to give up living outside the law, and at seventeen he went to sea as an able bodied seaman. Other chapters record his adventures at sea, working in a jute mill and as a furnance man back in Oakland, joining in a march of the unemployed on Washington, D.C., seeking more education, going to Alaska for gold, and, finally, marrying Bessie Maddern. The conclusion deals with his life as an adult writer, his further personal adventures, his second marriage, and his death at The Valley of the Moon at age forty.
Comment: London's many and varied experiences make the first half of this book fascinating for all readers. The second half, concentrating on his political and philosophical interests, his tangled personal life and his fiscal irresponsibility, would be of less interest to young readers.
Nonfiction: upper intermediate–junior high

CALIFORNIA ALMANAC, 1984-1985 edition. Edited by James Fay, Anne G. Lipow, and Stephanie W. Fay. Novato, Calif: Presidio Press and Pacific Data Resources, 1984. n.p. Index.

Content: This contains the usual kinds of statistical information found in general almanacs, but limited to California, such as: population, government, labor, business, communication and media, science, manufacturing, culture and the arts, consumers, women, minorities, and others. Each subject is listed in the table of contents with its own section number, and subtopic entries in the index give only section numbers. However, since the information is not crowded on the pages it isn't difficult to find what one is looking for. The print is a decent size, too. This is the first edition, and it will be published every two years.

Comment: The format is much easier to use and read than other almanacs, and there is much useful information here.

Reference: intermediate–adult

CALIFORNIA HISTORICAL MONUMENTS. Reprint. San Francisco: Pacific Gas and Electric Co., 1968. 47 p. Index.

Content: the background and importance of each of the designated historical monuments in California are explained in one page articles.

Comment: No matter where one goes in the state, some of the monuments will be old news, and some a total surprise! This reprint can hardly fail to interest Californians in visiting all the designated monuments and learning more. Compiled from a series of articles in *P.G. & E. Progress*. This softcover booklet is now out of print; the stapled, unbound manuscript is available, free, in limited quantities from P.G. & E.

Nonfiction: intermediate–adult

CALIFORNIA ORIGINALS: PROFILES OF PEOPLE WHO MADE AN ORIGINAL IMPRINT ON CALIFORNIA. Reprint. San Francisco: Pacific Gas and Electric Co., n.d., n.p.

Content: twenty-eight one-page biographies of people who had an impact on the history of California are included. Most of the profiles are of personages in northern California. Those included range from the quite well known—Jedediah Smith and Bret Harte—to the mostly forgotten—William Leidesdorff and Benjamin Lyford. The "warts" of the important are included along with their accomplishments: for instance, John Marsh is accused of being "The meanest man in California" by John Bidwell.

Comment: We can see this being used very satisfactorily in classrooms from the elementary level on up. The profiles are easy to read, informative, and present a rounded view of the people and their drives, successes, and failures. This stapled,

unbound reprint from *P.G. & E. Progress,* is available free in limited quantities from P.G. & E. in San Francisco.
Nonfiction: intermediate–adult

THE CALIFORNIA SENATE. Rev. ed. Sacramento: California Office of State Printing, n.p. Color photos and diagram.

Content: This short, soft-cover publication succinctly describes a branch of the legislature and tells the student what the California Senate does. Its sections are titled: "Composition of the Senate," "The Biennial Session," "Organization," "The Committee Structure," "The Senate Publications," "Bills and Resolutions," and "Rules and Regulations." The last section, "How a Bill Becomes a Law," is a simplified chart showing the route a bill takes through the California Legislature.
Comment: Available in classroom quantity, free, from one's representative in the California Senate. There is no table of contents or index. Pictures are of the present leaders, and the diagram shows where each senator sits during legislative sessions. It is meant as a study guide for those who are to visit the capital and is excellent to use in such preparations. It would be helpful, also, as an adjunct to any study of the state's history and government. See also the entry, *California State Assembly.*
Nonfiction: intermediate–adult

CALIFORNIA STATE ASSEMBLY. Rev. ed. Sacramento: California Office of State Printing: 1983. n.p. Color photos and diagram.

Content: This short, soft-cover publication, succinctly describes this legislative branch and tells the student what the California Assembly does. Its sections are titled: "The Members," "The Officers," "Rules Committee," "The Committee System," and "Sessions of the Legislature." The last part of the pamphlet has a page of history on California's capitals and descriptions of the background and meaning of the state seal, the bear flag, the state flower, and tree.
Comment: Available in classroom quantity, free, from one's representative in the California Assembly. Pictures are of the present leaders, and the diagram shows where each assemblyman sits during legislative sessions. There is no table of con-

tents or index. It is meant as a study guide for those who are to visit the capital and is excellent to use in such preparations. It would be helpful, also, as an adjunct to any study of the state's history and government. See also the entry, *The California Senate.*
Nonfiction: intermediate–adult

CALIFORNIA STATE PARKS. Sunset Books and Sunset Magazine. Lane Publishing Co.: Menlo Park, Calif.: 1972. 128 p. B/w illus., map, index.

Content: Included is information on state historic parks, other state parks, beaches, recreation areas, wayside camps, and scenic or scientific reserves. The historic parks range from small, single-point-of-interest parks to multiacred areas that include picnicking and hiking facilities. Five percent of the state's historical landmarks are in the state park system and included in the book. Arrangement is geographical in eight sections. Within each section, there is a map showing locations and types of parks. The entry for each park is annotated, giving hours, fees, addresses and access directions and, in the case of the historical parks, a brief historical background.
Comment: Although this book is out-of-print, it can be found in many public libraries. It could be used to plan group field trips as well as individual or family trips.
Nonfiction: intermediate–adult

979.4
CAL

3m (A)

CALIFORNIA THE GOLDEN STATE. Sacramento, Calif.: California State Senate, 1972. 24 p. B/w illus. and photos.

Content: Tells how we became a state, how we govern ourselves, our resources and our way of life. Also gives a brief history of capitals and capitols, descriptions of state seal and emblems. This is a handy review of the state. Especially useful are the short explanations of the duties of the various state elective offices, and the information on the emblems.
Comment: This booklet can be secured free by writing to one's state senator in Sacramento.
Nonfiction: intermediate–adult

19.4 CAL **CALIFORNIA YEARBOOK: BICENTENNIAL EDITION.**
LaVerne, Calif.: California Almanac Co., 1976. 384 p. Illus.,
photos, index. Foreword by March Fong Eu, Secretary of State
of California.

I A)REF **Content:** Everything one might want to know about the state of
California and then some! The contents include exploration and
settlement, political bodies and systems, education and the
community (including museums and libraries), native plants and
animals, physical history, geography and weather, uses of
forests, major crops and regions, mineral resources, energy
needs, resources in the ocean, fishing for food and sport, water
resources, parks and attractions, sports, history to 1976, transportation, economy and employment, manufacturing, banking
history, defense, population growth and distribution, cities, and
counties.
Comment: Found in the reference section of libraries, this book
contains numerous photographs, drawings, charts, graphs, and
statistical data. It is a fascinating compendium.
Nonfiction: intermediate–adult

Am Cameron, Eleanor. **JULIA AND THE HAND OF GOD.** New York:
E. P. Dutton, 1977. 169 p.

2 J/FICT **Content:** Whenever Julia went to meet Uncle Hugh in San
Francisco, she thought of earthquakes because she lived across
the bay from this city which had been devastated by earthquake
and fire in 1906. The day of her eleventh birthday was no
exception. At lunch, she heard once again how her uncle
survived what her grandmother had called "the hand of God
laying low the wicked city." For her birthday Uncle Hugh gave
her a leatherbound volume in which Julia, a budding author,
was to record her thoughts and which she promptly labeled
"The Book of Strangenesses."
   Later, when fire swept down out of the dry hills almost
leveling her own city, Julia asks her grandmother if the fire
happened because Berkeley was wicked. Gran, immensely
puzzled, cannot answer, as she cannot answer many of the
questions of the argumentative Julia. Difficult, headstrong, full

of ideas, Julia manages to get herself in the midst of the fire. This and much else is recorded in Julia's journal.

Comment: The author says the story is autobiographical, that she, herself, was engrossed by stories of the San Francisco earthquake as a child, and that the Berkeley fire did occur when she was eleven.

Fiction: intermediate

Carpenter, Allen. **CALIFORNIA.** Enchantment of America series. Rev. ed. Chicago: Childrens Press, 1978. 91 p. Color and b/w illus, index.

Content: In separate chapters the book covers briefly: history, natural resources, industrial resources, famous people, places of interest (going north, San Diego to Northern California.) The reference section includes: instant facts, a date line, a list of governors through 1975, and famous people.

Comment: The information is presented in a straightforward, uncomplicated style and is useful for state reports even though not entirely up to date.

Nonfiction: intermediate–junior high

Carrighar, Sally. **ONE DAY ON BEETLE ROCK.** New York: Alfred A. Knopf, 1956. 196 p. Illus. by Henry B. Kane. Introductory note by Robert C. Miller, Director of the California Academy of Sciences.

Content: This outstanding nature classic describes nine animals—a weasel and her brood, a lizard, a stellar jay, a deer mouse, a chickaree, a Sierra grouse, a coyote, a black bear and her cubs, a mule deer—as they act and interact on June 18 on and around Beetle Rock in Sequoia National Park in the High Sierra. June 18 is the day selected for viewing because wildlife is at the height of activity at that time.

Beetle Rock is an actual place, two acres of granite field, almost square, divided like a beetle's back. A chapter is devoted to each animal with that particular animal's perspective and through different periods of the day.

Comment: In the introduction, Robert C. Miller wrote, "This is a very dangerous book, full of disturbing possibilities. Should it

fall into the hands of the young, it is extremely likely to make naturalists of them." And he is so right! It combines an accurate scientific description of animal life with a richly textured poetic style to make an outstanding nature book. Excellent illustrations reinforce the text. The book can often be found at National Park bookstores.
Nonfiction: intermediate–adult

Castor, Henry. **THE FIRST BOOK OF THE SPANISH-AMERICAN WEST.** New York: Franklin Watts, 1963. 85 p. B/w illus. by Albert Micale, map, index.

Content: Gives an overview of the history of the region, with explorations by Spanish and Americans up to the end of the Mexican War and U.S. annexation. Includes a short chapter on the lasting Spanish influences such as place names, cowboy methods, words, and foods.
Comment: Although 300 years of history is so encapsulated, Castor manages to convey why the Spanish claimed the area, and how the U.S. took it. He also is sympathetic to the Spanish and Indian cultures while at the same time mentioning less-attractive aspects; he doesn't romanticize the Spanish West.
Nonfiction: upper primary–lower intermediate

Chamberlain, Newell D. **THE CALL OF GOLD: TRUE TALES ON THE GOLD ROAD TO YOSEMITE.** Fresno, Calif.: Valley Publishers, 1972. 180 p. B/w photos, appendix.

Content: The author gives recollections of old-timers or recounts events as described in the newspapers of the Yosemite-Mariposa area. Accounts of the arrival of goldseekers are followed by several chapters devoted to the activities, entanglements, and influence of Colonel John Fremont. The histories of several small communities—Hornitos, Coulterville, Mariposa, Indian Gulch—are related. There are biographical sketches of Lafayette Bunnell, J. M. Hutchins, Galen Clark, James Savage, John Muir, John Diltz, Angevine Reynolds, John Hite, Margaret Bigler, and a man known as Mariposa Al. Many of these biographical sketches include quotations from the person being described. Anecdotes of Indian, Mexican, and Chinese inhabitants of the area are woven into the story throughout the book. The roughness of life and the often cruel treatment of Indians and foreigners is very evident. The appendix contains The Miners' Ten Commandments.

Comment: This is very much a history of Mariposa County. Though written for adults, the very short chapters and the narrative style makes it feasible to use parts to get the flavor of the period for almost any age group.

Nonfiction: upper intermediate–adult

Chester, Michael. **FIRST WAGONS TO CALIFORNIA.** Sagas of the West Series. New York: G. P. Putnam's Sons, 1965. 96 p. Illus. by Steele Savage, index.

Content: The author tells of Elisha Stevens's wagon train starting west in 1844 and the problems and adventures along the way. The action then centers on California itself, early pioneers looking for a pass through the Sierra Nevada, wintering in the Sierra Nevada, how one group got into California's Great Valley, and where people settled. One chapter, "The Long Winter," records the time Moses Schallenberger spent alone in the mountains, and many anecdotes about him are included. These vividly recreate the temper of the times—rough camp humor, distrust between Indians and whites, the urgent need for cooperation between the races.

Comment: This title is part of the "Sagas of the West" series.

Nonfiction: intermediate

Chester, Michael. **FORTS OF OLD CALIFORNIA.** Sagas of the West Series. New York: G. P. Putnam's Sons, 1966. 95 p. Ink and wash drawings by Steele Savage, bibliog., index.

Content: The author writes about the presidios of San Diego, Santa Barbara, Monterey, and San Francisco, and the fort at Ballast Point, San Diego. Other chapters record pirate attacks in Monterey, events in the career of Mariano Vallejo, the defense of the north, the Russian occupation at Fort Ross, Sutter's Fort, John Fremont, and the story of the lost cannon found in Santa Barbara in 1848. Emphasis is on the attempts by many countries to establish military strongholds in California.

Information is included on Captain Vancouver, Jose Figueroa, Lieutenant Cordoba, James Pattie, General Vallejo and his bride Benicia, John Fremont, Jose Castro, Francisco Solano (chief of the Suisuns) and many others. The book abounds in names and anecdotes about colorful pioneers, explorers, and opportunists.

Comment: This title is part of the "Sagas of the West" series. A California chronology covering 1769-1858 is included.

Nonfiction: intermediate

Chester, Michael. **JOSEPH STRAUSS: BUILDER OF THE GOLDEN GATE.** Sagas of the West Series. New York: G.P. Putnam's Sons, 1965. 128 p. Illus. by Tom Humil, index.

624 C

2 m

Content: Joseph Strauss, the builder and designer of the Golden Gate Bridge, was often frustrated during his early working years. His designs were unusual and therefore, suspect. Seldom advanced any money, he built bridges and then was paid for them upon completion. Strauss also designed the bridge over the Tagus River in Lisbon, Portugal which is a replica of the Golden Gate but one foot longer.

Comment: The fairly complete story of Strauss is made even more interesting by the numerous drawings. They and the text enable the reader to understand what is required to build bridges of such magnitude.

Nonfiction: intermediate

Chu, Daniel, and Samuel Chu. **PASSAGE TO THE GOLDEN GATE: A HISTORY OF THE CHINESE IN AMERICA TO 1910.** Garden City, N.Y.: Doubleday, 1967. 117 p. Illus. by Earl Thollander, index.

25.251
CHU

I m

Content: Beginning with the history of Chinese-American clipper trade, the authors move on to the story of the Chinese roles in the gold rush and the building of the railroad. Anti-Chinese attitudes and actions are noted, and Chinatown settlements and the Six Companies organization are explained. Rebuilding by the Chinese after the 1906 San Francisco earthquake and fire concludes the book. In fairly simple language, the authors give much information about the Chinese in California. They include

background information on why the Chinese emigrated from their homeland, and remained a people apart for so long.
Comment: Discriminatory American laws and actions are noted, but not dwelt upon. There is a good description of the history of "coolie" labor on pages 19–21.
Nonfiction: intermediate

Clarke, James Mitchell. **THE LIFE AND ADVENTURES OF JOHN MUIR.** San Diego: The Word Shop, 1979. 318 p. B/w sketches, mainly by John Muir, photos, bibliog., index, appendixes.

Content: The author gives a very detailed account of John Muir's life from boyhood to his death. An outline of Muir's achievements includes his inventions, serious injury and subsequent redirection, geological findings in Yosemite, his study of the redwoods, and Alaskan adventures. Finally, we see him becoming an activist for preservation of the national forests, his role in the Sierra Club, and the establishment of Muir Woods.
Comment: Reading the entire book would be more an adult than a student undertaking, but reading portions of it could help a young reader to understand the genuis of a man who contributed much to California and to learning in general. The Muir sketches add to the interest. Appendix A gives advice "On Reading John Muir," and Appendix B advises "On Reading About John Muir."
Nonfiction: junior high–adult

Clifford, Eth. **GROUND AFIRE: THE STORY OF DEATH VALLEY.** Nature-Adventure Books. Chicago: Follett, 1962. 32 p. Photos by Ansel Adams, glossary.

Content: This Nature-Adventure book with color photos from *Arizona Highways* starts with a description of topography, the Shoshone Indian inhabitants, and the wildlife of the region. The author tells of Jayhawkers and families traversing the valley by wagon in the gold rush era, and finally of mineral wealth, prospecting in the area, and a geological description.
Comment: The text is very simply written and has large print. Reluctant readers in intermediate classes could readily use the

book to gain information on an interesting area and the history of California.
Nonfiction: primary–intermediate

Coerr, Eleanor. **THE BELL RINGER AND THE PIRATES.** New York: Harper & Row, 1983. 64 p. Color pictures by Joan Sandin.

Content: Pio, an Ahachmai Indian boy at Mission San Juan Capistrano, is worried about the pirates seen along the California coast. Later, while tending the sheep Pio hears the alarm that the pirates are on their way. He helps the padres and his parents pack up the valuables so all can hide in the hills but cannot bring himself to leave the mission. He is there when the soldiers arrive, and watches for the pirates, but because of the overwhelming numbers of pirates, the soldiers retreat. Pio stays and is briefly held captive by the pirates, but he is able to ring the mission bells to warn his people, and later, to inform them that the danger has passed. The book is based on the true story of the 1818 pirate raid of General Hypolite Bouchard's men at San Juan Capistrano Mission, as explained in the author's note. **Comment** In simple language, this "I Can Read" book tells about the life of the Indians at the mission and recalls an exciting episode in history.
Fiction: primary

Comstock, Esther J. **VALLEJO AND THE FOUR FLAGS, A TRUE STORY OF EARLY CALIFORNIA.** Grass Valley, Calif.: Comstock Bonanza Press, 1979. 135 p. Colored Illus. by Floyd B. Comstock, bibliog., index.

Content: The author tells in simple language and narrative style the life of Mariano Guadelupe Vallejo. Each of the book's four parts tells of a period under a different flag. The Spanish flag flew over California until Vallejo was fourteen. When as a boy, he saw Monterey attacked by pirates under the Spanish reign, he realized that control by an absentee government was hard on California. Under the Mexican flag from 1822 until 1846, Vallejo grew into a well–established thirty-six-year-old. Vallejo and other Californios became restive, wanting more home rule. The Bear Flag which caused Vallejo misery for several weeks brought revolution right to his home in Sonoma. Finally the American Flag raised in 1846, remained the flag to which Vallejo was faithful until his death in 1890. In the telling of Vallejo's life the author describes other people like Sutter and Fremont, and also the mission period, Indian troubles and policies toward Indians, the gold rush, the constitutional convention—all are woven into the tale.

Comment: Vallejo is shown as an ambitious, principled man who took every opportunity to learn. Fremont, on the other hand, is a villain in the tale. An interesting note: Vallejo served as a state senator and as a city mayor after statehood and also headed the committee which divided the state into counties. The original number of counties was only twenty-seven!

Nonfiction: intermediate

Conklin, Gladys. **JOURNEY OF THE GRAY WHALES.** New York: Holiday House, 1974. 40 p. Illus. by Leonard Everett Fisher, glossary, index.

Content: The story describes the birthing and mating of the gray whale in Scammon's Lagoon in Baja California then the long migration up the coast of California to the Bering Sea. There, the whale will spend about nine months before heading back down the coast to Baja. On their way north the whales stop at a shallow harbor just below the Canadian border to rub their bodies on the gravelly bottom to rid themselves of lice and barnacles.

Comment: This is simply and clearly written natural history.

Nonfiction: primary–intermediate

Conrat, Maisie, and Richard Conrat. **EXECUTIVE ORDER 9066: THE INTERNMENT OF 110,000 JAPANESE AMERICANS.** Los Angeles: Anderson, Ritchie, and Simon, 1972. 120 p. Photos.

Content: The days following the Japanese attack on Pearl Harbor were dark ones for the American spirit. Unable to strike back effectively against the Japanese Empire, Americans in the western United States lashed out at fellow citizens and resident aliens of Japanese ancestry. "Executive Order 9066", signed by President Roosevelt on February 19, 1942 was the instrument that allowed military commanders to designate areas "from which any or all persons may be excluded." Under this order, all persons of Japanese ancestry were removed from the western-coastal regions to guarded camps in the interior.

Comment: Through photographs from the California Historical Society which express more succinctly than words, Maisie and Richard Conrat compiled this book documenting one of America's tragic errors.

Nonfiction: all ages

CRE   Cretan, Gladys Yessayan. **SUNDAY FOR SONA.** New York: Lothrop, Lee & Shepard, 1973. 32 p. Illus. by Barbara Flynn.

I m   **Content:** Sona lived in San Francisco in the 1930s and was happy and loved by her Armenian-American relatives. Sundays were special because the whole extended family gathered at Sona's house. A large problem comes into Sona's life when she becomes vitally interested in the sailboat being restored by the friendly uncle of her pal, Tommy. Sona's grandmother doesn't think working on a sailboat is a ladylike endeavor, and Grandmother's word is law. She doesn't absolutely forbid Sona to continue, but what will happen when she finds out Sona is invited to go on the maiden voyage as a member of the crew— on a **Sunday?** Grandmother's belated understanding brings a happy ending to the real conflict Sona is experiencing.

Comment: The historical significance of this book is slight, but it does give an insight into the customs and conflicts felt by second and third–generation ethnic minorities being reared in the California-American culture.

Fiction: primary–intermediate

Crump, Spencer. **CALIFORNIA'S SPANISH MISSIONS: THEIR YESTERDAYS AND TODAYS.** Corona del Mar, Calif.: Trans-Anglo Books, 1975. 95 p. Sketches, maps, photos, bibliog., index.

Content: Starting with the times before mission days, the author describes Indian cultures and the contrasts between them and white cultures. He tells of the founding, flowering, and decline of the missions, and writes also of the preservation of the missions and the whole system in retrospect. Information is provided on each of the missions in the state. An excellent book for all, with an unusually complete picture of the entire mission era, and the political forces which led to the establishment of the missions.

Comment: Each chapter is short, concise, and well written, with all pertinent data presented in an uncomplicated manner. There are well-chosen photographs, sketches or maps on every page.

In the section on individual missions, there are sketches or photographs showing the original mission and the mission as it looks now. Though the author has presented a great deal of information, the result is not "crammed."

Nonfiction: intermediate–adult

Curry, Jane Louise, **DOWN FROM THE LONELY MOUNTAIN: CALIFORNIA INDIAN TALES.** New York: Harcourt, Brace, 1965. 128 p. Illus. by Enrico Arno.

Content: The first of the twelve tales tells of the beginning of the world and the making of California. Other tales explain the securing of light, dawn, fire and are traditional Indian legends.

Comment: The first tale would be of particular interest to the student studying California history. The other stories featuring Coyote, Fox, Mouse, would enrich the study of California Indians.

Fiction: intermediate

Dana, Richard Henry. **TWO YEARS BEFORE THE MAST.** 1840. Reprint. Cleveland: World, 1946. 415 p. Illus.

Content: A first-hand account of Dana's experience as a crew-man aboard the *Pilgrim,* sailing out of Boston in the 1830s around the Horn to California. The ship, on a two-year tour of duty, carried manufactured goods to trade for hides and tallow in California. Dana explains how the hides were prepared and brought out to the waiting ship. In one of the most extensive contemporary accounts by a non-Californio, he describes social customs and the pueblos of Los Angeles, San Francisco, and San Diego.

Comment: Dana expresses a very "Yankee" view of the people of California. While not unfriendly, it reflects a certain disapproval—common also to later American observers. Although generally considered an adult book, Dana's adventures can easily be read by interested students in junior high.

Nonfiction: junior high–adult

Deakin, Edwin. **A GALLERY OF CALIFORNIA MISSION PAINTINGS.** Edited by Ruth I. Mahood. Los Angeles: World Ritchie Press, 1967. 59 p. Illus.

Content: In addition to the mission studies, there is general information on California missions and on the artist, Edwin Deakin. The very simple and clear text enriches the beautiful paintings. There is a separate entry for each of the twenty-one missions. Produced by the staff of the History Division, Los Angeles County Museum of Natural History.

Comment: This book would complement nicely Helen Bauer's *California Mission Days* for classroom use.

Nonfiction: intermediate–adult

Degnan, Laurence, and Douglass Hubbard. **THE OLD STAGE DRIVER'S YOSEMITE YARNS.** Fresno, Calif.: Awani Press, 1961. 24 p.

Content: In folksy dialect, the authors tell twenty-four anecdotes reflecting the local color of Yosemite. Places mentioned include Wawona Road, Chinquapin, Half Dome, Glacier Point, Mariposa Big Trees, Bridalveil Meadow, Nevada Falls, Sonora, and Sentinel Bridge. There are stories about Galen Clark, Teddy Roosevelt, John Muir, George Anderson, Charley Leidig, John Degnan, Martin Sheehan, Leonidas Whorton, Nathan Phillips, Henry Frost, Johnny Brown, Hank Williams, John Lembert, George Ezra Benson, and Paiute George. The years covered are 1872 to 1910.

Comment: This is a collection of informal recollections of the

Yosemite area in the 1800s. It could provide local color to a study of California history and/or its national parks.
Nonfiction: intermediate-adult

Delgado, James P. **ALCATRAZ ISLAND: THE STORY BEHIND THE SCENERY.** The Story Behind the Scenery Series. Las Vegas, Nev.: KC Publications, 1985. 48 p. Color photos by Jeff Gnass.

Content: The text and pictures tell the history of Alcatraz, from its discovery in 1775 to its present day status as part of Golden Gate National Recreation Area. Of particular interest: the Alcatraz light has served as an aid to navigation since 1854; Alcatraz was used as a defense outpost for many years, most notably during the Civil War; it was a military prison from Civil War days until 1933 and a federal prison from 1934 to 1963; Alcatraz opened to the public in 1973 as part of the national recreation area.

Comment: Though this handsome soft-cover booklet was not written for students, capable readers from ages eleven and up could well use it. Younger readers, too, could benefit from the very fine color photographs and clear captions. There is no table of contents. The book is part of a series from KC Publications on park areas. Other "Stories Behind the Scenery" books of interest to Californians are *Channel Islands* (see title index), *Death Valley, Death Valley's Scotty's Castle, Sequoia-Kings Canyon,* and *Yosemite.* Many of these titles deal more with natural history than people and events.
Nonfiction: upper intermediate–adult

Delgado, James P., and Christopher C. Wade. **HOW CALIFORNIA ADOBES WERE BUILT IN THE 1830's: A SIMPLE GUIDE TO A LOST ART.** San Jose, Calif.: Smith-McKay, 1973. 9 p. Illus., bibliog.

Content: The few pages tell what adobe means and how adobe bricks are made. It describes how the foundations and walls of adobe structures are built and kinds of roofs used. Then it tells how to finish an adobe building. This simply written booklet contains much information of interest for a young reader learning about early California structures. Using it as a guide, students could construct a model of an early mission.

Comment: You'll have to find this in a library or through a friend as it's out-of-print.

Nonfiction: Intermediate.

Demarest, Donald. **THE FIRST CALIFORNIAN: THE STORY OF FRAY JUNIPERO SERRA.** New York: Hawthorne Books, 1963. 188 p. B/w illus., index, bibliog.

Content: A biography of Father Serra written for young people. Since the author had access to several critical biographies of Serra, his main task was to tell Serra's story so that students would be able to appreciate and be inspired by what Serra accomplished against great odds—human, geographical, and bureaucratic!

Comment: The stated reason for writing this book ". . . that there are few entirely adequate books about Fray Junipero Serra for young people . . .", in view of the wealth of material on Serra, has resulted in an easily read but not simplistically written biography. This would undoubtedly be the book of choice, over the biography by Wise, for intermediate and many junior high students as well, because of larger print and an easier writing style.

Nonfiction: intermediate–junior high

de Vries, Carolyn. **GRAND AND ANCIENT FOREST: THE STORY OF ANDREW P. HILL AND THE BIG BASIN REDWOOD STATE PARK.** Santa Cruz, Calif.: Western Tanager Press, 1978. 100 p. Illus., index.

Content: Andrew Hill was a talented artist and photographer, but even more important, a man of vision and the main force behind the creation of the beautiful Big Basin Redwoods State Park near Felton and Santa Cruz. Hill first became enamored of the magnificent sequoias soon after his arrival in California in 1867. Eventually he was to devote a large portion of his time and energies to their preservation. This book is the story of

Hill's life and the struggle of a dedicated group of people, who later founded the Sempervirens Club, to keep the loggers out of the few remaining virgin redwood forests in our state.

Comment: The publication of *Grand and Ancient Forest* coincided with the fiftieth anniversary of the establishment of the California State Parks Department. The book provides a glimpse into how one state park, in particular, was saved for the enjoyment of all—past, present, and future.

Nonfiction: Intermediate–adult

Dines, Glen. **GOLDEN CITIES, GOLDEN SHIPS.** New York: Mc-Graw-Hill, 1968. 48 p. Illus. and maps by the author.

Content: The book includes three separate stories of the Spanish explorers who came to the Pacific Coast from Mexico in the period between 1542 and 1770 including Cabrillo, Ferrelo, Vizcaino, Portola, and Ayala. Most were commissioned to find a passageway from the Pacific to the Atlantic but found instead good harbors at San Diego, Monterey, and San Francisco. The Spanish dream of a passageway did not come true, but in finding California they had access to a golden territory of another type.

Comment: This is a good book divided into three parts which can be read independently. The illustrations are interesting, and there are many dramatic moments related in the text. It can easily be further subdivided and used as a basis for art or dramatic projects in classroom or youth-group activities. The use of too many characters in each story often confuses one who wants to follow the progress of each explorer.

Nonfiction: intermediate

Dolan, Edward F., Jr. **DISASTER 1906—THE SAN FRANCISCO EARTHQUAKE AND FIRE.** New York: Julian Messner, 1967. 192 p. B/w photos, maps, index. bibliog.

Content: Describes what happened to San Francisco after the earthquake, including a north to south tracing of the earthquake line all down the San Andreas Fault with a brief explanation of how quakes happen and their effects. Along with the "blow-by-blow" account of the after-quake fires' progress are vignettes of what else was going on in the city, what officials were doing to alleviate the disaster, and how survivors and refugees were coping.

Comment: Mr. Dolan's style lends a sense of immediacy to the story of the 1906 earthquake and fire, and is quite readable even if the story is familiar. A number of small maps appropriately placed in the text make clear the extent of the fire.

Nonfiction: Senior high–adult

Donley, Michael W., *et al.* **ATLAS OF CALIFORNIA.** Culver City, Calif.: Pacific Book Center, 1979. 173 p. Color illus., gazetteer, index.

Content: This large book is divided into four main sections; the first, "The Human Imprint," contains most of the historical data. Historic maps, Indian groups and lands, mission information, land grants, gold rush districts, evolution of county and large city boundaries, and population growth are among the historical subjects. The other three sections deal with "Economic Patterns," "The Physical Environment," and "Reference."

Comment: This is an irresistible reference book. It has so much information on California's yesterdays and present. Teachers and students could well spend hours browsing through it although, of course, much particular information could be found when needed. The text is clearly written.

Nonfiction: upper intermediate–senior high

Douglas, William O. **MUIR OF THE MOUNTAINS.** Boston: Houghton Mifflin, 1961. 179 p. Illus. by Harve Stein, index.

Content: (Of this book and Silverberg's *John Muir: Prophet Among the Glaciers* and Swift's *From the Eagle's Wing, A Biography of John Muir.*)

All three of these detail the life of John Muir, "The Father of our National Park System," from his birth in Scotland in 1838 to his death in 1914. Muir's travels, which eventually led him to the Yosemite Valley, his marriage to Louise Wanda Strenzel, descriptions of the ranch in Contra Costa County, his publications, and travels to Alaska to see the glaciers—this information and more is covered. Muir's own words are often quoted to convey his feelings about the mountains, glaciers, trees, birds, and animals which he loved so much and fought to save for future generations. John Muir was one of the founders of the Sierra Club which continues to espouse his conservationist views.

Comment: All three biographies are commendable, but *Muir of the Mountains* by Douglas and *John Muir: Prophet Among the Glaciers* by Silverberg would appeal more to young readers than *From the Eagle's Wing* by Swift which is a bit too scholarly. Swift concentrates on Muir's publications and on numerous persons, places, and events which were part of his life using curiously few dates. The adult reader, however, would get a great deal from her book.

Douglas, on the other hand, offers the young reader Muir's world as Muir himself saw it, frequently using Muir's own words, in passages which enable the reader to feel his sense of wonder when viewing Yosemite, the Sierra Nevada, or Alaskan glaciers. Douglas takes care to explain bits of information to his young reader, as when he explains "stool pigeon" while describing the millions of now extinct passenger pigeons that used to inhabit the country.

Author Silverberg makes use of Muir's own words and includes other facts as well. He has a way of encouraging the reader to delve further into the biography in order to find out what happens next.

Of the three books, Douglas' would appeal most to the reader who had not read Muir's *The Mountains of California*. Silverberg's would appeal to the reader who had but wanted a bit more information. Swift's would satisfy those who are interested in even greater depth. All three are informative and enjoyable. Muir published extensively during a life-long campaign to save our environment. Among his publications: *Cruise of the Corwin* (1918), *My First Summer in the Sierra* (1911), *Our National Parks* (1901), *Steep Trails* (1918), *Stickeen* (1909), *The Story of My Boyhood and Youth* (1913), *A Thousand Mile Walk to the Gulf* (1917), *Travels in Alaska* (1915), *The Yosemite* (1912)—all published by Houghton Mifflin. (See Muir entries for other publications.)

Nonfiction: intermediate–junior high

Dowdell, Dorothy, and Joseph Dowdell. **THE JAPANESE HELPED BUILD AMERICA.** New York: Julian Messner, 1970. 89 p. Illus. by Len Ebert, photos, index.

325.252D

Im

Content: In nine chapters the authors trace the history of the Japanese in America from the first settlement—the Wakamatsu Tea and Silk Farm Colony in northern California—to the post-World War II period and the rise in prominence of many Japanese-Americans. One chapter follows the story of an immigrant in the late 1800s; one tells of the problems of farming and prejudice in California. There is information on the Japanese bringing new farming techniques and on Japanese-American culture. The relocation camps of World War II are described. A list of outstanding Americans of Japanese ancestry is included. **Comment:** There is much valuable information in the book. Chapters One through Four and Chapter Eight deal most directly with the Japanese in California.
Nonfiction: intermediate

Dowdell, Dorothy, and Joseph Dowdell. **SIERRA NEVADA: THE GOLDEN BARRIER.** Indianapolis: Bobbs-Merrill, 1968. 176 p. Photos, maps, charts, bibliog., index.

979.4 D

Im

Content: After describing the geological formation of the Sierra Nevada and prehistoric Indian life, the authors tell about the first American explorers of the mountains—Jedediah Smith, Joseph Walker, John Fremont. Then they describe the wagon trains—the Bartleson–Bidwell Party of 1841, the Stephens Party of 1844, the Donner Party of 1846. The stagecoach lines and the building of the railroad are noted, then the water developments—Owens River Project, Hetch Hetchy, Central Valley Water Project, California Water Project. The book concludes with natural history—the life zones, the forests, information about John Muir, and the national parks. **Comment:** Each chapter starts with a dramatization; sometimes the transition from it to the factual narration is abrupt and confusing, but overall the presentation is informative and effective.
Nonfiction: intermediate

Duque, Sally. **CALIFORNIA'S FATHER SERRA.** Portland, Oreg.:
921 SERR Binford and Mort, 1958. 40 p. Pen and ink wash illus. by the
author.

Im **Content:** Young Miguel Jose Serra, known to the world as
Junipero Serra, grew up on the island of Majorca off the coast of
Spain, in the small town of Petra. An intelligent boy, he went to
study with the Franciscan padres in the nearby town of Palma.
After he was ordained, he was finally granted his wish to go to
the New World to work with the Indians. He served first in
Mexico City and the missions of Baja California; later, he came
to Alta California to found the first nine of the twenty-one
missions: San Diego, San Carlos, San Antonio de Padua, San
Gabriel, San Luis Obispo, San Francisco, San Juan Capistrano,
Santa Clara, and San Buenaventura. Born November 24, 1713,
Fr. Serra died August 28, 1784. Although hampered by an often-
painful leg for most of his adult life, Father Serra courageously
and tirelessly sought to care for his beloved Indians. He is
buried at Mission San Carlos in Carmel.
Comment: This simply-told and well-written story is by an
experienced fourth-grade teacher who knew exactly what
would appeal to young readers.
Nonfiction: intermediate

Dutton, Davis and Judy Dutton, eds. **TALES OF MONTEREY:
SINCE THE BEGINNING.** New York: Ballantine Books, 1974.
171 p. Photos.

Content: This is a delightful collection of tales, excerpts from
novels and other works, and even poems by those whose lives
were touched by Monterey, Carmel, and the coast of Big Sur—
from Richard Henry Dana and Robert Louis Stevenson to Mary
Austin and George Sterling of the Carmel bohemia to Robinson
Jeffers, John Steinbeck, and Henry Miller. The editors introduce the area and explain important dates and names of the
Monterey coast. They also provide a brief, thorough biography
of each writer prior to the excerpt or entry. The photos are from
the collection of the Bancroft Library, University of California.
Comment: This often-nostalgic book has a great deal of charm,

and perceptive young readers will be made aware of the enchantment the area has had for so many people.
Nonfiction: senior high–adult

Ellis, Ella Thorp. **SLEEPWALKER'S MOON.** New York: Atheneum, 1980. 234 p.

Content: In 1942 when fourteen-year-old Anna's father went off to war, she came to live with the Raymond family in a small agricultural town near San Luis Obispo. Anna had spent summers there for years and yearned to be a "real" member of the happy family. Fifteen-year-old Paula was the sister she always wanted, and she had rapport with quiet ten-year-old Roger, too. Hans Raymond, the volatile, overworked town doctor, was her idol. She also appreciated the loving concern of Rosamund, mother of the family. So everything should be perfect! But it wasn't. Anna was growing up, noticing and being noticed by boys. Hans was more strict than her father had ever been, and Anna felt she was competing for the quality of love the family had for Paula. Anna was miserable and ecstatic by turns as she struggled with her adolescent sexuality. The day she got to ride around in the army tank selling war bonds was a high point. Realizing she really didn't know the soldier, Jimmy, when news came of his death in the Pacific was a low point.

With supporting love and budding maturity, and a great deal of confusion and pain, Anna starts making decisions about her life.
Comment: The 1942 setting in small-town California is accurately portrayed.
Fiction: junior high

Engle, Paul. **GOLDEN CHILD.** New York: E. P. Dutton, 1962. 127 p. Illus. by Leonard Everett Fisher.

Content: The story of a family who struggles out of the Sierra Nevada on foot, arriving at Sutter's Fort on Christmas Eve in time for their second child to be born, and how this affects the miners at the fort.
Comment: This was originally written as an opera libretto, and

it often reads as such. The story, a pseudo-Nativity, is rather dull and has an unrealistic plot. Even Fisher's illustrations seem dull.

Fiction: intermediate

Epstein, Sam, and Beryl Epstein. **THE SACRAMENTO: GOLDEN RIVER OF CALIFORNIA.** Champaign, Ill: Garrard, 1968. 99 p. Maps by Fred Kleim, photos, glossary, index.

Content: The eight chapters concern different aspects of this region's history and geography, particularly the Indians, explorers, discovery of gold and the gold rush, Sutter's empire, and the development of agriculture.

Comment: This is a good reference book for young readers who want to acquire specific information or who are writing reports. The book also lends itself to dramatizations. The glossary and index are helpful, the reading level sensible, and the makeup of the book attractive.

Nonfiction: intermediate

Erdman, Loula Grace. **A BLUEBIRD WILL DO.** New York: Dodd, Mead, 1973. 210 p.

Content: Pretty, sixteen-year-old Nancy Sullivan is orphaned in San Francisco with adequate gold, but some menacing and bewildering happenings are threatening her. The memory of the trip to the gold rush country and the tragedies of her parents' deaths are still fresh in her mind, and it seems wisest to go back to Aunt Matilda in New Orleans. Helped by some miner friends, Nancy boards the *Mary Pearl* and starts around the Horn. She becomes friends with the Porter family, but soon realizes that the menace she feared in San Francisco has come along with her. Nancy leaves the ship at Panama and makes her way with the Porters to New Orleans, only to find that Aunt Matilda has moved. The Porter family rallies round, and she plans her future with them.

Comment: This light novel does give some indication of living conditions in forty-niner days and the real hardships of traveling to and from California in the mid 1800s. The author's note at the end gives interesting supplemental information about the story. Recommended by the Association of Children's Librarians.

Fiction: intermediate–junior high

Evansen, Virginia Besaw. **NANCY KELSEY.** New York: David McKay, 1965. 238 p. Decorations by Paul Lantz.

Content: This is the story of a seventeen-year-old wife and mother who walked across the Sierra Nevada in 1841 carrying her baby. She was often frightened, hungry, and cold. Water was scarce, food more so, but she kept going following her husband, Ben. They went along the Platte River in their wagon, down the Bear River, across the blistering salt desert, and over high ridges into Nevada. There they had to abandon their wagon and began to walk along the acrid waters of the Humboldt, over the towering mountains into California, eventually settling in what is now Lake County. Nancy Kelsey was the first woman to make the long and terrible trek across the Sierra Nevada.

Comment: Obviously Nancy's spirit and determination would inspire young readers. Classified as fiction because dialogue has been included, the story's conversations are very believable and help make the story most enjoyable.

Fiction: junior high–senior high

Evansen, Virginia Besaw. **SIERRA SUMMIT.** New York: David McKay, 1967. 245 p. Decorations by Allen Thomas. bibliog.

Content: This is the story of the first successful crossing of the western mountains into California by wagons. The Stephens-Murphy party started from Missouri in March 1844 and arrived in California in December. The viewpoint is that of seventeen-year-old Moses Schallenberger, whose experiences matured him into manhood. Moses had thought the trip would be a lark, but he had reckoned without the dust and thirst, the fear of Indians, the agonizing difficulties of moving wagons across rivers and mountains, the responsibility of securing food, and of remaining behind to guard the wagons.

Comment: Moses Schallenberger eventually settled in San Jose, and became an important figure in California history. His story should be an inspiration to young people today.
Fiction: junior high

Evarts, Hal G. **JEDEDIAH SMITH.** New York: G. P. Putnam's Sons, 1958. 192 p. Pen and ink sketches by Bernard Krigstein.

Content: This is a fictionalized account of the life of Jedediah Smith, but, according to the author, ". . . as historically accurate as I could make it after much research." Smith, one of the mountain men, played an important role in the early nineteenth century history of California and led the first party of Americans overland to California in 1826.
Comment: The mountain men are endlessly fascinating to intermediate grade students.
Fiction: intermediate

Evarts, Hal G. **JIM CLYMAN.** New York: G. P. Putnam's Sons, 1959. 191 p.

Content: Clyman was the mountain man who brought James Marshall, the discoverer of gold, to Sutter's Fort in 1845. A poem written by Clyman is quoted from *James Clyman: American Frontiersman* by permission of the California Historical Society.
Comment: This fictionalized biography is a well-researched account.
Fiction: intermediate

Evarts, Hal G. **THE PEGLEG MYSTERY.** New York: Charles Scribner's Sons, 1972, 189 p.

Content: Two high school students seeking information for a school report excavate a portion of an Indian site on the California desert. Unexpectedly, they unearth a skeleton with a peg leg. In trying to find out the identity of their discovery, the students learn about a legend of lost gold treasure, and two peglegged men—Thomas "Pegleg" Smith, discoverer of the

West's most famous "lost" gold lode and El Cojo, a hero of the
Mexican Revolution of 1911.

Comment: This fast paced story vividly depicts the desert
setting. There is some history mixed with the fiction.

Fiction: intermediate–junior high

Ewing, Belle C. WHEN CALIFORNIA WAS YOUNG. Dallas: Banks
Upshaw, 1955. 243 p. Drawings by Laurence Read, glossary,
bibliog., index.

Content: Beginning with Indian life and legend, the book moves
on to Spanish settlement and the missions. The De Anza
Expedition which brought settlers leads into a description of the
first pueblos, presidios, and rancho life. Then the coming of the
adventurers is described—Jedediah Smith, Kit Carson, John
Fremont, John Bidwell, and also the Mormons. The importance
of John Sutter, as well as the Russian settlement at Fort Ross, is
included. There is information on the natural wealth of the
state; the different flags which have flown over it; the pony
express and the building of the railroad; and a geographic
overview of modern California is included. The final unit gives
dramatizations of early California history.

Comment: There is a summary at the end of each of the twenty-
four chapters, questions at the end of each of the seven units,
and suggestions for the teacher. Spanish and Indian words are
noted. Also included is a list of the missions and the dates of
their founding. The text is in narrative form, as a history told to
Nancy and Bob by an old Californio, Juan Del Rio. Interesting
inclusions are the story of the bridge at Bidwell Bar, the history
of the oldest orange tree, and the many uses of cattle.

Nonfiction: intermediate

Ewing, Norris. **TRAINS, TRACKS AND TRAILS: HOW THE
RAILROADS REACHED THE WEST.** Menlo Park, Calif.:
Lane Publishing Co., 1964. 64 p. B/w illus., glossary, bibliog.,
index.

Content: This is the story not only of how the Western Pacific and Union Pacific Transcontinental reached the West, but also how the other western railroads were built.

Comment: Even though this is a fairly "bare-bones" account, enough details are included to give a picture of the methods, difficulties, and effects of the westward movement of the railroads. The illustrations are plentiful, including many in the page borders that show details of railroad engines, cars and other equipment.

Nonfiction: intermediate–junior high

Falk, Elsa. **THE BORROWED CANOE: A STORY OF THE HUPA INDIANS OF NORTHERN CALIFORNIA.** Los Angeles: Ward Richie Press, 1969. 47 p. Color illus. by the author.

Content: Miskut had to learn to paddle a canoe and catch salmon before he could be included in the men's activities. When he decided to teach himself to paddle, he damaged his father's canoe, but was successful in trapping a salmon. He goes with his father to get a new canoe; he learns to paddle, and he is told he may join the men and other boys in a ritual dance.

Comment: A simple story to show what a boy must know in one Indian tribe to begin to grow up. ACL does not recommend this book because it doesn't convey the "complex vitality" of real Hupa people. Some facts are given in the text, and the illustrations show others—the inside of a dwelling, for instance. This could be a read-aloud to younger children.

Fiction: upper primary–beginning elementary

Felton, Harold W. **EDWARD ROSE: NEGRO TRAIL BLAZER.** New York: Dodd, Mead, 1967. 111 p. Photos, prints, maps, bibliog., index.

Content: Edward Rose, a tall black man with a scarred face, never mentioned in history texts, figured in almost every major activity associated with the early West. He was a trapper, guide, interpreter, Crow Indian leader, trailblazer, and treaty maker. He worked with such figures as William Ashley, Jim Bridger, Hugh Glass, Zenas Leonard and Ezekiel Williams. His knowledge of the rugged country, his skill with the Indians, and his expertise with a rifle made him an invaluable member of many expeditions.

Comment: This fast-moving story holds the attention and is interesting and informative reading for intermediate or higher-level readers.

Nonfiction: intermediate–junior high

Felton, Harold W. **JIM BECKWOURTH, NEGRO MOUNTAIN MAN.** New York: Dodd, Mead, 1966. 173 p. B/w illus., bibliog., index.

Place, Marian T. **MOUNTAIN MAN–THE LIFE OF JIM BECK-WOURTH.** New York: Macmillan, 1970. 120 p. B/w illus., bibliog., Index.

Content: Both of these books are based on Beckwourth's own account of his life published in 1856. Both tell many of the same stories although some details are included in one book and not the other, and Place's book uses more of Beckwourth's own words.

Comment: Although Beckwourth is often mentioned in connection with California history, most of his life was spent elsewhere. The amount of time he lived in California doesn't seem to be historically significant except for the discovery of the Sierra Nevada pass that bears his name. Both of these books treat this part of his life in a rather off-hand manner without much detail. Beckwourth's story could be read as an example of the kind of men who helped open up the West, including California, to later settlers. Place's book is easier to read for the younger student. Felton's book has photos and prints of the period and maps.

Nonfiction: intermediate–junior high

Fink, Augusta. **TO TOUCH THE SKY.** San Carlos, Calif.: Golden Gate Junior Books, 1971. 100 p. Map, glossary.

Content: This action–filled novel is the story of fourteen-year-old Cristobal's attempt to acquire Rancho Bernicita near the pueblo of Los Angeles, his rightful inheritance. Mexican rule has just been abolished, and corrupt politicians prevail. Cristo-

bal is befriended by Mactutu, an Indian whose people have been victimized both by politicians and by well-meaning padres. Mactutu teaches Cristobal the concept that there is more to land than the mere ownership of it.
Comment: Cristobal has a good many adventures during this quest. Life of the period in southern California is interestingly described.
Fiction: intermediate

Fisher, Anne B. **STORIES CALIFORNIA INDIANS TOLD.** Berkeley, Calif.: Parnassus Press, 1957. 110 p. Map and illus. by Ruth Robbins.

Content: These twelve authentic myths told to members of various Indian tribes by their storytellers include those on how California was made; the cause of earthquakes; how salmon became plentiful in the Klamath River; and why women talk more than men. A map shows the location of each tribe mentioned.
Comment: This is a great book for oral reading, for dramatizations, for mural making. I've read a story a day to fourth-graders, and they have used the ideas in numerous projects. Many children check out the book from the library. The illustrations are whimsical and colorful.
Fiction: intermediate

Fisher, Anne B. **THE STORY OF CALIFORNIA'S CONSTITUTION AND LAWS.** Palo Alto, Calif.: Pacific Books, 1962. 154 p. Illus. by Patricia Talbot, bibliog.

Content: After the gold rush, the need for law and order caused the calling of a constitutional convention in Monterey. This books tells of the work and social events of the convention, the signing of the constitution, and our first legislature. The fight over the location of the capital and the time of the vigilantes is also included along with information on the pony express, Judah's work for a railroad, and the building of the transcontinental railroad. Denis Kearney and the Working Men's Party lead to the call for a new constitution in 1879. The power of the railroads and water rights problems are discussed, as are

Mulholland, the Owens Valley, and the need for water for Los Angeles. Hiram Johnson's freeing the state from railroad control and the introduction of the initiative, recall, and referendum to government leads to a review of our first-hundred years as a state. The book ends with a chapter on citizenship and state officials.

Comment: The book is more readable than its title would indicate. However, it starts out very promisingly and then degenerates in style. Fisher has a penchant for such phrasing as, "Crash! Bang! Down went the trees from the forests for railroad ties!" Valuable information is included, but the reader must be aware that some is dated. According to the text, a state assemblyman earns $3,600 a year!

There are suggestions of "Things to Do" in connection with each chapter.

Nonfiction: intermediate

Fleischman, Sid. **BY THE GREAT HORN SPOON!** Boston: Little, Brown, 1963. 193 p. Line drawings by Eric von Schmidt. (published in paperback by Avon in 1967 as **BULLWHIP GRIFFIN**).

Content: This is a delightful gold-rush story featuring an unemployed butler, Praiseworthy, and the young man of the family of his former employers, Jack Flagg. They set off from Boston to recoup the family fortune in the gold fields. Their misadventures start when someone steals their ship tickets, and they are forced to stow away. The ever-resourceful, and impeccably-mannered Praiseworthy manages to find the thief and solve both an economic crisis and a mystery before San Francisco is sighted. The fast-paced action goes on to the gold country and an eventual happy ending.

Comment: Some real history is mixed with a Mark Twain type humor to produce a very readable tale. The Association of Children's Librarians recommended it, too.

Fiction: intermediate

Fleischman, Sid. **MR. MYSTERIOUS & CO.** Boston: Little, Brown, 1962. 152 p. Illus. by Eric von Schmidt.

Content: "Mr. Mysterious & Co." are really Mr. and Mrs. Andrew Hackett and children, heading for California in a covered wagon in 1884. Their magic shows and roadside adventures fill the story with fun. Their slogan is "San Diego for Christmas," and neither outlaws nor a lazy cow can deter them. **Comment:** Underneath Fleischman's zany yarn, the reader catches something of pioneer needs and worries as the family moves west. The Association of Children's Librarians liked this one, too.
Fiction: intermediate

Flory, Jane. **THE GOLDEN VENTURE.** Boston: Houghton Mifflin, 1976. 232 p. Illus.

Content: Minnie Weldon and her father lived in St. Joseph, Missouri, under the good, but strict, care of Aunt Addie. In order to earn enough money for two households—one for the hard-to-live-with Addie and another for himself, Minnie, and possibly a new wife—Pierce Weldon decides to join the rush to California. Minnie just can't stay behind, so she stows away in Pa's wagon and endures the long, hard journey to San Francisco. There she stays with Mrs. Stanhope and her daughters while Pa goes off to the goldfields.
Comment: The demand for services, the scarcity of necessities, the lawlessness of early San Francisco are central to the plot. The charming illustrations are not credited but add to the story. The Association of Children's Librarians recommend it.
Fiction: intermediate

Flower, Enola. **A CHILD'S HISTORY OF CALIFORNIA.** 1940. Rev. Ed. Caldwell, Idaho: Caxton Printers, 1964. 192 p. B/w photos, maps, bibliog., index.

Content: The text covers California history from days before Spanish discovery and settlement to the mid-1950s. In very simple language the author gives information about basic history such as early Indian life, the mission days of the late 1700s, and the changing of flags from Spanish to Mexican to the Star Spangled Banner in the 1800s.
Comment: First written in 1940 to be used as a school text, this

dated book still has something to offer the third to fifth grade reader—short chapters, questions and answers about each chapter at the back of the book, listings of Spanish and Indian words in use today, an attempt to involve the young reader, a chance for students of today to see pictures and description of "modern" California in the 1940s and 1950s. The attitude toward Indians demands an explanation to today's readers. It is often patronizing and condescending. There is no attempt to explain Indian actions from their cultural viewpoint.

Nonfiction: intermediate

Foltz, Mary Jane. **AWANI.** New York: William Morrow, 1964. 128 p. Illus. by Mel Silverman.

Content: Awani, an Indian boy from the Awani (Ahwanee) Valley, has come for the first time to the coast for the yearly trade of goods. On the return trip, Awani's parents are killed by a grizzly, and he is adopted by a Miwok tribe in the Point Reyes area. His struggle for acceptance, pitted against the village shaman who fears him, is finally victorious when it is he, Awani, who leads the others to the "ship of the gods"—Drake's *Golden Hind*.

Comment: This simple tale is fast paced and well told. The author weaves in Indian lore and a memorable account of one early European foray into California.

Fiction: primary–intermediate

Foltz, Mary Jane. **GABRIEL OF MISSION SAN JUAN CAPIS-TRANO.** Fresno, Calif.: Valley Publishers, 1979.

Content: Gabriel, a young Indian neophyte, has to come to terms with the conflict between what the padre tells him to do and what he wants to do.

Comment: This story, now out-of-print, shows what life might have been like at the seventh mission established in upper California.

Fiction: intermediate

Foltz, Mary Jane. **NICOLAU'S PRIZE.** New York: McGraw-Hill, 1967. 99 p. Illus. by Brinton Turkle.

Content: Set in 1870 at Pigeon Point, 50 miles south of San Francisco, the story centers on Nicolau, a recent Portuguese immigrant from the Azores. Nicolau, who works with his family in the whaling industry, is having trouble learning English and getting over homesickness; he is aware that his schoolmates object to the smell of whale blubber that clings to him. Nicolau's salvaging of an elegant carriage helps gain him acceptance, as does a school field trip to view whalers at work.

Comment: This short and easy-to-read story furthers understanding of immigrants' problems and of one of the early California industries. The Association of Children's Librarians recommends it with the reservation that the history is better than its literary quality.

Fiction: primary–intermediate

Forbes, Jack. **NATIVE AMERICANS OF CALIFORNIA AND NEVADA.** Happy Camp, Calif.: Naturegraph Publishers, 1982. 196 p. B/w photos, guide to resources and further reading, chart, appendix, index

Content: Six basic sections in addition to an introduction cover the significance of Indians and their heritage, their evolution in California and Nevada, the conquest by Spanish, Mexicans, and Americans, Indian awakening, concepts for understanding Indian history and culture, and a multicultural approach in Indian education. Each section has subheadings showing the specific topics addressed.

Comment: Though this book is definitely adult in approach, it contains such significant and little-known information that it is an important reference source for anyone learning about the Indian population of California. The author refers to both the Spanish and the American California settlements as invasions and conquests. He records from the Indian perspective and says, "The Indian experience in the Far West since 1769 has been an especially ugly one. The author has made no effort . . . to 'tone down' or soften the often harsh realities of native history."

Nonfiction: senior high–adult

THE FORTY-NINERS, by the editors of Time-Life, Inc. Text by William Weber Johnson. New York. Time-Life Books, 1976. 233 p. Color photos and paintings, bibliog., index.

Content: Divided into six sections, the text fully details events and people important to the gold rush. The book tells of Marshall and Sutter, the ordeals of coming to California, the destruction of the land caused by the mining in interesting detail. It also explains well many small, interesting points— what "seeing the elephant" meant, the importance of the general store in each community, and what E Clampus Vitus is. **Comment:** The text is complete and rich, but the illustrations are even better. The paintings and photographs provide a graphic history of the gold-rush period and can be instructive to readers of all ages. The book is highly quotable: "There was something about the gold rush that seemed to render rational considerations and careful planning and orderly organization null and void." Or, on what it was like to find gold, "Eureka! Oh how my heart beat! I sat still and looked at it some minutes before I touched it . . . When my eyes were sufficiently feasted, I scooped it out . . ."
Nonfiction: junior high–adult

Fradin, Dennis B. **CALIFORNIA IN WORDS AND PICTURES.** Chicago: Childrens Press, 1977. 44 p. Photos, index.

Content: This simple book about the history of California from its early beginnings to the crowded cities of today also includes listings of "Facts about California" and "Chronological Dates of California History." The geographical parts of the state and their rich products are described. The book also mentions some interesting historical characters such as Black Bart, Rattle-snake Dick, and Three-fingered Jack. **Comment:** The beautiful photographs add a great deal to this simplified history.
Nonfiction: primary–intermediate

Franchere, Ruth. **JACK LONDON: THE PURSUIT OF A DREAM.**

New York: Thomas Y. Crowell, 1962. 264 p. Photos, bibliog., index.

Content: An easily read, partial biography of Jack London from the age of seventeen to twenty-seven, when *Call of the Wild* was published and he became an established author. Those ten years were filled with poverty, discouragement, determination, and ambition.

Comment: London's daughter, Joan, shared memories, pictures, and other information with the author. The bibliography consists of secondary material including a book by London's daughter and one by his wife.

Nonfiction: junior high–adult

Fritz, Jean. **SAN FRANCISCO.** Chicago: Rand McNally, 1962. 128 p. Illus. by Emil Weiss, maps, index.

Content: Fritz starts by describing San Francisco—"A City of Magic"—and then goes back to give an overview of the city from 1769 to post–World War II. Then there are chapters on the areas of the city: Fleishhacker Zoo to the Wharf; Embarcadero to Rincon Annex to Candlestick; Twin Peaks to the Mission and Market Street to Golden Gate Park; the three hills—Telegraph, Russian and Nob; Chinatown and North Beach and Downtown. Montgomery and Market Streets get a chapter as does the 1906 quake. There is a concluding chapter on the new city from 1906 to the 1960s.

Comment: This is an informative and readable book that suffers from being dated. The format of encircling the city chapter by chapter would probably be best used with middle-grade students by coupling it with a large pictorial map of San Francisco. It's important to be aware that a student could read all about Chinatown without ever realizing he was learning about Americans.

Nonfiction: intermediate

Garthwaite, Marion. **COARSE GOLD GULCH.** New York: Doubleday, 1956. 217 p.

Content: Jonathan and his sister, Madie, arrive in San Francisco at the height of the gold rush. They had started with their mother and brothers from Vermont; all but Madie and Jonathan died crossing the Isthmus at Panama. Now the children were confidently planning to find their father, even though they knew little more than the name of the settlement where he had last been located, Coarse Gold Gluch. Befriended by the hearty Mr. Houlihan and bedeviled by the man in the yellow vest, the children have exciting adventures with Californios, Indians, and Chinese immigrants and eventually find their father.

Comment: A great deal of adventure is packed into these pages.

Fiction: intermediate

Garthwaite, Marion. **HOLDUP ON BOOTJACK HILL.** Garden City, N.Y.: Doubleday, 1959. 168 p. B/w illus. by Leo Summers.

Content: California (Callie) Dean is eleven years old in 1862 and lives in Hardpan, California. The only girl in a respected family of boys, she loves adventure and would love a friend her age. Unfortunately, the only nearby person her age is a boy who recently moved to town, Andy Jensen, and somehow they have become "sworn enemies." When a robbery occurs Callie and Andy find themselves working on the same side to defend the Indian, Winky Loosefoot. The week they work on proving Winky's innocence is full of adventure and the finding of new maturity.

Comment: Librarians say they keep a tight hold on Garthwaite's books, now out-of-print, because there just isn't that much well-written fiction which deals with California history. This tightly woven tale is an example. Its main historical contribution is good background on the prejudice confronting the Indian population in the post gold-rush era. Other than that, it's just a well–told tale!

Fiction: intermediate

Garthwaite, Marion. **SHAKEN DAYS.** New York: Julian Messner, 1952. 204 p. Illus. by Ursula Koering.

Content: Figuratively speaking, the "shaken days" are those that Megan Dyke lived through as her family uprooted from rural San Leandro to settle in the city of Oakland. They are shaken more literally by the 1906 earthquake.

Comment: This older book, now out of print, is worth looking for on library shelves. The main historical value of the book, besides its description of earthquake days, is the picture it gives of rural and urban life at the turn of the century. The problems of transportation and the consternation caused by the new automobile, middle-class life that includes a live–in maid, home-centered education and recreation—all are painted clearly in this pleasant story.

The author's style is somewhat uneven and some phrases are used without explanation which might mystify a young reader: "A white elephant," "a slobahonus," "bought for a song."

The Association of Children's Librarians recommended this book.

Fiction: intermediate

Gates, Doris. **BLUE WILLOW.** 1940. Reprint. New York: Viking, 1964. 172 p. Illus. by Ursula Koering.

Content: Janey Larkin is the daughter of an itinerant farm worker living in the San Joaquin Valley in the 1930s. Janey desperately wants a permanent home and settled friends. The one lovely thing Janey has is a blue willow plate. Janey's mother is sympathetic but also very busy washing, cooking, and cleaning for the family. At one point, Mr. Larkin finds work in a cotton field, and while living in a little shanty near the fields, Janey meets Lupe Romero and her family. The Romeros, Janey's teacher, the rent collector, and his boss all play important parts in Janey's life. After various hardships, the Larkins are happy at last when the blue willow plate is put in a place of honor in their new, permanent adobe home.

Comment: This tremendously interesting book, a Newbery honor book in 1941, should greatly broaden the horizon of any young reader. The author made each character come alive.

The Association of Children's Librarians liked it, too.

Fiction: intermediate

Gates, Doris. **THE ELDERBERRY BUSH.** New York: Viking, 1967. 160 p. Illus. by Lilian Obligado.

Content: This is a simple story of eight to ten year old girls who lived in the Santa Clara Valley during the early 1900s, and is written for a similar age group. The activities include a vacation at Santa Cruz, a Saturday shopping trip to San Jose, the last–day–of–school festivities, and a family Christmas.

Comment: Although this book could be read by a third-grader, it's pace and simplicity might not appeal to all. However, perceptive or mature readers would find it appealing, especially if they know the Santa Clara Valley. The Association of Children's Librarians recommended it.

Fiction: upper primary–intermediate

Gillespie, Charles B. **A MINER'S SUNDAY, FROM THE WRITER'S CALIFORNIA JOURNAL** 1849-50. Century, 1891. Reprint. Golden, Colo.: Outbooks, 1981. 16 p. B/w illus.

Content: "This story happens to be set in Coloma, the California gold discovery site of 1848. It might have happened in any of the gold-rush sites of the West . . . and it probably did, but only on Sunday." Thus does the author describe the gambling, drinking, and eating the one "elegant" meal of the week that seemed to be the main Sunday activities of the gold miners. Also included are two "Anecdotes of the Mines" by Hubert Burgess, one of which relates how claims were "salted" for prospective buyers, and the other, how indifferent men became to the ever-present violence in the mining communities.

Comment: There are great descriptions of the gambling games, and how the professional gamblers fleeced the miners, and one especially detailed account of how a young boy turned the tables on the dealer.

Nonfiction: senior high–adult

Goodman, Marian. **MISSIONS OF CALIFORNIA.** Redwood City, Calif.: Redwood City Tribune, 1962. 47 p. Illus. by the author.

Content: There is a separate entry with information about each mission.

Comment: Much information is available here which was not, in the past, found in mission histories for young people. The problems of mission life are documented. The padre at Soledad

dying of starvation, the clashes between Indians and Spanish soldiers, a mission father at San Luis Obispo charged with smuggling and then banished—these views of mission life can provide a contrast for young readers with the presentations of such authors as Helen Bauer and Helen Roberts.
Nonfiction: intermediate

Graves, Charles P. **JOHN MUIR.** New York: Thomas Y. Crowell, 1973. 40 p. Color illus. by Charles Levering.

Content: A short and simple-to-read biography of Muir.
Comment: "A simple, well–written portrayal of the naturalist and ecologist who led the fight for the conservation of America's forests . . . illustrations capture Muir's feelings for the beauty of the American wilderness." (School Library Journal)
Nonfiction: intermediate

Gray, Genevieve. **HOW FAR, FELIPE?** An I Can Read History Book. New York: Harper & Row, 1978. 64 p. Colored illus. by Ann Grifalconi.

Content: A small boy and his burro go on the de Anza expedition from northern Mexico overland to Alta California in 1775.
Comment: This short, simple story traces why families might have made this difficult, six-month trip to escape great poverty and the dangers encountered: unfriendly Indians, lack of food and water, death of pack animals until their eventual arrival at Misson San Gabriel. A final author's note adds that all but twelve of these families went on to found the pueblo of San Francisco and that the descendants of all these families live in California to this day.
Fiction: primary

Gudde, Erwin G. **1000 CALIFORNIA PLACE NAMES: THEIR ORIGIN AND MEANING.** 3d rev. ed. Berkeley, Calif.: University of California Press, 1969. 96 p.

Content: Ths soft-cover booklet is based on the second printing (1962) of the etymological-geographical dictionary, *California Place Names*. It lists, in alphabetical order, the meanings of

1000 place names in California. Foreign names are translated, and a brief biographical sketch is given when the place name was originally a person's. Not apparent from the title is the inclusion of commonly-used words which often are part of a place name or otherwise important to Californios: *adobe, alta, arroyo, redwood, estero.*

Comment: Who could resist looking up the names of familiar places to find out or check up on the reasons and meanings of their names? This would be of interest to anyone with California connections. It's a good reference book to have and could be used for a mini-history lesson and help in determining the origins of local place names.

Nonfiction: all ages

Hanna, Phil Townsend. **CALIFORNIA UNDER TWELVE FLAGS.** Revised by Anna Marie Hager. Los Angeles: The Automobile Club of Southern California, 1969. n.p. Illus.

Content: This title includes twelve one-page chapters with the opposing page showing the flag and a scene of the period. The flags are those of the Spanish Empire, England, the Spanish National Ensign, Russia, the Russian-American Company, a privateer, the Mexican Empire, the Mexican Republic, the Fremont Flag, the first Bear Flag, the American Flag of 1846, and the official Bear Flag.

Comment: The why and wherefore of each flag is simply explained. The colored illustrations are good, particularly the large flag shown in each chapter. There is a lot to be learned from this very small book.

Nonfiction: all ages

Hannau, Hans W. **CALIFORNIA IN COLOR.** New York: Doubleday, 1977. 127 p. Illus.

Content: Gives a very brief history of the state in sections of one to several paragraphs. Two sections cover northern California and southern California by cities, with descriptive text that runs from one short paragraph to several pages for San Francisco and Los Angeles. Other sections cover national parks and monuments, geology, plant and animal life, climate, economy, agriculture, manufacturing, labor, and population.

Comment: There are books giving the same information in a better-organized format. The colored photos are adequate, but, as in the text material, there is no logical arrangement.
Nonfiction: intermediate–adult

Harrison, C. William. **THE FIRST BOOK OF MODERN CALIFOR-NIA.** New York: Franklin Watts, 1965. 66 p. Photos, bibliog., index.

Content: Following a chapter on California statistics, "Varieties and Extremes," the author deals with exploration and early settlement. Then he gives information on the gold rush, the transcontinental railroad, oil, and migration west during the depression. Chapters are devoted to agriculture and water, commerce and industry, education and culture. Northern and southern California are each explained, and there is special coverage of San Francisco and the Bay Area.
Comment: This slim volume is jam-packed with information. Succinct paragraphs describe aspects of California from the freeway system to the attitudes of residents.
Nonfiction: intermediate

Harte, Bret. **THE LUCK OF ROARING CAMP AND OTHER TALES.** Great Illustrated Classics. New York: Dodd, Mead, 1961. 309 p. Brown and white illus. Photos of the author.

Content: twenty-three stories of Harte's are included. The plots of seven of these are summarized in the annotation for the title, *Tales of the Gold Rush.*
   The remaining titles in this edition are: "High-Water Mark," "A Lonely Ride," "The Man of No Account," "Mliss," "The Right Eye of the Commander," "Notes by Flood and Field," "The Mission Dolores," "John Chinaman," "From a Back Window," "Boonder," "Wan Lee, the Pagan," "Two Saints of the Foothills," "The Fool of Five Forks," "A Ghost of the Sierras," "My Friend the Tramp," and "The Office-Seeker."
Comment: Harte's stories are published in many different editions. For comment on the stories, see the annotation on *Tales of the Gold Rush.* The strengths of this collection are the inclusion of illustrations, pictures of the author, and clear,

good-sized print. Younger students would probably respond better to the shorter collection, *The Luck of Roaring Camp and Three Other Stories,* annotated below.
Fiction: junior high–adult

Harte, Bret. **THE LUCK OF ROARING CAMP AND THREE OTHER STORIES.** New York: Franklin Watts, 1968. 84 p. B/w illus. by Leonard Everett Fisher.

Content: This collection of Harte's stories includes "The Luck of Roaring Camp," "The Outcasts of Poker Flat," "Tennessee's Partner," and "The Idyl of Red Gulch"—all summarized below in the annotation of *Tales of the Gold Rush.*
Comment: The strengths of this collection of Harte's stories are the wonderful illustrations by Fisher, the clear, large print, and the slim volume itself—not intimidating for younger readers. For comments on the stories themselves, see the annotation under *Tales of the Gold Rush.* The Association of Children's Librarians recommended this, noting it is now out-of-print.
Fiction: Upper elementary-adult

Harte, Bret. **TALES OF THE GOLD RUSH.** New York: The Heritage Press, 1944. 223 p. Illus. by Fletcher Martin.

Content: This collection of Bret Harte's short stories contains thirteen tales. Summaries of the eleven found to be included in other Harte anthologies are printed below.
"The Luck of Roaring Camp." A baby is born to a prostitute, who succumbs shortly after childbirth, in an otherwise all male mining camp. Named Thomas (Tommy) Luck, he brings tenderness and love to a rough lot and begins the regeneration of a more civilized society. He and his male "nanny" die in a flood.
"The Outcasts of Poker Flat." Four no-goods, two male and two female, are exiled from Poker Flat. Caught on the road in a storm, they are befriended by an innocent, young couple. The freshness of youth and the couple's devotion bring out the best in three of the four exiles. The fourth deserts taking the mules, their only transportation. Finally, the young man is sent for help; all the rest die in the storm.
"Miggles." Seeking haven from a storm, soaked stagecoach

riders stop at the home of a beautiful, young recluse, Miggles. She lives with Jim (a mute, paralyzed, older man) a talking bird, and a tame, half-grown grizzly bear. Miggles, a former saloon owner, left society to care for Jim, who'd spent his money on her and then lost his health.

"Tennessee's Partner." This story is based on the friendship of an inarticulate man for his gambling, ne'er do well, partner, Tennessee. After the partner tries, unsuccessfully, to save Tennesse from being hanged, he pines away and joins his friend in death.

"Brown of Calaveras." Brown—a man weak with money, drink, and women—suddenly is joined by his gorgeous wife from the East. Suave gambler, Jack Hamlin, seeing her on the stagecoach before knowing she was the wife of a friend, is smitten. The clandestine love affair of Hamlin and Mrs. Brown ends when Hamlin values love for friend over love for woman.

"The Idyl of Red Gulch." Miss Mary, the prim schoolmistress, becomes the romantic idol of the drunken reprobate, Sandy. Reformed, he woos her with flowers and gentleness. As the school year ends and Miss Mary is about to leave, the "overdressed mother of a pupil whose paternity was doubtful" visits her. The mother begs Mary to take her son away from the rough mining camp to San Francisco, where he can have good schooling and the influence of a proper woman. The mother names the child's father as Sandy. The stricken Miss Mary takes the child and leaves for San Francisco.

"The Iliad of Sandy Bar." Scott and York, long-time partners and friends, part after a mysterious quarrel, becoming implacable enemies. They spend years destroying each other's efforts and reviling each other without ever divulging the reason for their estrangement. York returns from a long absence to find Scott dying and cares for him in his final week. Scott's last words are, "Old Man, thar *was* too much saleratus in that bread!"

"How Santa Claus Came to Simpson's Bar." Some rough miners carousing on Christmas Eve end up at the home of a sick boy, Johnny. In the middle of their revels they pause to listen as his father massages the boy's aching limbs, and the boy asks about Christmas and Santa Claus. The miners secretly hatch a plan, and their leader goes on a wild, midnight ride to the nearest town to bring back some toys for the sick Johnny.

"An Ingenue of the Sierras." The riders and driver of a stagecoach, fearful of being robbed by the notorious Ramon Martinez gang, get involved instead in the elopement of a beautiful, innocent, young girl. Helped by all, the girl meets and marries her lover, and they're sent off with their luggage. Only later do the helpers learn that the groom was Ramon Martinez, and the luggage contains his ill-gotten gains.

"A Protegee of Jack Hamlin's." Gambler Jack Hamlin saves a young girl who is considering suicide following a disastrous romance and then takes over her care and education. Gradually, the worldly Jack falls in love with her. A former amour of his turns out to be her sister, and he flees the scene.

Comment: Bret Harte is credited with developing the short story of local color mainly based on these tales of the gold rush. His stories abound in sentimental characters—besotted miners, heart-of-gold gamblers, fallen women with good instincts—and also reflect the racial tenor of the times: " 'And this yer's the cattle,' (speaking of, and to, a Chinese person), said the Colonel, . . . 'that some thinks oughter be allowed to testify agin a White Man! Git—you heathen!' " ("The Iliad of Sandy Bar".) "How Santa Claus Came to Simpson's Bar" contains a cruel joke directed at Chinese and in "An Ingenue of the Sierras," Harte has a character refer to "Greasers."

Though the vocabulary would certainly challenge many in junior high, the short-story form and direct story line, the action, and the humor would make most of the tales comprehensible to average or above young readers.

Harte weaves in some wonderfully descriptive language: "Meanwhile the shadows of the pine-trees had slowly swung around until they crossed the road, and their trunks barred the open meadow with gigantic parallels of black and yellow."

Bret Harte gained world renown as the chronicler of gold-rush life and humor. Students would gain understanding of the times and some literary appreciation, too, by reading or hearing these stories.

Harte's stories are available in many different collections with differing titles. Two other collections precede this one.
Fiction: junior high–adult

Haslam, Gerald W., and James D. Houston, eds., **CALIFORNIA HEARTLAND**. Santa Barbara, Calif: Capra Press, 1978. 224 p.

Content: This book written for adults describes the Great Central Valley through the words of residents and visitors from the eighteenth century to the 1970s. It quotes Yokut Indians, the mission priest Fray Juan Crespi, characters from *The Grapes of Wrath,* Mark Twain, John Muir, William Saroyan, and many others. (Adapted from *Sunset Magazine.)*
Comment: Selected quotes from this book could help students visualize California as others saw it long ago.
Nonfiction: upper intermediate–adult

Havighurst, Walter. **THE FIRST BOOK OF THE CALIFORNIA GOLD RUSH.** New York: Franklin Watts, 1962. 61 p. Color illus. by Harve Stein, maps, index.

Content: Traces the history of the discovery of gold in January 1848 until the end of the big returns, when the miners moved on to silver and gold discoveries in Nevada, Colorado, and Montana. Includes accounts of trips overland and around the Horn, mining towns and mining methods, and life in San Francisco. The last chapter gives a brief analysis of the effects of the gold rush on western settlement and growth.
Comment: Descriptions are lively, even though very brief, and give a flavor of life and activities in mining settlements and in San Francisco. The map shows how the rivers flow out of the Sierra Nevada into the Sacramento and San Joaquin Rivers. Gives a good picture of the mining areas in relation to pre-1848 communities.
Nonfiction: intermediate

Heiderstadt, Dorothy. **MORE INDIAN FRIENDS AND FOES.** New York: David McKay, 1963. 146 p. bibliog., index.

Content: Two chapters are of particular interest to Californians:

"Pasquala: Who Saved the Mission," and "Captain Jack: Modoc Warrior."

Comment: This book is a sequel to *Indian Friends and Foes.* Although the author is making a sincere attempt to be objective, she still writes from a white person's point of view; the Indians come in second best, as usual.

Nonfiction: intermediate

Higgins, Marguerite. **JESSIE BENTON FREMONT.** Boston: Houghton Mifflin, 1962. 174 p. Illus. by B. Holmes, index.

Content: After a privileged childhood in Washington, D.C., as the daughter of U.S. Senator Thomas Hart Benton, Jessie Benton eloped with Fremont and by age nineteen was taking an active role in helping with Fremont's expeditions and career. She suffered through his court-martial and moved with him to California, where she filled a role as the "first lady" of the West—in San Francisco, San Jose, Monterey, and then back to Washington, D.C. After Fremont's unsuccessful campaign for the presidency, they came back to California to live in Mariposa County, and finally, Los Angeles.

Comment: This is the romantic story of a remarkable pair. The biography makes it clear that Jessie was a formidable force in the struggles and victories of her father, Senator Benton of Missouri, and her husband. She knew and enjoyed politics and intellectual pursuits. Besides writing the chronicles of Fremont's surveying expeditions, she helped support her family by writing several other books. Author Marguerite Higgins was a well-known journalist during World War II. A listing of other books about the Fremonts is included.

Nonfiction: intermediate

Hoexter, Corrine K. **FROM CANTON TO CALIFORNIA: THE EPIC OF CHINESE IMMIGRATION.** New York: Four Winds Press, 1976. 304 p. Photos, bibliog., index.

Content: Part One, "The Golden Magnet", investigates the presence of Chinese immigrants from the mid-nineteenth century on. The economic and social conditions in their provinces of origin are examined with the motives and prospects of the

emigrants. Chapters cover their involvement in the gold rush; their work in building the Union Pacific Railroad across the Sierra Nevada; the growth of "Chinatowns;" their opportunities in business, agriculture, and domestic service. The author explores prejudice and harassment of the Chinese by the white communities. Part One concludes with the burning of Chinatown in the 1906 disaster. Part Two is an extended biography of Dr. Ng Poon Chew, born in China in 1866, who emigrated to California in 1881 and founded the first Chinese-American daily newspaper. A distinguished editor and lecturer, he was dubbed the "Chinese Mark Twain" and was awarded numerous honors. **Comment:** This sober history is a careful, readable account of the reluctant acceptance of Chinese immigrants and the injustices they suffered.
Nonfiction: junior high–senior high

Holland, Ruth. **THE ORIENTAL IMMIGRANTS IN AMERICA: FROM EASTERN EMPIRE TO WESTERN WORLD.** New York: Grosset and Dunlap, 1969. 60 p. Pictures by H. B. Vestal, index.

Content: The author explains the emigration from the homeland; why Orientals were needed in California; why emigration from China was desirable. Then she tells of the growth and expression of prejudice, followed by the Burlingame Treaty. She explains the Oriental contribution to American culture and Japanese immigration to Hawaii and California. Information on World War II, the relocation camps, and the use of Japanese during the war makes up one chapter, and, finally, the postwar improvement in relations is described.
Comment: The book is full of information and well organized as a reference for young readers. The changing attitudes of third generation Chinese-Americans and Sansei are not reflected and would have to be sought in more recent literature.
Nonfiction: intermediate

Holt, Stephen. **WE WERE THERE WITH THE CALIFORNIA RANCHEROS.** New York: Grosset & Dunlap, 1960. 178 p. B/w illus. by William Reusswig.

Content: Using the example of one Californio family, the book tells the story of the end of the large ranchos and the beginning of American settlement of these lands in the 1850s. Some details of rancho life are given. Noted anthropologist, Oscar Lewis, is named as historical consultant for this work.

Comment: Although the purpose of the story was to give the reader a sense of the changeover to American occupation of the land, the story and dialogue are contrived and the characters stereotyped.

Fiction: intermediate

Howard, Robert West. **FLAG OF THE DREADFUL BEAR.** New York: G. P. Putnam's Sons, 1965. 127 p. Illus., maps, bibliog., index.

Content: Basically a history of California between 1837 and 1846, the book starts with information about General Vallejo and then tells about sailors jumping ship and becoming Californios. The story moves on to John Sutter and his fort, and the trailmakers John Bidwell, Thomas Fitzpatrick, and Benjamin Kelsey. There are chapters about the request sent to the president of Mexico for an honest, strong-willed governor and about Thomas Larkin and the goodwill he engendered. The arrival of wagon trains and Captain Fremont led to the defying of the California government by Americans and the "Flag of the Dreadful Bear." There are chapters on The Osos Battalion and on California becoming a state.

Comment: This is an interesting book for young readers. One tidbit new to me was that the flag invented for California was called the "Dreadful Bear" derived from grisly bear, not grizzly bear, because the numerous bears were horrifying to the people.

Nonfiction: intermediate

Howorth, Peter C. **CHANNEL ISLANDS: THE STORY BEHIND THE SCENERY.** Story Behind the Scenery Series. Las Vegas, Nev.: KC Publications, 1982. 48 p. Color photos.

Content: Text and pictures tell of the Channel Islands from geological development to designation as a national park in

1980. There is information about the prehistoric mammoths, whose bones have been found on two of the islands. The "ghost forests" are also explained, as is the present-day plant and animal life. The last section deals with man's activities on the islands, from habitation 11,000 years ago, through Chumash settlers and Spanish explorers, sea otter hunters, a possible convict colony in 1830, Chinese fishing camps, to the "real settlers"—the sheep ranchers—of the last half of the nineteenth century.

Comment: Though this handsome soft-cover booklet was not written for students, capable readers from ages eleven and up could well use it. Younger readers, too, could benefit from the very fine color photographs and clear captions. There is no table of contents. The book is part of a series from KC Publications on park areas. Other Story Behind the Scenery books of interest to Californians are *Alcatraz Island* (see title index), *Death Valley, Death Valley's Scotty's Castle, Sequoia-Kings Canyon,* and *Yosemite*. Some of these titles deal more with natural history than with people and events.
Nonfiction: upper intermediate–adult

Hoyt, Edwin P. **LELAND STANFORD.** New York: Abelard-Schuman, 1967. 160 p. B/w photos, bibliog., index.

Content: This traces Stanford's life and career from farmer–innkeeper's son (fifth son in a family of seven surviving sons) to railroad builder, governor of California, and the state's senator in Washington, D.C. His lasting monument is Stanford University founded after the death of his only son.

Stanford was apparently a man of integrity and principle, shy, not a powerful speaker, and in spite of his connection with the much-disliked railroad monopoly, he was personally well liked. The author illuminates these qualities as well as his love of wealth and ostentation.

Comment: As a book for young readers, there is too much unnecessary detail given when broader outlines would have sufficed. The best chapter is near the end when the author deals with Stanford and his family. A minor, but annoying inconsistency—the author keeps using "Leland" when referring to

Stanford even though other men are referred to by their surnames.
Nonfiction: junior high–senior high

Hubbard, Douglass. **GHOST MINES OF YOSEMITE**. Fresno, Calif.: Awani Press, 1958. 37 p. Photos.

Content: Douglass Hubbard, chief park naturalist of Yosemite National Park, gives a very detailed study of one particular mining enterprise. Tioga Hill is the setting and the time is the early 1880s. All the things associated with mining—speculation, explosions, famous mining men, tunnels, machinery, human-interest stories, deserted settlements, inadequate communication and transportation—come into this story.
Comment: There are many quotes from accounts of the period. Research usage will be hampered by the lack of an index.
Nonfiction: junior high

Hubbard, Fran. **A DAY WITH TUPI—AN AUTHENTIC STORY OF AN INDIAN BOY IN CALIFORNIA'S MOUNTAINS.** 1955. Reprint. Fresno, Calif.: Awani Press, 1966. 17 p. Color illus. by Ed Vella.

Content: Tupi was a Mi-wok Indian who lived in the valley called A–wa–ni, and during this day with him we learn what his name means, the habits of some animals in the valley, how the Indians use animals aside from food, two legends, how a game is played, how acorns are made edible, and what's eaten at a feast.
Comment: This is a nice little story and quite informative. The author lived in Yosemite where her husband was chief park naturalist.
Fiction: upper primary–beginning intermediate

Hunter, Vickie, and Elizabeth Hamma. **STAGECOACH DAYS.** Menlo Park, Calif.: Lane Publishing, 1963. 63 p. Illus. by Randy Steffan, glossary, bibliog., index.

Content: Starting in 1849 with the first stage lines in California, the book goes on to tell of the Concord Coach, the stagecoach

drivers, the guns and horses used, and the stagecoach robbers. There is a story of "The Longest Stagecoach Ride Ever" (the overland stage) and what happened to stagecoaches after the railroad came.
Comment: There is a lot of simply written information.
Nonfiction: intermediate

Huntington, Harriet E. **THE YOSEMITE STORY.** Garden City, N. Y.: Doubleday, 1966. 90 p. B/w photos and drawings by J. Noel, glossary, bibliog., geological timetable, index.

Content: This geological history begins with a chapter on the discovery and development of Yosemite, telling of how it became a park, and the early recognition of its significance by John Muir and Francois E. Matthes. The photographic work of Ansel Adams is also noted. Most of the book deals with the geological development of Yosemite—the uplift of the Sierra Nevada, glaciation, and the escarpment.
Comment: This slim volume would be for students more interested in geology than in history though the first chapter does have historical data. There are many large and beautiful pictures of the area.
Nonfiction: intermediate–senior high

Hurd, Edith Thacher. **SAILERS, WHALERS AND STEAMERS— SHIPS THAT OPENED THE WEST.** Menlo Park, Calif.: Lane Publishing, 1964. 64 p. Illus. by Lyle Galloway, bibliog., glossary, index.

Content: This book is described as being the first-written maritime history of the Pacific Coast. It covers water transportation of people and goods from the time of clipper ships to motor-driven ships, whalers, and steamers—both paddle wheel and river. Several of these old ships are permanently docked at the Maritime Museum or North Beach area of San Francisco.
Comment: This very interesting book reminds us how much California state history is rooted in ships and all that is connected with them. Small illustrations in page margins, in addition to the larger ones, are helpful in augmenting the text; also

included are a two-page map of whaling and sailing routes and illustration of two types of ships mentioned.
Nonfiction: intermediate–junior high

Jackson, Charlotte. **THE KEY TO SAN FRANCISCO.** Keys to the Cities. Philadelphia: Lippincott, 1961. 128 p. B/w illus., map, index.

Content: This seems to be a retelling of Jackson's *Story of San Francisco* with two chapters added to tell about the Panama-Pacific Exposition of 1915, the building of the two bridges, the 1939 San Francisco World's Fair, and a descriptive tour of various areas of the city.
Comment: A chatty, easily read chronicle. Obviously, since it was published twenty-five years ago, the contemporary section is itself "history." At least one dating error was noted—Portola didn't discover San Francisco Bay in the sixteenth century. Too much stress is put on the easy going life-style of the Californios as lazy and fiesta-loving.
Nonfiction: grade 5–junior high

Jackson, Charlotte. **THE STORY OF SAN FRANCISCO.** New York: Random House, 1955. 175 p. Drawings by Kurt Werth, index.

Content: This book chronicles the growth of San Francisco from a little Spanish hamlet of about 300 pioneers from Mexico to the present, describing Yankee traders in their clipper ships, prospectors, and shiploads of Chinese from across the Pacific. Information is included of the early Vigilante Committee, the gold-rush days, the building of the cable cars, the first luxurious theater, and then the fateful year, 1906, when the great earthquake and fire nearly destroyed the town.
Comment: It is a colorful story of fascinating people—Italian fishermen, opera stars, and financiers. It gives a vivid picture of early days and of the determination of the people to rebuild after the disasters of 1906.
Nonfiction: intermediate

Jackson, Helen Hunt. **RAMONA.** 1884. Reprint. Boston: Little, Brown & Co., 1939. 424 p. Illus. by N. C. Wyeth.

Content: The very romantic story of Ramona, first published in 1884, is set in southern California in the postmission era after California had become part of the United States. Ramona, daughter of a socially outcast Scots father and an Indian mother is reared as the ward of a widow, Senora Moreno, a landed aristocrat, who lavishes affection on her son Felipe but has none for the loving, gentle Ramona. The foster daughter engenders even more of Senora Moreno's antagonism by choosing an Indian for her husband. The sad trials of Ramona and Alessandro end only with his tragic death. Ramona is then reunited with the loving Felipe, whose domineering mother has died.

Comment: The unjust seizure of Mexican lands and the inhumane treatment of Indians by the United States government are subplots interwoven with the stories of the main characters. Americans and the U.S. administration are the villains. The few colored illustrations highlight the sentimentalized clash of good and evil, but the descriptions of California in the 1800s would be of interest to a young reader.

Fiction: junior high–adult

Johnson, Annabel, and Edgar Johnson. **A GOLDEN TOUCH.** New York: Harper & Row, 1963. 230 p.

Content: Set in the gold country at the turn of the century, this story concerns a boy and his attempts to "reach" his father, a gambler accused of cheating.

Young Andy Brett is sent out to live with the father he didn't remember when his maternal grandfather became too old to care for him. Andy arrives to find that his father had just been banished from the community of Black Hawk for cheating at cards and goes with his taciturn father and jovial Uncle Hep to establish themselves in a new mining community.

They join forces with old Misery Jones, the Frenchman Remi, and his fiery little sister Josey to try to make an old mine pay. But trouble follows them; the sheriff from Black Hawk is on their trail, Andy is plagued with doubts of his father's honesty, and the partners in the mining venture begin to distrust each other. The climax comes deep in the tunnels of the old mine.

Comment: This good story gives a picture of mining after the gold-rush days. The Association of Children's Librarians recommended this book.
Fiction: intermediate

Johnson, Annabel, and Edgar Johnson. **TORRIE.** New York: Harper & Row, 1960. 217 p. Maps.

Content: Fourteen-year-old Torrie Anderson had underrated the abilities of her parents to make the overland trip to California through dangerous territory. Watching them cope with illness, hunger, and the hardships of the journey forces Torrie to reevaluate her own ideas.
Comment: Torrie's father is a teacher and all he can do is read, or so Torrie thinks. An interesting look at teachers of the day! The Association of Children's Librarians recommended this book.
Fiction: intermediate–junior high

Johnson, Paul. **THE GOLDEN ERA OF THE MISSIONS 1769-1834.** San Francisco: Chronicle Books, 1974. 63 p. Color paintings by Chesley Bonestell, map.

Content: There are two pages for the history of each mission with a painting of the mission as it looked in its prime. Six pages of introduction give concise, historical background of the establishment of the mission system, its workings and eventual goal, its secularization, abandonment, and restoration. Each mission is described at its peak, in contrast to what can be seen today, and the standing of each, in terms of agricultural output, numbers of neophytes, and degree of success or failure is indicated. Bonestell's paintings are based on contemporary evidence and are considered to be authentic portrayals.
Comment: Gives good factual information about the missions, and ties to historical events where appropriate. This is a good source for information on the mission chain.
Nonfiction: intermediate–adult

Johnson, William Weber. **THE STORY OF SEA OTTERS.** New York: Random House, 1973. 89 p. B/w photos, index.

Content: The sea otter's appearance, habitats, foods, relatives, near extinction, and reappearance are all briefly described. The history of Russian expansion across the Bering Strait down to California and the entrance of English, Spanish and Americans into fur trade with China are traced with the help of a map on the back endpapers. Dangers to the sea otter, efforts for its conservation, and its place in the marine ecosystem are included.

Comment: This is an interesting story, nicely told, with lots of charming photos. It can give an added dimension, if read beforehand, to a trip to the Monterey Aquarium.

Nonfiction: intermediate–junior high

Jones, Claire. **THE CHINESE IN AMERICA.** Minneapolis: Lerner Publications, 1972. 95 p. Photos, index.

Content: Starting with life behind the Great Wall of China, the author takes us to California, the "Land of the Golden Mountains." She tells of the welcome of the early Chinese settlers and their roles in the goldfields and working on the railroad. The growth of prejudice against the Chinese led to their confinement in "Chinatowns" and the restriction of further immigration. The largest Chinatown, in San Francisco, experienced the devastation of the 1906 earthquake and fire and was rebuilt. Chinatowns in other American cities are also described. The changing attitudes toward Chinese-Americans, and the individual achievements of some, as well as the rising assertiveness of Chinese youth, are all covered.

Comment: Though this book deals with Chinese in all of America, two parts are almost exclusively centered on the Chinese in California. Much straightforward factual information is given, and, in another chapter, the reader is invited to simulate the experience of an immigrant Chinese.

Nonfiction: intermediate

Karney, Beulah. **THE LISTENING ONE.** Scranton, Penn.: John Day, 1962.

Content: The focus is upon Victoris Bartholomea Comicrabit, called Lomea, who becomes head of a group of San Gabriel

Indians during the time at which Mexico is achieving its independence from Spain. Lomea is mission-educated and with the help of her new husband, Pablo, is able to retain for her people some of the land and the rights that had long been theirs but which were in danger of being lost to greedy newcomers.
Comment: The Association of Children's Librarians recommended this book.
Fiction: junior high

Katz, William Loren. **BLACK PEOPLE WHO MADE THE OLD WEST.** New York: Thomas Y. Crowell, 1977. 181 p. Illus., photos, letters, and other documents.

920
KAT

I BE
J m

Content: Biographical sketches of thirty-five black men and women, rarely mentioned in history texts, who explored and settled the frontiers of the early United States. Among those who came to California were James Beckwourth, a Crow chief and trapper; William Leidesdorff, a public-minded San Franciscan; Biddy Mason, a California freedom fighter, and Mifflin W. Gibbs, a crusader for black equality.
Comment: The lively descriptions and amusing anecdotes about these neglected contributors to the development of the United States and of the Old West make this book informative and easy to read. There are suggestions for further reading.
Nonfiction: intermediate

Kemble, John Haskell. **SAN FRANCISCO BAY: A PICTORIAL MARITIME HISTORY.** Cambridge, Md.: Cornell Maritime Press, 1957. 195 p. B/w photos, drawings, paintings, maps, index.

Content: The book is arranged by topics and covers the history of each one, such as "Port of San Francisco," "Carriers of Bay Rivers," "The Navy in the Bay." Each chapter opens with a brief, introductory overview, and all other text is in the form of captions for the illustrations.
Comment: The book is particularly interesting because of the pictures of San Francisco and other areas around the bay before the advent of bridges, high rises, and extensive suburbs.
Nonfiction: junior high–adult

Knill, Harry. **DOS CALIFORNIOS.** Santa Barbara, Calif.: Bellerophon Books, 1978. n.p. B/w drawings by Gregory Irons. Text in English and Spanish.

Content: The text deals mainly with the attacks of Hipolito Bouchard along the California coast in late 1818. The illustrations and captions also tell of the foundings of the missions.
Comment: This is a sad jumble of English and Spanish text, oddly placed captions, and advertisements for other Bellerophon publications! It's also a peculiar mix of historical data and storytelling.
Nonfiction: intermediate

Knill, Harry. **EARLY LOS ANGELES.** Santa Barbara, Calif.: Bellerophon Books, 1984. 48 p. Illus.

Content: The text deals with major leaders and main events in the history of the Los Angeles area from the entry of the Franciscan friars into Alta California in 1769 to the southern California land boom of 1887.
Comment: By trying to compress many events and leaders into few pages, the author has created a hard–to–follow text. That, coupled with the lack of a table of contents and index, would make this a difficult title to use in classrooms. However, the illustrations are interesting, rarely seen paintings. The accompanying captions could make a skimming of this title instructive for younger, as well as older, readers.
Nonfiction: junior high–adult

Knill, Harry, Editor. **GREAT INDIANS OF CALIFORNIA.** Adapted from the writings of Vallejo, and Padre Francisco Palou; commentary by H. H. Bancroft. Santa Barbara, Calif.: Bellerophon Books, 1986. 46 p. Reproductions of historic drawings, in black and white.

Content: This is a collection of stories of Indians and Indian battles with the Californios, adapted from original manuscripts mainly written by Mariano Vallejo. Corrections and comments are offered by the historian, H.H. Bancroft. The Indian attack on San Diego mission in 1775, one on the Colorado River settlements in 1781, and one with the Suisuns in 1810 or 1817 are amongst the ones described. Indians chiefs Palma, Pomponio, Malaca, Motti, Chalpinich, Pacomio, and Estanislao (Stanislaus), Marin and his comrade Quintin are accorded brief biographies.

Comment: This is an interesting and informative account, simply written, which could well be of value to those of any age interested in early California history.

Nonfiction: intermediate–adult

Kroeber, Theodora, and Robert F. Heizer. **ALMOST ANCESTORS: THE FIRST CALIFORNIANS.** San Francisco: Sierra Club, 1968. 168 p. Photos.

Content: This photographic essay on California-Indian faces shows young and old Indians, identifying them by name and tribe. The authors relate Indian history, interspersing pictures and lore. The photographs form the basic structure with some narrative and legends added. There are sections on the Indians of the Central Valley, the southern coastal area, the Colorado River, the north coast. Also, there is a section on the reduction of the Indian population in California, and several sections on the Indian way of life.

Comment: This is a magnificent collection of character portraits.

Nonfiction: all ages

Kroeber, Theodora. **DRAWN FROM LIFE: CALIFORNIA DAYS IN PEN AND BRUSH.** Socorro, N.Mex.: Ballena Press, 1977. 275 p. Illus.

Content: This very complete collection of paintings and drawings of California Indians is done by artists of pre-photography days. There are 322 reproductions as well as text on the work and customs. (adapted from Booklist)

Comment: Booklist called this title a full-scale report.

Nonfiction: all ages

Kroeber, Theodora. **THE INLAND WHALE.** Berkeley, Calif.: University of California Press, 1963. 203 p. Illus. by Joseph Crivy, foreword by Oliver LaFarge, appendix, bibliog.

Content: This is a collection of nine interesting and distinctly different tales which California Indians told. Among them is a delightful love poem, several fables concerned with tribal mores and ambitions, a travel story, a romantic depiction of the courtship of a late bloomer, a novelette involving intrigue and revenge, and a tale of a man who followed his wife to heaven. **Comment:** The appendix offers a discussion of the literary merits of the stories and describes the California-Indian tribes by whom the stories were told. The bibliography lists fifteen different authors, including many stories by each.
Fiction: intermediate–adult

Kroeber, Theodora. **ISHI, LAST OF HIS TRIBE.** Berkeley, Calif.: Parnassus Press, 1964. 209 p. Illus. by Ruth Robbins, glossary of Yahi Indian words.

Content: Mrs. Kroeber presents for young readers a memorable version of the life of Ishi, the "last wild North American Indian," based on her anthropological study, *Ishi in Two Worlds*. Beginning with the early years of Ishi's life, the reader follows him and his people from the time when they hid in caves during the day and hunted at night to escape the detection of the "saldu" (the white man), through the deaths of his grandparents and his friend; his separation from his sister and uncle, and finally, the death of his mother. Ishi, now the last of his tribe, wanders distractedly into the town of Oroville in northern California.

After Ishi was found, he agreed to live in San Francisco at the University of California Anthropology Museum, where he stayed until his death in 1916. In telling the story, Mrs. Kroeber describes the Yahi—their customs, religious rituals, medicines, food, clothing, and folklore. She tells how animal skins were prepared, tools made, what foods were prepared and how, and other aspects of their lives.
Comment: This is an immensely readable book for young and old. Respect, kindness, and knowledge pass between Ishi and the "saldu" around him as they learn about each other. Ishi taught the world much, and his adjustment to the wilds of

civilization was a remarkable feat. The Association of Children's Librarians recommended it, too.

Nonfiction: upper intermediate–adult

L'Amour, Louis. **THE CALIFORNIOS.** New York: Saturday Review Press, E. P. Dutton, 1974. 186 p.

Content: Set shortly before gold-rush days in the then-rural Malibu area, the story centers on the efforts of the landed Mulkerin family—part Irish and part Mexican—to retain their ranch in the face of serious indebtedness. The strong and beautiful Senora Mulkerin relies on, and yet leads, her two sons as they fight powerful and evil men who have the legal right to evict them unless they can produce some cash. One son, Sean, complicates the struggle by helping a lovely young girl to run away from an arranged wedding to a rich and vengeful young man.

A mystical Indian whom the Mulkerin family have long befriended and respected leads them to a small supply of gold, which, with the Senora's ingenuity, saves the ranch.

Comment: The slim, historical value of this western adventure is its revelation of the cashless basis of the economy prior to the gold rush. The protagonists, a prominent family with friends among the leaders of the province, can't raise $2500. Also, the draw of a social event—the Senora's fandango—in a society where people yearn for opportunities to get together is made evident. Some historical figures—Pio Pico, Micheltorena, Abel Stearns—and the politics of the period play a minor role.

Fiction: junior high–senior high

Lampman, Evelyn Sibley. **THE BANDIT OF MOK HILL.** New York: Doubleday, 1969. 254 p. B/w drawings.

Content: Angel, a young orphan, is rescued in San Francisco by an eccentric singing teacher and travels with him, his wife, and daughter to the goldfields. Angel's secret wish is to join the outlaw band led by Joaquin Murietta. Gradually, the boy realizes that his picture of the outlaws is distorted, and he is torn by loyalties to old and new friends.

Comment: Great for preteens. Many real problems of the gold-

rush times are woven into the plot. The Association of Children's Librarians recommend it.
Fiction: Intermediate

Lasky, Kathryn. **BEYOND THE DIVIDE.** New York: Macmillan, 1983. 251 p.

Content: In April of 1849 Will Simon, a Pennsylvania Amish, rebels against the rigid constraints of his faith and leaves for California; his fourteen-year-old daughter, Meribah, chooses to go with him. The story is of their trip and its hardships; it portrays characters strong and weak, selfish and generous, tolerant and intolerant. When Will sickens in the Sierra Nevada, Meribah must manage to cross the passes into the California valley. She is aided by Mr. Goodnough, a kindred, artistic soul, who joins her to his party. More hardships and the death of Will leave Meribah on her own and starving. She is befriended and saved by a small tribe of California Indians. Recovered in body and surer of her other needs, Meribah decides to head back to a beautiful valley in the Oregon Territory (now Idaho) where she knew she could live in peace.
Comment: The California historical importance of this book is not great, but the segment dealing with Meribah's interlude with the Mill Creek-area Indians is informative about a vanished culture. Students familiar with Kroeber's *Ishi: Last of His Tribe* might compare the two. Teachers and librarians will want to be aware of a candidly handled rape scene in the story.
Fiction: upper intermediate–senior high

Latham, Frank B. **JED SMITH, TRAILBLAZER AND TRAPPER.** A Discovery Book. Champaign, Ill.: Garrard Publishing Co., 1968. 80 p. Illus.

Content: Traces highlights of Smith's career as a trapper and explorer in the Rocky Mountains and California. The emphasis is on his adventurous spirit, his survival skills, and his "firsts"—including traveling from the Missouri River to the California coast, crossing the Sierra Nevada west to east, and traveling by land from southern California to the Columbia River.

Comment: Large print and a fairly simple narrative make this a good choice for the younger student to learn about the role the mountain men played in opening up the West, even though California history is mentioned only briefly.
Nonfiction: upper primary–beginning intermediate

Laurgaard, Rachel Kelley. **PATTY REED'S DOLL.** Caldwell, Idaho: Caxton Printers, 1957. 140 p. Bibliog.

Content: Patty Reed's four-inch wooden doll tells of the Donner Party's trek from Springfield, Illinois to Sutter's Fort, California. The initial high hopes of the participants, descriptions of the prairie, the hardships, the snowed-in winter (minus accounts of possible cannibalism) at Donner Lake, and the rescue are included.
Comment: This well-written narrative is an interesting and catchy way to relate the Donner Party tragedy to young people. The doll is displayed in the museum at Sutter's Fort.
Fiction: intermediate–junior high

Lauritzen, Jonreed. **COLONEL ANZA'S IMPOSSIBLE JOURNEY.** New York: G. P. Putnam's Sons, 1966. 217 p. Ink and wash drawings by Steel Savage, index.

Content: This is a detailed account of De Anza's life as a great Spanish explorer who did more than any other to establish Spanish settlement in California. After his father's untimely death at the hands of the Apache, De Anza left his studies for the priesthood in Mexico City to return to his native Sonora and help his country. With full appreciation for its difficulties, he accepted the commission to explore the regions between Sonora, Mexico and the early missions established in southern California and to proceed to San Francisco Bay—and then lead colonists over the route. He carried out his mission and returned home to accept the governorship of New Mexico.
Comment: An inspiring and exciting account of one who gave unstintingly of his best efforts to maintain the Spanish settlements in what is now the southwestern United States. It would appeal to hero worshipers of all ages. An excellent adventure

narrative which can be used for recreational, as well as reference, reading.
Nonfiction: intermediate

Lawrence, Isabelle. **WEST TO DANGER.** Indianapolis: Bobbs-Merrill, 1964. 207 p.

Content: Tom Tucker of Boston was young, easygoing, pleasure loving. His mother and little sister couldn't really count on his help even though Mr. Tucker was far off in California seeking his fortune. When Mrs. Tucker decided to sell all they owned to finance a trip to California to reunite the family, Tom was delighted. After a very exciting shipboard trip through the Isthmus of Panama and up to San Francisco, Tom, now separated from mother and sister, sets out to find his father in the goldfields. Tom survives living with the Indians of Yosemite and being the victim of holdups; he finds his father, and the family is reunited in San Francisco.

Comment: This fast-moving tale gives an idea of the fears and hardships suffered by families trying to reach California in gold rush days.
Fiction: intermediate

Laycock, George. **DEATH VALLEY.** New York: Four Winds Press, 1976. 113 p. Bibliog., map, photos, index.

J979.4 87
LAY
1 m

Content: This book tells the history of Death Valley—the Jayhawkers of 1848, the goldseekers, and the Indians of the desert. It also tells what a desert is, how it was formed, and the use of the borax which is found there. It concludes with suggestions for fun in the desert—walking trips, photography tips, ghost towns.

Comment: This book contains much precise information. There is an emphasis on concerns for the present, such as the need to remove invading trees and the recent research on the endangered bighorn sheep. An index makes all the information readily available.
Nonfiction: intermediate

Leadabrand, Russ. **THE SECRET OF DRAKE'S BAY.** Los Angeles: Ward Ritchie Press, 1969. 46 p. Illus. by Don Perceval.

Content: Ten-year-old Mary and eleven-year-old Michael live with their grandfather at Drake's Bay during the summer. They meet and befriend David, curator of a San Francisco museum, who is trying to gather evidence authenticating Drake's landing at the bay 400 years before.

Comment: The author establishes a dreamlike quality in this simple tale, interweaving history, fantasy and the natural science of the Drake's Bay area.

Fiction: intermediate

Lee, Hector. **TALES OF CALIFORNIA: FROM THE HISTORY AND FOLKLORE OF THE FAR WEST.** Logan, Utah: Utah State University Press, 1974. 124 p. B/w drawings.

Content: Well-known and not-so-well-known stories drawn from folklore and the local history of California make up the book. Set from the 1830s to the early twentieth century, they are mostly about real people, and basically factual, but embellished in the retelling through the years.

Comment: These short, easily read stories are adapted from television and radio programs offered by the author some years ago. The style is similar to that of Ralph Rambo's little books.

Fiction: intermediate–junior high

Lenski, Lois. **SAN FRANCISCO BOY.** New York: Lippincott, 1955. 176 p. Illus. by the author.

Content: When Felix, a Chinese boy, moved with his family from Alameda, then a somewhat-rural island in San Francisco Bay, to San Francisco's Chinatown, he found it hard to adjust to the crowds and faster-living pace. The story tells of extended-family living, celebrations of holidays, work and school activities, and most of all, how Felix's family became part of a wider community which included those of many ethnic backgrounds.

Comment: Though the book is somewhat dated, it is a good story for the interpretive reader who can sense the feelings and attitudes which are being changed by a new environment. Felix grows up indeed! It is not a book to read aloud to a class because the action is too simple and slow-moving for television-oriented youngsters.

Fiction: intermediate

Leong, Russell. **MY CHINATOWN A TO Z.** San Francisco: Chinatown Adventures, 1966. n.p. Color illus. by the author.

Content: The fifteen-year-old author describes San Francisco's Chinatown from the abacus to the zodiac of Chinese years. In between he uses letters of the alphabet and simple line drawings to describe his native home. *K* tells of Kong Chow, the oldest existing temple in Chinatown, first built in 1851 and destroyed in the 1906 earthquake and fire. *P* for Portsmouth Square tells of it as the heart of the city in gold rush days. *Y* stands for the *Young China Daily,* a historic old newspaper founded by Dr. Sun Yat Sen in 1910.

Comment: This would be a good browsing book for those interested in knowing more about San Francisco Chinatown. Though the ABC format and very simple drawings might make it seem primary, the reading level and information are appropriate for older students.

Nonfiction: intermediate–junior high

Levitin, Sonia. **THE NO-RETURN TRAIL.** New York: Harcourt, Brace, 1978. 160 p.

Content: "In California oranges grow on trees! The land's so rich, why, if you poke a fence post, it'll sprout leaves in a week!" With this dream, seventeen-year-old Nancy Kelsey with her young husband, Ben, and their tiny daughter, joins a wagon train journeying to the West Coast. Along the trail the group encounters disease, death, Indian attacks, and the savagery of the elements. Nancy faces fear, self-doubt, and waning love for her husband, but she finds strength to fight and endure. The love and passion for life that grow between Nancy and Ben spur them on and reach out to encourage other members of the expedition.

Comment: From the historical facts of the Bidwell-Bartleson Expedition of 1841, the author weaves an unforgettable story of two young people who brave uncharted territory to carve out a new home. It is also the story of the first overland journey by a woman. The Association of Children's Librarians reviewed it and recommended it, too.
Fiction: junior high–adult

Lewis, Oscar. **THE SACRAMENTO RIVER.** New York: Holt Rinehart & Winston, 1970. 90 p. Pencil sketches, index.

Content: In eight self-contained chapters the author gives information on the river from its geographical importance in the Sacramento Valley to the irrigation projects from the 1850s to the 1960s. He also includes information about the people—the Yana Indians and Ishi, the Spanish explorers to the American trappers, Sutter and his fort. He notes the changes that came to the whole valley from the gold rush. Finally, he views the river as a transportation system and recounts the attempts by man to tame the flooding.
Comment: This is an excellent book, informative and useful.
Nonfiction: intermediate

Lewis, Oscar. **SAN FRANCISCO: MISSION TO METROPOLIS.** Berkeley, Calif.: Howell-North Books, 1966. 259 p. B/w photos, bibliog., index.

Content: In twelve chapters, each with subheadings in the table of contents, the author gives a detailed history of San Francisco from the European discovery of the site to the mid-1900s. Discovery and settlement, Yerba Buena as a village, the effect of the gold rush, the struggle for law and order are chapter topics. Then, a chapter each is devoted to the events of the 1850s, the 1860s, and the 1870s. Another chapter deals with the turn-of-the-century days, and, of course, one chapter deals with the 1906 earthquake. The problems of rebuilding the city, the 1920s—40s, and a look at the city at midcentury are covered in the remaining chapters.
Comment: This is twenty years old and, obviously, dated—old St. Mary's Church was still standing and the Wells Fargo Bank

Building was the newest skyscraper in town. However, it is as complete a history of San Francisco as can be found. To find the less well known information, and find it in detail, use this book.
Nonfiction: upper intermediate–senior high

Luce, Willard and Celia. **SUTTER'S FORT: EMPIRE ON THE SACRAMENTO.** Champaign, Ill.: Garrard, 1969. 95 p. Illus. by Paul Frame, map, glossary, index.

Content: This life of Sutter describes in detail how his empire began, grew, and fell, and the everyday life of Sutter's Fort. Included are animal hunts, cattle roundups, and encounters with grizzly bears.
Comment: This interesting look at Sutter depicts him as fair and kind to both Indian and white workers in a time not noted for such behavior.
Nonfiction: intermediate

Ludwig, Edward W. **GUMSHAN—THE CHINESE-AMERICAN SAGA.** Los Gatos, Calif.: Polaris Press, 1982. 35 p. B/w illus. by Jack Loo. Photos.

Content: In color-book format and size, this tells about the Chinese in America from the fourth century B.C. to the present. The double-page spread has text on one page and a matching illustration across from it. Some of the illustrations are original drawings by Mr. Loo; others are reproduced from photographs.
Comment: Except for the pages on early Chinese visits to America, this includes much of the same information as Betty Sung's Chinese in America (see index), but is not quite as well organized. The three pages on early Chinese presence in America are the most interesting and fascinating. The illustrations, especially the photos, didn't reproduce too well.
Nonfiction: intermediate–junior high

Luger, Harriet. **THE LAST STRONGHOLD, A STORY OF THE MODOC INDIAN WAR, 1872-1873.** Reading, Mass.: Addison, Wesley, 1972. 212 p. B/w photos, bibliog.

Content: The paths of three teenage boys—a Modoc Indian, a white settler, and a young soldier—cross during the Modoc-Indian War in the early 1870s when several army units were sent against Captain Jack and his Modoc stronghold, now part of Lava Beds National Monument in northeastern California. **Comment:** There's a feeling of tragedy from beginning to end of this book. It shows the contempt of whites for Indians and their culture, the anger and misunderstanding of Indians for whites and their culture, the agony of a Russian-Jew separated from family and his culture. The story is definitely a "downer," but probably presents a real picture of the time of the Modoc-Indian War. There is a note included on what is fact and what fiction. **Fiction: upper intermediate–junior high**

Lyngheim, Linda. **THE INDIANS AND THE CALIFORNIA MISSIONS.** Van Nuys, Calif.: Langtry Publications, 1984. 115 p. B/w illus. by Phyllis Garber, bibliog., glossary, index.

Content: Briefly explaining the discovery of California, the author moves to the time of Spanish settlement and describes life for the California Indian before and after the mission development. The history of the twenty-one original missions is recorded. In each case, something unique about the mission and a description of it as it is today is included. The problems amongst the padres, the soldiers, and the Indians are carefully explained, not just glossed over. The "little missions" or asistencias, the end of the missions, and Father Junipero Serra each get a chapter, too. There is a listing of the missions and their locations. **Comment:** The author wrote this book to fulfill the need for fourth-graders to have a book on the missions written at their reading level. Some third-graders could use it too. **Nonfiction: upper primary–beginning intermediate**

McCall, Edith. **GOLD RUSH ADVENTURES.** Frontiers of America. Chicago: Children's Press, 1962. 127 p. Illus.

Content: The publisher's note states that in this series McCall writes, in simple language, true stories of real people; the purpose is to make "stories of our country available to younger readers and interesting to a wide age range." These accounts tell of the trip west via the Panama Isthmus by a newspaper reporter; a group of men organized as soldiers and led by a navy captain, who made the long trip across the Rockies and Sierra Nevada; and an artist who found that his artwork brought more return than actual prospecting, as well as accounts of John Sutter, and Governor Colton's visit to the goldfields.

Comment: Except for those of John Sutter and Governor Colton, these descriptions are of individuals or groups not familiar to readers of other gold-rush accounts. This brings a certain freshness to the stories. The print is large, the language not too complicated, and the narrative is spirited; the stories move at a good pace. Could be a read aloud for its easy narrative style.

Nonfiction: upper primary–junior high

McDonald, Cawley. **CALIFORNIA IN PICTURES.** New York: Sterling Publishing, 1979. 63 p. B/w photos, index.

Content: With text and pictures the book covers the topics of land, history, government, people, and economy. The land section includes attention to the cities of Sacramento, San Diego, Los Angeles, and San Francisco. The history section includes exploration, settlement, the Russians, covered wagons, the secret messenger (Archibald Gillespie, bringing orders to John Fremont), Mexican war, gold rush, and pony express. In the people section there is brief mention of many figures in past and present California history. Black Bart and George Fisher, an escaped slave turned pirate, are featured in more detail than others.

Comment: Despite its name, this slim, attractive volume has quite a bit of text and an ample proportion of pictures. The compressed text occasionally leads to awkward, confusing sentences and the omission of important information—the Big Four are discussed without connecting them with the transcontinental railroad, and Fort Ross jumps into the text without any explanation of its being established by the Russians. Also, one should question a few of the facts presented, several of which we believe to be inaccurate.

Nonfiction: intermediate–junior high

McGiffin, Lee. **RIDERS OF THE ENCHANTED VALLEY.** New York: E. P. Dutton, 1966. 158 p.

Content: A young boy, after journeying from Kentucky to Sonoma County in the 1850s, becomes involved in a number of dangerous adventures including one with the notorious bandit, Joaquin Murietta.
Comment: The conflict between the Californios and American gringos is portrayed. Luke, the young hero, fights for the rights of his Californio friends. The Association of Children's Librarians recommended it.
Fiction: junior high

McGlashan, M. Mona. **GIVE ME A MOUNTAIN MEADOW.** Fresno, Calif.: Valley Publishers, 1977. 248 p. Illus.

Content: The book portrays the life of a remarkable Californian, Charles Fayette McGlashan (1847-1931), who is credited with saving the story of the Donner Party from oblivion. "A crack investigative reporter, formidable criminal lawyer . . . and historian who produced a classic account of the Donner Party tragedy. 'Mac' was also a gifted inventor and astronomer, progressive legislator and editor, an enthusiastic butterfly collector . . ., a spellbinding orator, and a zestful sportsman credited with being the father of winter sports in the California Sierra." (from *Contemporary Quarterly*).
Comment: This is a stirring biography of a pioneer whose life was filled with an amazing variety of achievements. Unhappily, it is now out-of-print. The author is the granddaughter of C. F. McGlashan.
Nonfiction: senior high–adult

Mack, Gerstle. **1906: SURVIVING SAN FRANCISCO'S GREAT EARTHQUAKE AND FIRE.** San Francisco: Chronicle Books, 1981. 123 p. Illus., maps, index, bibliog.

Content: In a brief, opening chapter, Mack, as a twelve-year-old in April 1906, writes of his own experiences during and immediately after the earthquake. The rest of the book consists of

descriptions of what happened in various parts of the City, as a result of the 'quake and subsequent fire.
Comment: The value of this book is its first-hand observation. Also worthwhile is the map showing the San Andreas fault line from San Juan Bautista to Fort Bragg, Mendocino Co., Calif.
Nonfiction: junior high–adult

McNeer, May. **THE CALIFORNIA GOLD RUSH.** New York: Random House, 1950. 184 p. Pen and ink sketches.

Content: The news of Marshall's discovery slowly spread worldwide, to Chileans, Chinese, Dutch, English, French, and Greeks. The American alcalde, Walter Colton, sent a formal report to the United States government about the find, and gold fever grew wildly. Some came around the Horn, as did those in the *Edward Everett,* and some through Panama. Some came overland in Conestoga wagons; they all came to dig for gold. When they arrived in the little town of adobe homes called San Francisco, they entered a lawless environment. It was every man for himself in the gold country, and wild stories abounded. Eventually law began to reassert itself and normalcy return. The songs and dances, the miner's recreations, are some of the memories that remain of the early gold-rush days.
Comment: This old, but easily read book is still on many school library shelves. It has good anecdotal records of personal experiences. Studebaker, Armour, Mark Hopkins, and Mark Twain are some famous individuals mentioned. The book can be read quite quickly.
Nonfiction: intermediate

Margolian, Malcolm. **THE OHLONE WAY: INDIAN LIFE IN THE SAN FRANCISCO-MONTEREY BAY AREA.** Berkeley, Calif.: Heyday Books, 1978. 182 p. Illus. by Michael Harney, bibliog., maps, index.

Content: The author tells in some detail about the Ohlones and their land, life in a small society, the world of the spirit, and modern times.
Comment: Not only is the text informative and well written, but

the intricate detail of the various aspects of Ohlone life shown in the illustrations convey more to me than any other illustrations I have seen.
Nonfiction: intermediate–adult

Martin, Patricia Miles. **ROLLING THE CHEESE.** New York: Atheneum, 1966. n.p. Color and b/w illus. by Alton Raible.

Content: Maria, a little Italian-American girl, is visiting her uncle in San Francisco. She watches the men in the Italian community play a game called "rolling the cheese" and wants to take part. How Maria entered the contest one Sunday and managed to beat all of the men is the focus of the story.
Comment: This delightful story is set in and about the produce market of early San Francisco. The Association of Children's Librarians liked it, too.
Fiction: primary

Martinez, Carmel. **SUSAN PECK, LATE OF BOSTON.** New York: G. P. Putnam's, 1962. 187 p.

Content: Seventeen-year-old Susan Peck leaves her home in Boston to join her widowed father who has just remarried in San Francisco. In 1821 San Francisco is still a tiny frontier village—and foreign as well. Susan is very mindful of her independent American heritage and not too accommodating to Spanish customs and laws. How she learns to love her nineteen-year-old Spanish stepmother and adjust to San Francisco is the essence of this story.
Comment: Susan is portrayed as a brat and stubbornly strong-minded in her Americanisms, but she does express introspective adolescent confusion as well. As is common with most "growing up" novels, there isn't much action to the plot, but the historical descriptions are interesting.
Fiction: junior high–senior high

Masson, Marcelle. **A BAG OF BONES: THE WINTU MYTHS OF A TRINITY RIVER INDIAN.** Happy Camp, Calif.: Naturegraph Publishers, 1966. 130 p. B/w illus., maps.

Content: The Wintu Indians lived in the Central Valley between the Sacramento River and the Coast Range. These stories of creation, legendary Indians, and animals were told to the author by a Wintu who had been a boyhood friend of her husband's. The stories are written as he told them, the sentences short, the language used by one whose mother tongue wasn't English, and the repetitions often found in cultures with orally-transmitted legends. There is a short chapter on Wintu life that is informative and interesting.

Comment: I didn't find these stories very interesting or easy to read. Repetitions that might be all right in storytelling slow down the reading, and the stories are not too exciting. Not much checked out from the local public library. Use it to learn the stories, and then retell them in your own words.

Fiction: junior high–senior high

Meltzer, Milton. **THE CHINESE AMERICANS.** New York: Thomas Y. Crowell, 1980. 170 p. B/w photos, bibliog., index.

Content: In eleven chapters, Meltzer carefully records the history of Chinese immigrants in America, mainly in California. A chapter titled "What's Wrong with this Picture?" describes the celebration of the completion of the transcontinental railroad. Nine-out-of-ten workers on the Central Pacific portion of the railroad were Chinese; they were paid less than white workers, given the most dangerous and grueling jobs, and then not given credit at the completion.

Then the author tells of Chinese gold miners, farmers, and fishermen. Chinese contributions to mining techniques and in reclaiming land for agriculture are well explained. Information is included on where in China most immigrants came from and why they came, Chinatown in San Francisco, prejudice and its effects, and the situation with Americans of Chinese descent today.

Comment: Reading this book would really help a student understand the background of early Chinese pioneers in California as well as the reasons for their life-style.

Nonfiction: intermediate–junior high

Meltzer, Milton. **THE HISPANIC AMERICANS.** New York: Thomas Y. Crowell, 1982. 140 p. B/w photos by Morrie Camhi and Catherine Noren, bibliog., index.

Content: The fourteen chapters deal with the entire Hispanic–American picture in the United States—the early explorers such as Columbus, Ponce de Leon, Cabeza de Vaca, Coronado; the Hispanics of New York City and Miami; the continuing problems of Hispanics throughout the country today.

The sections of the book that deal specifically with California and the Hispanic–American are: recollections of the experiences of a young boy coming to Sacramento in the 1920s; descriptions of the effects of major events on California's Mexicans such as the Treaty of Guadalupe Hidalgo, the discovery of gold, and the completion of the railroad; and sections which tell about Cesar Chavez and the development of the United Farm Workers.

Comment: The portions dealing directly with California are very informative and would be useful for students trying to understand the history and present–day problems of Hispanic-Americans. Reading the whole book would give a broader picture of similar history and problems throughout the country. **Nonfiction: upper intermediate–junior high**

Meyer, Kathleen Allan. **ISHI.** Minneapolis: Dillon Press, 1980. 70 p. B/w photos.

Content: In eight chapters the author delineates the life and times of Ishi, the last of the Yahi Indians. From his desperate entry into the much feared white man's world in 1911 until his death in 1916, the man known as Ishi revealed much about the life and culture of northern California Indians. Tribe territoriality, the attempts to adjust to the incursion of white men into their world, the desperate attempt to wrest a living from an ever-decreasing area, the dignity and humor of a culture much different from our own—all these issues are addressed in this slim volume.

Comment: After a rather slow start, the author really pulls the reader into the world of a California Indian. The mistreatment

of Indians and whites by each other is told from both the Indian and white points of view.
Nonfiction: intermediate–junior high

Miles, Miska. **THE PIECES OF HOME.** Boston: Little, Brown, 1967. 60 p. Illus. by Victor Ambrus.

J mil

I m

Content: Farley and John Hamilton are enjoying life in San Francisco with their parents in the early 1900s. Farley likes his Victorian home on Filbert Street and being able to explore his city, especially fascinating Chinatown. After the earthquake and fire the family must camp–out with thousands of others in the park. Farley takes an unbidden trip back to Filbert Street to rescue a bowl his mother treasures and returns with a kitten lost by a young friend from Chinatown.
Comment: The book gives a good portrayal of people in a frightening situation. The vocabulary and concepts are aimed at about fourth–grade maturity level, though the format is more appealing to a slightly younger reader.

The Association of Children's Librarians recommended it, also noting it was now out-of-print.
Fiction: primary–intermediate

Miller, Helen Markley. **THE SAN FRANCISCO EARTHQUAKE AND FIRE.** New York: G. P. Putnam's Sons, 1970. 95 p. Pen and Ink sketches by Albert Orbaan, maps, bibliog., index.

Content: Helen Miller tells a fast-paced story of the earthquake, which did extensive damage, but from which the city could have recovered fairly soon had the fires not started. At first the authorities thought they could be contained, but with the water mains broken, fire ravaged the city for three days. The author describes the attempts to fight the fires, of the several-hundred thousand made homeless, of the aid that poured in from all over the country and the world. (Of foreign nations, Japan contributed most.) But, above all, Miller tells of the San Franciscans themselves—how they helped each other, rich and poor alike, and how they managed to keep up their spirits in the days following one of the worst disasters ever to hit the United States.

Comment: Good description, but perhaps a few too many names, facts and figures for the younger reader. Twelve-year-olds and up could learn a lot as they are introduced to tenor Enrico Caruso, actor John Barrymore, and the photographer, Arnold Genthe, whose pictures best recorded the disaster.
Nonfiction: junior high

Miller, Henry. **ACCOUNT OF A TOUR OF THE CALIFORNIA MISSIONS & TOWNS—1856: THE JOURNAL AND DRAWINGS OF HENRY MILLER.** Santa Barbara, Calif.: Bellerophon Books, n.d. 63 p. B/w illus.

Content: The sketches and text in this book are from material in the Bancroft Library at University of California, Berkeley. The pictures show the missions just before they were in near-total ruin; there are also sketches of some of the communities (Alviso, Monterey, San Luis Obispo, Santa Barbara, Los Angeles) that had grown up by, or near the Missions. There are no pictures of Missions San Rafael or Sonoma, because they were not in this collection although Miller had visited these areas. The journal is an account of Miller's trip from San Francisco to San Diego, as he visited and sketched each of the missions en route. The text has been edited—deleting some accounts of murders and other nefarious activities—so as to include more pictures. The book is in Bellerophon's usual soft-cover color book format.
Comment: This is quite interesting and easy to read; especially fascinating are Miller's descriptions of various towns, from the tiny community of Redwood City, a "little town of about 50 houses," to the thriving town of Los Angeles (pop. about 4,000). His descriptions of the countryside he travelled are very evocative of the still rural and unsettled nature of California, and which can be seen—in a few places!—even today.
Nonfiction: intermediate–adult

Montgomery, Jean. **PASSAGE TO DRAKE'S BAY.** New York: William Morrow, 1972. 192 p.

Content: A high-adventure tale of the voyage of Drake and his men to the New World as seen through the eyes of the fictional orphan Tom. Tom escapes the punishing life of the poor in sixteenth-century England to sail on the *Pelican* (later renamed the *Golden Hind*) to raid Spanish ships. The meanness of shipboard life is somewhat balanced for Tom by the adventure itself, the hope of bettering his condition, and the friendship of the seaman, Dorgan. The enmity of the dandy, Brian Salsbury, however, causes Tom constant grief. Incitement to mutiny and its bloody consequences form part of the action. Tom comes to realize that the widespread contempt for the Indians is misplaced, as the Indians at Drake's Bay nurse him back to health and befriend him in time of great need.

Comment: This is a macho, but well researched, fictional account of life at sea. The references to homosexuality are historically accurate. There is a note on Drake's Plate of Brasse. The Association of Children's Librarians recommends this book with reservations because of the violence in it.

Fiction: upper intermediate–junior high

Montgomery, Jean. **SEARCH THE WILD SHORE.** New York: William Morrow, 1974. 221 p.

Content: Russians and Spanish are vying for territory on the West Coast in 1818. A Russian boy, Zakhar Petrov, looking for his long-absent father, experiences the collision of cultures in a new land. Zakhar hoped to find his father at the Russian-American Fort Ross but was disappointed. He shipped out on an otter-hunting boat captained by a cruel Boston skipper. Troubled though this time was, Zakhar's greatest trial occurred when he and an Aleut companion were captured and enslaved by Spaniards. At first an awkward, groping youth, Zakhar matured by the time he reached safety, and his new self-reliance was, perhaps, his most important discovery.

Comment: This is an action-filled novel. The Association of Children's Librarians reviewed this book and recommended it.

Fiction: intermediate

Montgomery, Jean. **THE WRATH OF COYOTE.** New York: William Morrow, 1968. 280 p. Illus. by Anne Siberell, glossary.

Content: The legendary Chief Marin, called Kotola by his Miwok people, was a boy when the Spanish first came to the shores of the San Francisco area. From the day Kotola first spotted the tall, white-sailed ship, he and his tribe were locked in an inescapable struggle with the white men. In the beginning he was drawn to the strangers, attracted to their new ways, but as their impingement on the Miwok world became more evident, he developed a bitter hatred for them. Filled with this spirit, he led his group in a long, but doomed, effort to avoid annihilation.
Comment: The Association of Children's Librarians reviewed this book and recommended it.
Fiction: intermediate

Morrison, Dorothy Nafus. **UNDER A STRONG WIND: THE AD-VENTURES OF JESSIE BENTON FREMONT.** New York: Atheneum, 1983. 176 p. B/w illus.

Content: Using primary, and well known secondary, reference sources, Morrison has written a lively account of Jessie Benton Fremont's life. No use was made of fictional conversation or action, nor was any necessary, for Jessie wrote prolifically in her later years, and her ideas and thoughts on many subjects were well documented.
Comment: Although this account seems slightly more scholarly than the other biographies of Jessie noted herein, it is not difficult to read and gives more of an account of what social and political forces influenced the Fremonts' adventurous life. Excellent contemporary engravings and photographs.
Nonfiction: intermediate–junior high

Muir, John. Outbooks, of Golden, Colorado, (See Supplier listings) has reprinted a number of John Muir's nature writings, including:

IN THE HEART OF THE CALIFORNIA ALPS. 1872. 24 p.
THE MAMMOTH TREES OF CALAVERAS. 1872. 24 p.
THE HUMMINGBIRD OF THE CALIFORNIA WATER-FALLS. 1878. 24 p.

SIERRA BIG TREES. 1878. 80 p.
THE WILD SHEEP. 1881. 32 p.
A RIVAL OF THE YOSEMITE—THE CANYON OF THE SOUTH FORK OF KING'S RIVER. 1891. 24 p.

These booklets are all illustrated with engravings contemporary with the writings.

Comment: The print in four of the titles (numbers 1, 2, 3, 6) is quite small, and would be a turn-off to some students. These are good samplers of Muir's descriptions of the plants and creatures he observed in his California travels.

Nonfiction: junior high–senior high

Muir, John. **THE MOUNTAINS OF CALIFORNIA.** 1894. Reprint. Natural History Library. Garden City, N.Y.: Doubleday, 1961. 300 p. B/w photos, index.

Content: This is John Muir's first book, originally published in 1894; the current edition was published in cooperation with the American Museum of Natural History as part of the Natural History Library. The book contains photos of California's National Parks.

Comment: Some details do not jibe with modern usage or findings, such as scientific names of plants, altitudes, and distances, but Muir's descriptions are marvelously poetic, graphic, and detailed.

Nonfiction: high school–adult

Murphy, Marion Fisher. **SEVEN STARS FOR CALIFORNIA: A STORY OF THE CAPITALS.** Sonoma, Calif.: Marion Fisher Murphy, 1979. 75 p. Brown/white illus. by Scott William Sherman.

Content: The author tells in detail the many changes of site and the complicated maneuverings that determined the seat of government for California.

Monterey was the capital under Spanish rule and alternated with Los Angeles as the capital during much of the Mexican rule. In 1825, Echeandia, governor of both Baja and Alta

California, centered his government in San Diego. Later, Monterey regained the capital, but as the population center shifted from north to south, Los Angeles began a long-term effort to become the capital and did for short periods. By the late 1840s the now predominant American influence favored a northern choice, and the gold rush suddenly shifted the population north. Statehood was imminent, and the Constitutional Convention met, naming San Jose the permanent capital. A wet winter later, Vallejo became the permanent capital. After difficulties there and an interim in Sacramento, Benecia was designated the third permanent capital in 1853. By 1854 the fourth permanent capital was Sacramento, where it has been ever since—though not without efforts to have it moved to Oakland, San Jose, Monterey, San Francisco, and Los Angeles.

Comment: This is a most complete accounting of the moves of the capital site and the reasons for the moves. The text makes plain that agitation for separating California into two states started as early as the 1830s. It would be more useful if it contained an index, and a table of contents.

Nonfiction: intermediate–adult

Murphy, Virginia Reed. **ACROSS THE PLAINS IN THE DONNER PARTY.** A personal narrative of the overland trip to California 1846-47. 1891. Reprint. Century. Golden, Colo.: Outbooks, 1980. 64 p. B/w illus. by Frederic Remington and others, photos, map.

Content: This is an account of the Donner Party's trek to California and its tragic fate as recalled by Virginia Reed Murphy forty-five years later, and published in *Century* Magazine in 1891. Since Virginia was twelve years old at the time of the original event, she was old enough to observe and remember events in a less-prejudiced way than adults more involved in the decision making. Murphy gives excellent descriptions of starting—supplies, wagons, meeting Indians—and the four months camped at Donner Lake. Also included are rosters of family groups, giving places of origin, names and ages of family members, who died and where, names of survivors and when rescued, names of the dead and when they died, and a list of relief parties.

Comment:This is an excellent alternative to George Stewart's *Ordeal by Hunger,* which would be difficult for younger students. The account is vivid and moving, and Murphy's memories quite clear. The illustrations are excellent and contemporary, or close to it. Could be read aloud.

Nonfiction: intermediate–adult

Mylar, Isaac L. **EARLY DAYS AT THE MISSION SAN JUAN BAUTISTA: A NARRATIVE OF INCIDENTS CONNECTED WITH THE DAYS WHEN CALIFORNIA WAS YOUNG.** Rev. ed. Fresno, Calif.: Valley Publishers, 1970. 204 p. Photos, index.

Content: Mylar's personal memoirs of people, places, and events in and around the mission between 1855 and 1880 are told in a chatty and rambling style, easy to read and enjoy. It gives a good picture of life in northern California.

Comment: This book, first published in 1929, was out-of-print, then reissued. The newer edition has a revised table of contents, new pictures from the historical society files and an index ". . . designed to correct significant errors . . ." found in the first edition.

Nonfiction: junior high–adult

NEW HISTORICAL ATLAS MAP OF SANTA CLARA COUNTY. Reprint. San Jose, Calif.: Smith-McKay Printing, 1973. 110 p. Maps, etchings.

Content: In 1876 Thompson & West of San Francisco compiled an *Historical Atlas Map of Santa Clara County.* In 1973 Smith-McKay republished it. The early pages of the book contain a short history of Santa Clara County and descriptions of political and physical features of the valley, including such diverse topics as common schools and artesian wells. This is followed by several pages of selected statistics (Santa Clara County produced 1,537,632 bushels of wheat in 1875, and San Jose boasted a Handel and Haydn Musical Society). The balance of the book is devoted to reproductions of city maps and etchings of the show–places and business buildings of the time.

Comment: This book is good for many hours of enjoyable browsing through an idealized picture of Santa Clara County in 1876.

Nonfiction: intermediate–adult

Nickelsburg, Janet. **CALIFORNIA FROM THE MOUNTAINS TO THE SEA,** 4 vols. New York: Coward-McCann, 1964. Illus. by Robert Gray, photos.

Content: All four volumes have a short introduction, a conclusion, and an index.

California's Climates. Introductory chapters on where climate comes from and "Summer and Winter: the Equator and the Poles." Then the book deals with the climates of various regions of California—coast, Coast Ranges, Central Valley, four separate regions of the Sierra Nevada, desert, and Los Angeles Basin.

California's Mountains. Introductory chapters on what mountains are made of and the chain of volcanic mountains. The volume deals with individual mountains—Diablo and Whitney—and mountain ranges—Sierra Nevada, Transverse Ranges, Peninsular Ranges, and desert mountains.

California—Water and Land. The chapters deal with the Sacramento River, stream erosion and silting, canals and aqueducts, underground water, lakes, dry lakes, the ocean, and shore.

California's Natural Resources. The natural resources discussed are the forests, citrus fruits, prunes, dates, wine, raisins, field crops—barley, alfalfa, rice, cotton. Also included are livestock—cattle and sheep—tuna fishing and petroleum.

Comment: In the series *California From The Mountains to The Sea,* the author has done an extraordinary job of describing California's resources, giving brief historical backgrounds where pertinent, and writing in a clear, easy to understand style. Anyone reading these books can pick up all kinds of information. For example, instead of sheep being—well, just sheep—there are two main types of wool-producing sheep—the short, fine wool breeds and the long, medium wool breeds. Fine wool makes smooth cloth, but it cannot take hard wear.

Also included are charts, such as the one showing the formation of oil, which very clearly shows the process involved. There is also a chart showing how ground fog is formed. Altogether, these books are very instructive and informative. The pictures, charts, and diagrams add to one's understanding. Some information is dated, obviously; nonetheless, it's a fine series.

Nonfiction: intermediate

Noble, Iris. **COURAGE IN HER HANDS.** New York: Julian Messner, 1967. 190 p.

JNOB

Im

I br

Content: A story of the trials faced by the gently reared, sixteen-year-old daughter of a Boston sea captain during her stay at Fort Ross in 1815. First, she undergoes a long, arduous voyage around Cape Horn. At Fort Ross, she is fearful of both the Indians and the Russians because she is unfamiliar with their languages and customs. Finally, through personal courage she overcomes her fears and learns some of the language, customs, and superstitions of the Pomo Indians. In the end, she even becomes a heroine.

Comment: I found the story delightful and charmingly written, but the Association of Children's Librarians does not recommend it, calling it "sexist and racist."

Fiction: intermediate—junior high

Nordhoff, Charles. **C.P.R.R. THE CENTRAL PACIFIC RAIL-ROAD.** 1882. Reprint. *California for Health, Pleasure, and Residence—A Handbook for Travelers and Settlers.* Golden, Colo.: Outbooks, 1976. 32 p. B/w illus.

Content: This slender paperback tells mainly of the Sacramento merchants, especially Huntington, who built the Central Pacific Railroad. The two Crockers, Stanford, and Hopkins also figure in the volume; the business genius and practicality these men brought to the overwhelmingly complicated task is emphasized. The part played by Theodore Judah is briefly acknowledged.

Comment: This could be a fine read-aloud during a study of the

transcontinental railroad and also is of sufficient interest to capture motivated readers from upper elementary on.
Nonfiction: upper intermediate–adult

Norman, Charles. **JOHN MUIR—FATHER OF OUR NATIONAL PARKS.** New York: Julian Messner, 1957. 191 p. Bibliog., index.

Content: This biography draws on Muir's own writings from his letters and publications. This is a chronological biography, but the emphasis is on Muir's love of nature and how it led to his explorations of wilderness areas in California and Alaska. It shows Muir also as a practical inventor. Muir's role in having national forest areas set aside and in the founding of the Sierra Club are interesting in the light of today's continuing fight for conservation.

Comment: The many quotations from Muir's writings are a good introduction for the younger reader and can provide incentive for older readers to pursue their sources. The descriptions of wilderness areas with their plants, storms, and vistas are very evocative. In today's crowded California, it's especially interesting to read reactions to a more natural condition of the land. Muir's quotations make good read-alouds.
Nonfiction: upper intermediate–high school

O'Dell, Scott. **CARLOTA.** Boston: Houghton Mifflin, 1977. 153 p.

Content: Carlota, the sixteen-year-old heroine, is reared by her father, the Spaniard Don Saturnino de Zubaran, on the Rancho de los Dos Hermanos near the present city of San Diego. Carlota could ride as well as, or even better than, any vaquero on the ranch; she knew how to throw lances and was responsible for a weekly inspection of all ranch buildings. Don Saturnino, having lost a son, taught Carlota all the business of the ranch, much to the disgust of the Don's mother, who firmly believed that Carlota should be taught a more traditional female role. Carlota's training becomes valuable when Don Saturnino dies of a wound received at the Battle of San Pasqual, the last conflict between the Californios and the gringo Americans who were swarming over the countryside in their search for land and gold. The story ends with romance for Carlota in the offing, but whether marriage to a Californio or to one of the new Americans is left to the reader to decide.

Comment: O'Dell's usual fast pacing, putting many factual details into few words, is evident. Carlota is a delightful heroine, and many young readers can identify with her in her struggle to be herself in a world full of equally strong-willed men. It's a well-told story; the Association of Children's Librarians liked it, too.

Fiction: intermediate

O'Dell, Scott. **THE CRUISE OF THE ARCTIC STAR.** Boston: Houghton Mifflin, 1973. 199 p. Maps by Samuel Bryant.

ANF
910.45 0
I m

Content: Using a present-day cruise from San Diego north as the setting, O'Dell reminisces about the people and events which have made history along the coast. He tells about Cabrillo, Vizcaino, Bering, Father Serra, Portola, Kate Sessions—then recaps the Mexican War in California before he comes back to the present day as the cruise reaches Dana Point. He recollects the story of Richard Henry Dana and the life of Jedediah Smith. As the *Arctic Star* pulls into San Pedro, the history of Dead Man's Island is recounted. More about the early explorers is recalled as the ship moves on to Santa Barbara. At Point Conception history jumps forward to the 1923 naval disaster in that area. Nearing Monterey and San Francisco Bay, O'Dell tells more about Father Serra, early Spanish days, and gold discovery. He talks about Sir Francis Drake when Drake's Bay is near and then moves along the northern coast and up to Astoria, Oregon.

Comment: This fascinating narrative gives the reader a good grasp of the California coast today and the people of many yesterdays who shaped its history. O'Dell even weaves in a subplot featuring his relations with his young crewman, his fisherman friends, and his able navigator-wife. Young readers might have trouble with the time jumps, but they would be rewarded if they persevered; among the unusual historical tales O'Dell unfolds are the English sailor's version of Dead Man's Island and the work of Kate Sessions in San Diego.

Nonfiction: upper intermediate–adult

O'Dell, Scott. **ISLAND OF THE BLUE DOLPHINS.** Boston: Houghton Mifflin, 1960. 184 p.

Content: Karana, a young Indian girl, sees her father and many others killed in a conflict between her island people and the Russian fur hunters. Then, a ship comes from the California mainland to take survivors away to the mainland. Karana jumps off the ship and swims to shore as she realizes that her brother has been left behind. When her brother is killed shortly thereafter, Karana is alone. For the next eighteen years she lives there taming the wild dogs that killed her brother—because her need for companionship is so great—and learning the essentials for survival.

Comment: This beautifully written novel weaves an exciting, spellbinding tale showing a girl's indomitable spirit, courage, self-reliance, and acceptance of fate.

The novel is based on the true story of an Indian woman who spent eighteen years alone on the Island of San Nicolas, known to the Indians as the Island of the Blue Dolphins, the outermost of the eight Channel Islands. History records her as "The Lost Woman of San Nicolas." She really was rescued, as in the book, and taken to the mission at Santa Barbara in 1853. The book won a Newbery Award, was recommended by the Association of Children's Librarians, and is loved by all the children who read it!

Fiction: intermediate

O'Dell, Scott. **JOURNEY TO JERICHO.** Boston: Houghton Mifflin, 1969. 40 p. Illus. by Leonard Weisgard.

Content: Nine-year-old David Moore lives in Big Loop, West Virginia where his family and all the others in the village are employed in coal mining. David is attracted to, and frightened of, the mine; his near-miss injury, plus the all-too-frequent accidents at the mine, impel his mother to insist that the family seek another line of work. David's father gets work in the lumbering industry in far-off Jericho, California. The family has to communicate via the mails as there is not enough money for all to move. Eventually, David leaves with his mother and sister to join his father and become a Californian.

Comment: The very slight historical significance this tale might

have is in illustrating to the young reader one of the reasons why people emigrated to California.
Fiction: primary–intermediate

O'Dell, Scott. **ZIA.** Boston: Houghton Mifflin, 1976. 179 p.

Content: Zia and her brother move to Santa Barbara Mission hoping to find their aunt, Karana, who was left on an island *(Island of the Blue Dolphins)* eighteen years before. Zia and her brother find a boat and begin a hazardous journey against the sea. They eventually help rescue Karana, and in so doing, Zia, caught between the world of her tribal past and the world of the mission, finds her own freedom.
Comment: By no means as exciting or as well written as *Island of the Blue Dolphins,* this story does show some aspects of mission life from the Indian point of view. The Association of Children's Librarians recommended it.
Fiction: intermediate

Ogan, Margaret, and George Ogan. **NUMBER ONE SON.** New York: Funk & Wagnalls, 1969. 127 p. Ink and wash illus. by Vic Donahue.

Content: This is an unusual story about a San Francisco–Irish family—strong, warm-hearted people with a zest for living. The father is a commercial fisherman with little formal education. Fourteen-year-old Paddy Costello aspires to be "number one son" in his father's esteem and replace his older brother, Jerry, who really dislikes fishing. Paddy gets his chance when Jerry announces he is going to quit, move out of the house, and go to college. Paddy and his Japanese friend, Ken Nakamura, lend a hand and soon learn what hard work it is to snatch a living from the sea, as well as how hazardous the daily life of a commercial fisherman is.
Comment: This is a lively enough adventure to engage even reluctant readers. It is set in San Francisco's Fisherman's Wharf area in the 1960s.
Fiction: intermediate

Oliver, Rice D., and Barbara Paff. **STUDENT ATLAS OF CALI-**

FORNIA. Costa Mesa, Calif.: California Weekly Explorer. 1982. 61 p. B/w maps and photos, glossary, index.

Content: There are five main sections. The first, untitled, tells about the state emblems, describes the coastline, and gives information on how to use a map. At the end of this section and three others, there is a student activity sheet. The next section deals with specific regions such as the Los Angeles Basin, mountain ranges, desert areas, rivers and drainage, wilderness areas, natural harbors, and earthquake faults. History is the focus of section three. Pictorial maps and text describe Indian groups, sea and land explorations, a California time line using historical stamps as the motif, missions and ranchos, explorations of Jedediah Smith, the Mexican War, the gold rush, and pioneer routes west. Section four covers the use of land—counties, agriculture, national parks, forestry, the port of Long Beach. And section five gives information about water, climate, wildlife, places to visit, Bay Area cities, and the 1980 population of cities.

Comment: There is much of interest in this booklet. Study of the first section would certainly help students with map skills. And the history section gives good graphic maps to help students see where events occurred. The time line is very helpful. Each page, however, reminds the user that the material cannot be reproduced by any means so a discouraging number of copies is needed to use with any group.

Nonfiction: intermediate

Ortiz, Simon J. **THE PEOPLE SHALL CONTINUE.** San Francisco: Children's Book Press, 1977. 24 p. Color illus. by Sharol Graves.

Content: An epic story of Native American survival, the tale begins with the creation of the People. Earth, their Mother, takes care of them, and they take care of her. But the People are settled on reservations, and their children are removed to boarding schools. The old life is virtually destroyed. Now, after many years, the young of the People are listening once again, and they are telling the story of their survival.

Comment: "I have just read *The People Shall Continue,* and it

is so good I just could not stop reading it." (Scott Simon, then a fifth-grader in San Francisco.)
Nonfiction: primary–intermediate

Palmer, John Williamson. **PIONEER DAYS IN SAN FRANCISCO.** Reprinted from various 19th century sources. Olympic Valley, Calif.: Outbooks, 1977. 32 p. B/w illus.

Content: The story of San Francisco from 1846, when the first American flag was raised, to the mid-1850s. Covers a wide variety of topics, including the early days of the Mormon settlement, the effects of the gold rush, prices of goods, nationalities of inhabitants, descriptions of streets and buildings, locations of early businesses, law and order, fires and reconstruction, religious growth.

Comment: The small print and little or no narrative would probably discourage the younger or poor reader, but the contemporary descriptions bring early San Francisco to life. Could be read aloud in small doses to expand textbook readings. Many contemporary prints are included, as is a view of the city in 1847 on the cover.
Nonfiction: junior high–adult

PARKS OF CALIFORNIA. Reprint. San Francisco: Pacific Gas and Electric Co. 1974. n. p.

Content: This series compiled from articles published in *P.G. & E. Progress* from 1972 to 1974, gives historic information about many well known California parks. It describes some municipal parks, state parks, national parks, national monuments, and regional parks.

Comment: The short articles are fairly easy reading and contain much information to interest. As with the other P.G. & E. booklets the original of this one is out of print; a stapled, unbound photocopy is available, free, in limited quantities from P.G. & E.
Nonfiction: intermediate–adult

Pinchot, Jane. **THE MEXICANS IN AMERICA.** Minneapolis: Lerner, 1973. 99 p. Photos, index.

Content: The author deals with identifying Mexican-Americans, telling of their origin and history, showing the way in which the Mexican-American community has emerged, and then noting some specific individuals and their achievements.

Comment: Though this book is not focused specifically on California, it gives a detailed picture of the problems, concerns, and contributions of Mexican-Americans in the Southwest, including California. Studying the text would help a student achieve an understanding of the history affecting the lives and attitudes of Mexican-Americans in our culture today. The writing is detailed and intense; it requires careful reading.

Nonfiction: intermediate–junior high

Place, Marian T. **MOUNTAIN MAN—THE LIFE OF JIM BECK-WOURTH.** New York: Macmillan, 1970. 120 p. B/w illus., bibliog., index.

Content: See Felton, Harold W. *Jim Beckwourth, Negro Mountain Man.*

Pohlmann, Lillian. **MYRTLE ALBERTINA'S SECRET.** New York: Coward-McCann, 1956. 128 p.

Content: Myrtle Albertina, born about 1881 in the Grass Valley-Nevada City area of the mother lode country, had two problems: finding a special gift for her mother's birthday and proving to her father that she could keep a secret. The accomplishment of both involves her and her dog with a traveling photographer and his son, a "highgrader" (gold thief), the local sheriff, and making what seemed to her very grown-up decisions.

Comment: The pleasant story set in a California mining town has an authentic historical background.

Fiction: intermediate

Pohlmann, Lillian. **MYRTLE ALBERTINA'S SONG.** New York: Coward-McCann, 1958. 218 p.

Content: Set in the Grass Valley-Nevada City area of the mother lode in the late nineteenth century, the story relates the further adventures of Myrtle Albertina, her dog, and her friend Tuley. Upset because Tuley's father feels that he cannot continue to live in a town where some still regard him as a "highgrader" (gold thief), Myrtle Albertina figures ways to keep him there, involving in the process her friends in the many ethnic groups to be found in early California mining towns.

Comment: The author has a nice way of blending the interests of the various ethnic groups in her stories. However, the Association of California Librarians says it's a mediocre story with an unrealistic, gold-town setting.

Fiction: intermediate

Pohlmann, Lillian. **OWLS AND ANSWERS.** Philadelphia: Westminister, 1964. 175 p. Illus. by Al Fiorentino.

Content: Margaret is a shy and unhappy young girl living with her mother in San Francisco in the late 1800s while her father is off gold mining. Margaret's mother remains and tends the family store because she believes that living with her husband in Grass Valley would be too rough for her and their daughter. Margaret convinces her mother that she can go off alone to visit her father. When she arrives in Grass Valley, the friendly Butler family is there to welcome her, but her father has disappeared. Two weeks with the Butlers offer Margaret lots of new adventures and time to grow. By the last page, the family is reunited.

Comment: A good "girl growing up" story that would help a young reader envision life in the northern California of the 1890s.

Fiction: intermediate

Pohlmann, Lillian. **THE UNSUITABLE BEHAVIOR OF AMERICA MARTIN.** Philadelphia: Westminister, 1976.

Content: America, a strong-willed, resourceful girl of the 1870s, has no wish to live the rich, southern-plantation life her aunt and uncle expect. So when her friends, Bird and Roy, decide to go west, she goes with them to test herself and to find Ned Massie who had recently left the South to seek gold near Nevada City. Journeying by paddle-wheeler, train and stage-coach, she experiences new places and new faces. On her arrival in Nevada City, she finds that Ned is not there. Working out the trials of being on her own through long months of fulfilling and unfulfilling relationships, she feels herself richly changed, at last, into a mature women.

Comment: This is not a very plausible story of life in the frontier west.

Fiction: junior high–senior high

Politi, Leo. **PICCOLO'S PRANK.** New York: Charles Scribner's Sons, 1965. 44 p. Illus. by the author.

Content: Piccolo, a pet monkey, hopped and skipped to Luigi's lively organ music. One day the high-spirited monkey jumped into mischief that almost brought disaster.

Comment: The vivid illustrations and light-hearted story, set in the Bunker Hill section of Los Angeles, will amuse young readers while recalling an earlier period in one area of the southern-California metropolis.

Fiction: primary

Potts, Marie. **THE NORTHERN MAIDU.** Happy Camp, Calif.: Naturegraph Publishers, 1977. 46 p. B/w photos, map.

Content: The author, a Maidu Indian herself, gives the what, how, why of Maidu daily life—homes, baths, clothing, marriage, religion, doctoring, midwives, toys and games, and others—in short sections. The Maidu lived in present–day Lassen, Butte, and Plumas Counties.

Comment: This is a useful, interesting, and easily read book. One can get a good idea of how these Indians lived and worked.

Nonfiction: intermediate–junior high

Pourade, Richard S. **THE CALL TO CALIFORNIA.** San Diego: Calif.: Union-Tribune Pub. Co., 1968. 194 p. Illus., maps. Index.

Content: The subtitle (The Epic Journey of the Portola-Serra Expedition of 1769.) says in a nutshell what this book is about. Approximately half of the book traces the journey up Baja California to San Diego; the rest is an account of Portola's attempt to find Monterey Bay and his discovery of San Francisco Bay. The format consists of a two-page spread of each stop of the expedition, one page of a photo of the stopping point, the other page of historical narrative and excerpts from diaries of some of the company. Picture maps at the beginning of each chapter pinpoint locations mentioned. The modern location of the stops is given.

Comment: The value of this book is that the photos are close to actual stopping points of the expeditions, and along with the diary accounts, give a vivid picture of what this trip entailed. Rewarding reading to those who want to know what it was really like in the early days, but are not up to the complete diaries.

Nonfiction: junior high–adult

Preble, Donna. **YAMINO KWITI.** A Story of Indian Life in the Los Angeles Area. 1940. Reprint. Berkeley, Calif.: Heyday Books, 1983. 224 p. B/w illus., glossary of Indian words, bibliog.

Content: *Yamino Kwiti* is the story of a Gabrielino Indian boy living in California in the mid-1700s, just before the establishment of the missions. The young protagonist has adventures with bears, and conflicts with neighboring tribes; he dreams of being a courier like his father. He is frustrated by being trained as a member of the priesthood against his will. His agile brain and intense curiosity get him into scrapes; the same qualities bring him into contact with the first white men to come into his southern California domain.

Comment: When this story was first published in 1940, the noted anthropologist, Alfred Kroeber, wrote the foreword and praised the authenticity of the portrayal of Indian life. The tale would hold a child's interest. The use of Indian words adds richness but might also make it harder for younger students to read independently.

Fiction: intermediate

Pritchard, Alan. **CALIFORNIA BEFORE 1776.** Sacramento, Calif.: Creative Editions, 1975. 34 p. B/w illus. by Ric Hugo.

Content: In nine short, breezy chapters the author deals with the very early history of California and the United States. The chapters that deal specifically with California cover information on the bristlecone pine, the origin of man according to Miwok legend, Ishi, Sir Francis Drake and early Spanish explorers, a little on the establishment of the missions, and Ayala's entry into and exploration of San Francisco Bay.

Comment: This soft-cover reprint, based on material published in the *Sacramento Bee,* was originally written in celebration of the 1976 bicentennial. It's definitely an informal approach. When talking about Ishi's world, for example, the author says, "As nations go, Yana wasn't much." The book does contain interesting information. One feature that looks especially interesting is the comparison of what was going on in the thirteen colonies at the same time as specific events that were happening in California.
Nonfiction: intermediate–adult

Putnam, George Palmer. **DEATH VALLEY AND ITS COUNTRY.** New York: Duell, 1957. 231 p. Bibliog., index.

ANF
973.01
PUT
Im

Content: Following a general description of the valley, the author gives several possible reasons it got its name and then deals with some historical anecdotes. He goes on to include information about the emigrants of 1849 and 1850, borax, the climate, the geology, the local Indians, the plants, Death Valley Scotty and Scotty's castle, prehistoric and present animal life, and the rocks and gems. Toward the end of the book, the author describes various nearby areas—Amargosa country, Stovepipe Wells, the Panamint Valley, ghost camps, and the Owens Valley.

Comment: The writing style varies from anecdotal to personal to scientific. Elementary students might have problems staying with it for many chapters, but it could be used for reference.
Nonfiction: intermediate

Putnam, Vii. **HARD HEARTS ARE FOR CABBAGES.** New York: Crown, 1959. 285 p.

Content: Eight-year-old Vanita recounts episodes of her life as a youngster in a big gypsy tribe which decided to settle down near Stockton after a lifetime of wandering throughout Europe and sojourning in New York City. All the members of the large, extended family have their special activities and pursue their interests fearlessly. The neighboring "wofude" man (one who hates gypsies) and the conservative townspeople try to discourage the settlement, but the gypsies observe their customs and their ceremonies. We see them befriend a Chinese parolee and an Indian; we see them steal, dance, sing, and above all, teach their children their pattern of living.

Comment: An unusual, rather-complicated novel. Parts of it would appeal to children, especially if read aloud.

Fiction: upper intermediate–adult

Radlauer, Ruth. **YOSEMITE NATIONAL PARK.** Chicago: Children's Press, 1975. 48 p. Color illus.

917.94
RAD

IBr
I BKm
2 m

Content: A description of how the valley was formed, the numerous sights—lakes, waterfalls, trees, animals, Pioneer History Museum, Indian Village—a bit of history and various activities available, with matching color photographs on the facing page. A mini-tour of the park.

Comment: A good introduction to the park, with wonderful illustrations, and good advice regarding feeding animals, heeding the rangers, and general good park manners.

Nonfiction: upper elementary–junior high

Rambeau, Nancy, and John Rambeau. **LONG AGO STORIES OF CALIFORNIA.** Sacramento: California State Depart. of Education, 1957. 192 p. Illus. by Sabina and Jean Yates, glossary, bibliog.

uc6

OP

Content: "Chumash Boy" tells of Chumash Indian life at the time of Cabrillo's voyage in 1542. "The Black Pearl of La Paz" is about a boy who came from Baja California in 1795 when Spain was entrenched in both Alta and Baja California. "The Magic Door" is set in the rancho days of 1836 and has a Mexican girl as protagonist. "Go West for Gold" features an American family in 1850. "China Boy" tells of an immigrant

Chinese boy of the 1860s. "Stranger at Cherry Hill" is the story of an Italian family who arrives in 1890.

Comment: The reading is easy for students of fourth-grade level and above; knowledge about the feelings of the people and the problems of the times can be found.

Fiction: primary–intermediate

Rambo, Ralph. **ADVENTURE VALLEY: PIONEER ADVENTURES IN THE SANTA CLARA VALLEY.** San Jose, Calif.: Rosicrucian Press, 1970. 48 p. Illus. by the author, bibliog. Map.

Content: This contains short vignettes of early residents of Santa Clara Valley—Indians, Americans, Mexicans. Special features include a list of early valley residents, giving their place of origin and the year they arrived; a map of ranchos in the valley with their names, the owner's names, whether the ranchos were Mexican grants or American awarded, and the year of granting.

Comment: The writing style in a number of instances isn't as light hearted as in Rambo's other books, possibly because he is relating more secondhand material.

Nonfiction: intermediate–adult

Rambo, Ralph. **ALMOST FORGOTTEN: CARTOON PEN AND INKLINGS OF THE OLD SANTA CLARA VALLEY.** San Jose, Calif.: Rosicrucian Press, 1964. 48 p. Illus. by the author, index.

Content: This is a collection of one-page histories from Indian times through Spanish settlement, the forty-niners to memories of the author's childhood *circa* 1900. It includes a dictionary of names—people, places, things—who, why, and how they were.

Comment: This is the first of Rambo's marvelously chatty "memory books." Several of the subjects have subsequently been more fully treated in his later works. The text is hand lettered. There is a list of sources used for historical background.

Nonfiction: intermediate–adult

Rambo, Ralph. **LADY OF MYSTERY.** San Jose, Calif.: Rosicrucian Press, 1967. 16 p. Sketches by the author.

Content: This is a short history of the Winchester Mystery House and of Sara Winchester who built it. It includes descriptions of materials used, rooms, and oddities. The book is based on personal recollections of the author and on stories of contemporaries.
Comment: The house has long been a mystery even to those who live near it. This book should clear up many of the stories surrounding Mrs. Winchester and her unusual home. Rambo stresses fact and refutes legend.
Nonfiction: intermediate–adult

Rambo, Ralph. **"LO, THE POOR INDIAN" OF THE SANTA CLARA VALLEY.** San Jose, Calif.: Rosicrucian Press, 1967. 16 p. Sketches by the author.

Content: This is ". . . a short collection of fact and anecdotes to describe in words and pictures the environment and lives of the Indians . . ." of Santa Clara Valley from the time of Spanish settlement to near extinction during American settlement.
Comment: The author used the writings of contemporary historians and sociologists found in local university collections as sources. He includes a glossary of Spanish and Indian words in the hand-lettered text.
Nonfiction: intermediate–adult

Rambo, Ralph. **ME AND CY.** San Jose, Calif.: Rosicrucian Press, 1968. 48 p. Illus. by the author.

Content: These are reminiscences of the author as a youngster in San Jose, *circa* 1905. Cy was an older neighbor of Rambo's who befriended the nine-year-old boy, took him to visit the residents of a "retirement colony" in the Alviso garbage dumps, and told wonderful tall tales based on local history.
Comment: The hand-lettered text and informal anecdotal style will appeal to good readers at the elementary level and up.
Nonfiction: intermediate–adult

Rambo, Ralph. **PIONEER BLUE BOOK OF THE OLD SANTA CLARA VALLEY.** San Jose, Calif.: Rosicrucian Press, 1973. 48 p. Illus. by the author, bibliog.

Content: This is an alphabetically arranged "Who Was Who," *circa* 1849. ". . . brief and casual biographies about certain typical pioneers of the Santa Clara Valley . . . chosen for their prominence or historical contributions." Many entries are familiar as present-day street and place names. The information includes place of origin if not native born, date of birth (but not death), date of arrival in California for self or ancestors, and claim to fame. The addenda includes additional names with dates of arrival in the valley, origin, and a few remarks about each; a list of elementary schools in 1887; pioneer towns and places, and their origins.
Comment: This would be a good book to "dip into." Santa Clara Valley students could browse for names they know as place names and find out about the persons they commemorate.
Nonfiction: intermediate–adult

Rambo, Ralph. **REMEMBER WHEN . . . A BOY'S-EYE VIEW OF AN OLD VALLEY.** San Jose, Calif.: Rosicrucian Press, 1965. 56 p. Sketches by the author.

Content: Rambo discusses schools, entertainments, area characters, the Chinese community, and other remembrances of his childhood.
Comment: This is the sequel to the author's *Almost Forgotten,* and he uses the same hand-lettering, cartoon illustrations, and chatty style to make the past come alive again.
Nonfiction: intermediate–adult

Rambo, Ralph. **TRAILING THE CALIFORNIA BANDIT, TIBUR-CIO VASQUEZ 1835–1875.** San Jose, Calif.: Rosicrucian Press, 1968. 40 p. Bibliog. Illus. by the author.

Content: This very short biography of Vasquez includes contemporary accounts in newspapers, magazines, and local county records.
Comment: This is an interesting and easy to read booklet; the style is informal, but factual. Hand-lettered text with many drawings by the author, some of which are portraits copied from contemporary pictures of the subjects.
Nonfiction: intermediate–adult

Randall, Janet. **BRAVE YOUNG WARRIORS.** New York: David McKay, 1969. 182 p.

Content: The story highlights the hostility between the Yankees coming into California and the Californios. Young Mark Tyler and Gil Estrada, although enemies at the beginning of the story, become good friends after being lost off a ship near one of the Channel Islands, being rescued, and enduring the long trip south to the Estrada ranch.

Comment: There is a lot of action in this novel, and young readers would absorb a good bit of history while enjoying the story. Be aware that the Association of Children's Librarians recommended the book with reservations, ". . . a good adventure story . . . (but) the author used words such as "lazy" and "indolent" to describe Californios . . ."

Fiction: intermediate

Randall, Ruth Painter. **I JESSIE.** Boston: Little, Brown, 1963. 223 p. B/w illus., index.

Content: This story of Jessie Benton Fremont, wife of John Charles Fremont, is based on Jessie's letters and autobiographical writings as well as other biographical materials. Many quotations from her own writings are used throughout.

Comment: What an extraordinary woman Jessie Fremont was, and what an extraordinary life she had! This is brought out very effectively by Randall, and the Fremonts' lifelong devotion to each other is well pictured. If one was originally biased against Fremont, reading this story might bring one to a less-critical viewpoint.

Nonfiction: junior high–senior high

Raphael, Ray. **AN EVERYDAY HISTORY OF SOMEWHERE.** New York: Alfred A. Knopf, 1974. 193 p. Pen and ink drawings by Mark Livingston, bibliographical essay.

Content: "Being the true story of Indians, deer, homesteaders, potatoes, loggers, trees, fishermen, salmon, and other living things in the backwoods of northern California" is the subtitle. In the introduction, the author says, "The everyday history of anyplace (sic) is just talking about what's been happening there over the centuries—nothing more, nothing less.'' And talk about it he does. There are few dates or facts. Instead, the reader wanders along through paragraphs about the life of the early coastal Indians, into some Indian folk tales, and then to the everyday life of a deer. Tales weave in and out, drifting from vignettes of people into stories of animals, and on into present-day people and creatures.

Comment: This attractively designed and illustrated book wanders pleasantly. When you finish, you don't know all the facts of those coastal counties, but you will feel you know what's been happening over the centuries. Having students read excerpts from this and comparing it to a straightforward history could help them learn the differing perspectives of books.

Nonfiction: junior high–adult

Reece, Daphne. **HISTORIC HOUSES OF CALIFORNIA.** San Francisco: Chronicle Books, 1983. 121 p. B/w illus., index.

Content: The houses are grouped by general geographical areas from north to south—north coast, Sacramento Valley and Tahoe, Wine Country, Bay Area, gold country, central coast, southland. Each entry gives the name of the house and, usually, the original builder, the year it was built, and a brief history of the house and builder and/or owners. Also listed are the historical or preservation societies responsible for preservation, restoration and upkeep of the houses. Addresses, phone numbers, hours, and admission charges, if any, are also included. There are numerous photos but not of every house listed.

Comment: This would be a useful resource for teachers interested in having their students gain insights into postmission, daily living. The houses range in size and style from fairly simple adobe or wood frame to the elaborate ostentation of San Simeon. Many of the houses contain furnishings of the original owners, as well as later acquisitions that are contemporaneous with their period.

Reference: intermediate–adult

Reinstadt, Randall. A. **GHOSTLY TALES AND MYSTERIOUS**

HAPPENINGS OF OLD MONTEREY. Carmel, Calif.: Ghost Town Publications, 1977. 64 p. Illus. by Antone A. Hrusa, maps.

Content: Forty-three tales in a vein similar to *Ghosts, Bandits and Legends of Old Monterey* reviewed below.
Comment: See general comment after last Reinstadt entry.
Nonfiction: intermediate–adult

Reinstadt, Randall A. **GHOSTS, BANDITS AND LEGENDS OF OLD MONTEREY.** Carmel, Calif.: Ghost Town Publications, 1974. 48 p. Illus. by Thornton Harby, map.

Content: The individual stories recount tales of ghosts and phantoms associated with old houses of Monterey, Pacific Grove and Carmel, as well as stories set in the forests, caves, and coastal spots. The tales range in time from Indian days to the present.
Comment: See general comment after last Reinstadt entry.
Nonfiction: intermediate–adult

Reinstadt, Randall A. **MONTEREY'S MOTHER LODE.** Carmel, Calif.: Ghost Town Publications, 1977. 96 p. Photos, maps.

Content: Nineteen pages of text recount the history of local mining, focusing on the Los Burros district, Santa Lucia Mountains, and lower Monterey County. Stories, legends, and mysteries of individual miners and mines associated with this inhospitable territory are recorded. Some sixty-five pages of captioned photographs follow. The first section has old photos of mines, buildings, people, and artifacts. The second section has more recent photographs, including many of the damage of a disastrous 1970 fire in the Los Padres National Forest.
Comment: See general comment after last Reinstadt entry.
Nonfiction: intermediate–adult

Reinstadt, Randall A. **SHIPWRECKS AND SEA MONSTERS OF CALIFORNIA'S CENTRAL COAST.** Carmel, Calif.: Ghost Town Publications, 1975. 168 p. Illus. by Antone A. Hrusa, photographs, maps.

Content: Some forty-one shipwrecks along the central coast are reported, including an account of the ill-fated dirigible *Macon* in 1935.
Comment: These stories are copiously illustrated with historic photographs. The section dealing with real, imagined, or alleged sea monsters is also rich with photographs and drawings of these wary denizens of the deep.
Nonfiction: intermediate

Reinstadt, Randall A. **TALES, TREASURES AND PIRATES OF OLD MONTEREY.** Carmel, Calif.: Ghost Town Publications, 1976. 72 p. Photographs, maps.

Content: This book recounts the numerous tales and legends of lost mines, caches of Indian gold, buried treasure, banditry associated with various valuables, and attacks from the sea by pirates and American warships. Details of the finding of a bottle enclosing a lead plate in which Sir Francis Drake had inscribed his claim to this land are also included. Thirty rare historical photos are included.
Comment: See general comment after last Reinstadt entry.
Nonfiction: intermediate–adult

Reinstadt, Randall A. **WHERE HAVE ALL THE SARDINES GONE?** Carmel, Calif.: Ghost Town Publications, 1978. 168 p. Photos, maps.

Content: Thirteen pages of text recount the growth and decline of the fishing industry in Monterey. The individuals and structures, the fires and accidents, the romantic interpretation of the area by John Steinbeck, and the contemporary state of the tourist-supported area—all is included. About 140 pages of captioned photographs follow, unfolding the history of a remarkable town.
Comment: Reinstadt is a Monterey teacher and lecturer on California history, who teaches a college course on "How to Turn Children on to California History." The six Reinstadt books annotated here are randomly organized collections of stories, legends, and pictures of the Monterey area. They would be interesting for a student to dip into, rather than to read cover

to cover. Indexes and line maps would be useful additions. The historical photographs are well chosen and well reproduced.
Nonfiction: intermediate–adult

Rife, Joanne. **WHERE THE LIGHT TURNS GOLD, THE STORY OF THE SANTA YNEZ VALLEY.** Fresno, Calif.: Valley Publishers, 1977. 151 p. Bibliog., index.

Content: Starting with a chapter on the problems and concerns of the Santa Ynez Valley, the author then moves back to explain the history of the area. She tells of the Chumash Indians, the coming of the Spanish and the missions, and then details the stories of the pioneer towns—Ballard, Santa Ynez, Los Olivos, Buellton, and Las Cruces. "The Outlanders" is a chapter on the people who lived in the valley outside those pioneer towns. "The Danish Influence" tells about the history of Solvang.
Comment: This book was written for adults, but parts of it could be useful with young readers. The chapter on the Chumash tells of the local Indians from prehistory to the present. In the chapter on the Spanish and the missions, there is more detail about the long-term restoration than is usually found. The history of the individual towns and people would be interesting and helpful in regional studies; the chronology at the end—four and one-half pages of dated listings of important historical events of the area—would be fun for young readers to study as they tried to learn more about their own area.
Nonfiction: junior high–adult

Ritter, Ed, Helen Ritter and Stanley Spector. **OUR ORIENTAL AMERICANS.** St. Louis: McGraw-Hill, 1965. 104 p. Illus., photos, bibliog., index.

Content: An easily read overview of the history of the Orientals in the United States, mainly in California. The Chinese and Japanese receive the greatest coverage as the most-numerous Asian minorities. The last chapter, "Filipinos and Others," is mainly about Filipinos and is only a cursory look.
Comment: This is more of an introductory book than a complete study.
Nonfiction: junior high–adult

RIVERS OF CALIFORNIA. San Francisco: Pacific Gas & Electric Co., n.d. 47 p.

Content: Twenty-six rivers in California are described in texts of one-full page or more. Fifty-eight more California rivers have shorter entries. In each case, the location, length, and importance of the river is described. In most cases, some history is included as well, a significant amount in the descriptions of the following rivers: American, Colorado, Cosumnes, Feather, Kern, Klamath, Kings, Noyo, Russian, Sacramento, Salinas, San Lorenzo, San Joaquin, Smith, Stanislaus, and Yuba.

Comment: There is much natural and political history in this stapled unbound photocopy of material first compiled from a series of articles in *P.G. & E. Progress*. Limited quantities are available free from P.G. & E. As many of the rivers were named after Indian tribes, there is a good deal of Indian lore, too.

The photographs are not well reproduced.

Nonfiction: upper intermediate–adult

Roberts, Helen. **MISSION TALES: STORIES OF THE HISTORI- CAL CALIFORNIA MISSIONS.** Rev. ed. 7 vols. Palo Alto, Calif.: Pacific Books, 1962. Illus. by Muriel Lawrence, Endpaper maps.

Content: *Vol. 1.* Mission San Diego. "The Miracle Ship." A tale of the first critical year of the California missions.

Mission San Luis Rey. "Father Peyri's Shadows." The priest's surprising reward to two Indian students.

Mission San Juan Capistrano. "The Two-Tailed Comet." The struggle of a young Indian against the terrifying superstitions of his people.

Vol. 2. Mission San Gabriel. "The Artist of San Gabriel." The charming story of Gabriel, a young Indian who yearned to be a painter, and the fulfillment of his dream.

Mission San Fernando Rey. "A Gift for the Padre." A touching story of the Christmas gift Father Ibarra receives.

Mission San Buenaventura. "The Garden of San Buenaventura." An Indian boy's rise from kitchen helper to chief gardener.

Vol. 3. Mission Santa Barbara. "The Lone Woman of San

Nicolas." The rescue of an Indian woman after eighteen years of exile on a lonely island.

Mission Santa Ines. "Pasquala of Santa Ines." The true story of a courageous native girl who saved the mission.

Mission Purisima. "The Anger of Chupu." The effect of a disastrous earthquake upon an Indian youth, his grandfather, and his palomino horse.

Vol. 4. Mission San Luis Obispo. "The Tilemaker." A young Indian's contribution to the perfecting of the tiles.

Mission San Miguel. "The Wishing Chair." The legend of the Wishing Chair and what happened to a Tulare Indian girl who sat in it.

Mission San Antonio de Padua. "The Bear Hunter." An exciting account of the bear hunt that saved the mission from starvation.

Vol. 5. Mission Soledad. "Clemente's Christmas." Showing how a lonely sheepherder found friends through the Nativity play.

Mission San Carlos. "Juan of Carmel." An Indian boy's adventure in the early days of Carmel Mission.

Mission San Juan Bautista. "The Magic Barrel Organ." A young Indian singer lost his voice but found it in time to stop the enemy.

Vol. 6. Mission Santa Cruz. "Miguel and the Pirates." An Indian girl found happiness in her mission home.

Mission San Jose. "The Music Maker." About an Indian boy who loved music.

Vol. 7. Mission San Francisco de Asis. "Chamais and Li-lote." The romantic story of the first Indians at Mission Dolores.

Mission San Raphael. "The Warrior of San Rafael." A lame Indian boy's victory over a dreaded kidnapper.

Mission San Francisco Solano. "Big Chief Solano." The story of a powerful Indian chief and his decision for peace with the white man.

Comment: Each volume of this classic seven-volume series contains three stories (except #6 which contains two) about individual missions in the same geographical area. For each story, the author establishes the locale, provides a brief history of the mission, describes the local Indians, and gives a chronol-

ogy of important events in which the mission figured. The fictional part concerns the interaction between the padres and young Indians who learn in varying ways to accept mission culture. The biased treatment of the padres presents only their positive aspects, stressing how much the mission culture did for the Indians in "civilizing and Christianizing" them. Despite this, the series is valuable for presenting some accurate historical information and insights into Indian tribes and cultures. The volumes were originally published in 1948 and are approximately ninety pages each.
Fiction: intermediate

Roberts, Margaret. **PIONEER CALIFORNIA—TALES OF EX-PLORERS, INDIANS AND SETTLERS.** San Luis Obispo, Calif.: Padre Productions, 1982. 226 p. B/w illus., maps, bibliog., index.

Content: A history of California from the Spanish arrival to the gold rush that focuses on specific people at different periods within this span. The characters include an Indian of the Monterey area, Jedediah Smith, the Donner Party, John Charles Fremont, the Death Valley Party, and John Sutter. The bibliography is a mix of primary and secondary sources mostly for adults. There are some children's and young people's histories of California cited; but they are not always identified as such.
Comment: The stories are well researched and crammed with facts and details. Since the chapters are self-contained without linking narrative, they can be read as individual stories rather than cover to cover—in fact, for younger intermediate readers, this would be an easier approach.
Nonfiction: intermediate–junior high

Robinson, W.W. **THE KEY TO LOS ANGELES.** Keys to the Cities. Philadelphia: Lippincott, 1963. 128 p. Photos, map, index.

Content: A history of the city from its pueblo days through the ranchos, the American "invasion," its opening up with railroad access, the building of San Pedro harbor and aqueducts, to the present.
Comment: Since this book is twenty years old, its contempo-

rary sections are historical, but as a short and easily read history of Los Angeles's beginnings and growth, this has value.
Nonfiction: intermediate–junior high

Ross, Dudley T. **DEVIL ON HORSEBACK.** Fresno, Calif.: Valley Publishers, 1975. 212 p. Illus., index.

Content: Jack Powers came to California as a private in the New York Volunteers during the war with Mexico in 1847. Mustered out in 1848, he tried mining along the Stanislaus River and became one of the terrorizing Tammany Hall "Hounds" in San Francisco. He attempted to make his fortune in cattle driving, became involved in land ownership and was fleeced in a land fraud. He, thereafter, became notorious as Jack Powers, desperado, continually in trouble with local vigilante groups. His most famous exploit was riding a string of relay horses 150 miles in less than seven hours to win a $2500 wager. Two years later in 1860, he was killed in a remote corner of Arizona.
Comment: Power's ten-year California career is still marked by mystery, but the author has done a good job of gathering, arranging, and interpreting the available materials and creating a biography of one of California's mid-nineteenth century outlaws. (adapted from *Los Angeles Times*.)
Nonfiction: senior high

Rowland, Florence Wightman. **PASQUALA OF SANTA YNEZ MISSION.** New York: Walck, 1961. 111 p. Pen and ink illus. by Charles Geer.

Content: Pasquala, a Tulare Indian, and her family were content to live at the Santa Ynez Mission. The story recounts the events of mission life—school and church, festivals and games, the work of the Indians, and the leadership of a kindly priest. When a warlike Tulare chief who wished the defectors to return to his tribe kidnapped Pasquala and others, her bravery saves the mission from Indian attack.
Comment: The book gives an overview of mission life and an idea of the basic struggle between Spanish and Indian cultures. The kidnapping episode clearly contrasts life in a Tulare settlement with that of the mission. Fourth-grade classes hearing this

read aloud were clearly interested and asked for it later at the library.

The Association of Children's Librarians, however, does not recommend it, saying it is biased in favor of the mission system.
Fiction: intermediate

Sanderlin, George. **THE SETTLEMENT OF CALIFORNIA.** New York: Coward-McCann, 1972. 223 p. Photos, bibliog., index.

Content: Beginning with the Spanish discoverers between 1492 and 1757, the author moves to Father Serra and the development of the mission system, concentrating on the years to 1775. Then attention is given to the Russian settlement in California, which ended in 1841, followed by the story of the growing American involvement—through Boston clipper ships and the mountain men. The next emphasis is on the change over to American rule between 1845 and 1847, the gold rush starting in 1848 and 1849, and the successful drive for statehood which spanned the years 1848 to 1851.

Comment: This clearly and simply written history contains pertinent excerpts from many first-hand accounts from the 1700s through 1850. Excerpts from such sources as the diaries of the Franciscan friars, *Two Years Before The Mast,* and *The Shirley Letters* make California history live.
Nonfiction: intermediate–junior high

Saroyan, William. **THE HUMAN COMEDY.** New York: Harcourt, Brace, 1943. 246 p. Revised, 1971. Illus. by Don Freeman.

Content: This novel relates the activities, joys, sorrows, and problems of a fatherless family of four children and their mother during World War I. The setting is a Central Valley farm community called Ithaca in the story. Here fourteen-year-old Homer Macauley learns about life as he attends school with the Italians, Armenians, Chicanos, the slum dwellers, and the elite. He also has glimpses into the lives of the businessmen, the vintners, the wealthy landowners and, especially, that of the old heavy-drinking telegrapher with whom he works as the fastest messenger the company ever had. Since Marcus Macauley, Homer's older brother, is away at army camp, the family experiences with the whole community the frustrations of wartime living and the fears of that final telegram.

Comment: This excellent story is told with sincerity and simplicity, but it may take a sensitive and thoughtful young person of today to read it with understanding.
Fiction: junior high–adult

Saroyan, William. **MY NAME IS ARAM.** New York: Harcourt, Brace, 1937. 219 p. Illus. by Don Freeman.

Content: This series of episodes in the life of the author relates memories of his life as the son of an Armenian-immigrant family living in Fresno. He runs away from school to attend the circus; he defies his irate and frustrated teachers; he helps his uncle with his dream orchard; he chauffeurs an oil-rich Indian. The book gives us a glimpse of the ideas and ideals of a poverty-stricken family during the Great Depression.

Comment: An easy-to-read, interesting book telling of the early life of a celebrated American author. Many young readers could enjoy the action, but it would take a sensitive reader to appreciate its depth.
Nonfiction: junior high–adult

Sasek, M. **THIS IS SAN FRANCISCO.** New York: Macmillan, 1962. Color illus. 60 p.

Content: In simple text and colorful illustrations, the author-illustrator gives some basic information about San Francisco up to 1962. Places of interest mentioned include Lombard Street, the Broadway Tunnel, Telegraph Hill, Fisherman's Wharf, the bridges, Mission Dolores, Steinhart Aquarium, and Chinatown.

Comment: This title seems most suitable as a book to read aloud and discuss with young children. Those who know San Francisco will recognize many of the pictures.
Nonfiction: primary

Scott, Bernice. **JUNIPERO SERRA, PIONEER OF THE CROSS.** Fresno, Calif.: Valley Publishers, 1976. 224 p. Bibliog., index.

Content: The preface carefully explains that this work, though historically accurate, must be classified as fiction because the conversations and detailed descriptions are the creations of the author. Its framework is the true story of Miguel Serra of Majorca, who was to become Father Serra, the founder of the California mission system.

After becoming a member of the Franciscan order, he won recognition and following as an inspired speaker and leader. He rejected the opportunity to pursue scholarship and prominence in the church hierarchy to become a missionary in the New World, bringing with him his friends, Francisco Palou and Juan Crespi. After some service in Mexico, he was sent briefly to Baja California and then on to Alta California as president of the missions to be established. Arriving in Alta California in 1769—fifty-six years old and lame—Father Serra, helped by Padres Palou and Crespi, spent fourteen years founding the first nine missions and fighting zealously to convert the Indian population. Though he had trouble with the governing military figures—notably Pedro Fages, Rivera, and de Neve—he died at age seventy knowing he had established a foothold for Christianity.

Comment: This very readable account of the life of Serra is one of the few full-length biographies of him written simply and clearly enough for young, as well as older, readers to enjoy. Unfortunately, it is out of print. However, check your library; copies can be found.

Fiction: intermediate–junior high

Seidman, Laurence I. **THE FOOLS OF '49. THE CALIFORNIA GOLD RUSH 1848-1856.** New York: Alfred A. Knopf, 1976. 217 p. Maps, prints, photos, bibliog., index.

Content: Simply, yet in vivid detail, the author tells of the discovery of gold, the rush it precipitated, the travail of the travelers, and the California land and inhabitants affected. Quotes from actual letters and diaries, as well as songs, depict the hopes and woes, humor and prejudices of the motley group of seekers for treasure that suddenly became the major factor of California life.

Comment: There are many dramatic excerpts to read aloud to fourth-graders. The author has a knack for choosing telling examples to make readers understand the impact of historical events. Throughout the book, Mr. Seidman is careful to project the viewpoint of all cultures concerned. In his chapters on the miners' harsh treatment of foreigners and on the native California Indians, the author paints a grim picture of life for those whom the miners didn't understand or value.

This would be a good reference book for anyone interested in California history.

Nonfiction: junior high–adult

Selvin, David F. **THE OTHER SAN FRANCISCO.** New York: Seabury, 1969. 169 p. Drawings by Joseph Papin, index.

Content: This history of San Francisco from the time of the Costonoan Indians to the 1960s is full of people, events, and dates.

Comment: The author knows his history and has facts and figures galore. For the San Francisco-history buff, the book is a delight; but for the young reader, there is too much information. The author apparently intended to record the melting pot of peoples who contributed to the founding and growth of San Francisco, and comments about the varied ethnic groups are found throughout.

Nonfiction: intermediate

Seton, Ernest Thompson. **MONARCH, THE BIG BEAR OF TAL-LAC.** 1902. Reprint. Olympic Valley, Calif.: Outbooks, 1978. 167 p. B/w illus.

Content: The story of a grizzly bear cub who was captured and kept as a pet and then escaped into the Tahoe Sierra region. Because he kills sheep and cattle, he is hunted—at first to be killed and then to be trapped alive—by the man who originally raised him. Included are details of grizzly life and habits.

Comment: Because California grizzly bears are extinct, this knowledgeable story is especially interesting. The author, a noted wildlife writer, says that though the adventures related are not of one particular bear, they are based on true events. The story was originally published in 1902, but is still a good, suspenseful adventure. It could be read aloud, allowing for some "flowery" passages.

Fiction: intermediate–adult

Shannon, Monica. **CALIFORNIA FAIRY TALES.** 1926. Reprint. New York: Stephen Daye, republished 1957. 298 p. Illustrated by C. E. Millard.

Content: This is a collection of twenty-three thoroughly Californian fairy tales. In "Mariposa" a sprite lives in a redwood stump and watches ". . . the wind bring fogs in from Monterey Bay, hiding them in trees as if they were sails stolen from old ships." In "An Unbelieving King" a princess breaks out of a watermelon and dries her damp tresses while sitting comfortably on a cantaloupe. "Little Pagan Beggars" gives a fictional accounting of the pirate raid at Mission San Carlos, while "Pajaro" deals with the hides sold to sea captains during Mexican days—all written in fairy tale fashion.
Comment: Selected readings from this book could provide contrast with the factual historical accounts.
Fiction: intermediate

Shannon, Monica. **MORE TALES FROM CALIFORNIA.** 1928. Reprint. New York: Stephen Daye Press, 1960. 311 p. B/w drawings.

Content: This is a collection of fairy tales, tales of gods and giants, and here-and-now stories. Some of the tales explain natural history phenomena in California: "Ana Josepha" tells a legend of how California woodpeckers got their red heads. Several of the fairy tales have authentic-sounding, old California settings. "The Merchant's Daughter" takes place in old Monterey, and "More than a Bullfight" is set in the southern San Joaquin Valley. The Kaweah River area and the Yokut Indians are included in several tales. The most interesting tale, historically, is "The Luckless Pigwidgeon," a legendary explanation of how gold came to be in the Sierra Nevada.
Comment: These tales seem of limited use for students of California history, though the story about gold and the settings of some of the others could prove interesting. "More than a Bullfight" provides a gorily realistic look at the gold-rush-era bull and bear fights. Be aware of racist slurs about Indians.
Fiction: intermediate

Shapiro, Irwin. **THE GOLDEN BOOK OF CALIFORNIA, FROM**

THE DAYS OF THE SPANISH EXPLORERS TO THE PRESENT. New York: Golden Press, 1961. 97 p. B/w and color illus., maps, geographical supplement, index.

Content: The title tells it all. In eighty pages of text and pictures, the basic history of California is covered. The geographical supplement includes maps of counties, temperature, rainfall, growing season, state and national parks, land use, water supply, transportation routes, and photos showing the wide scenic diversity of the state.

Comment: For a survey history, this is quite good. The language is lively, and the material includes not only the important names, but interesting details. The illustrations are excellent contemporary drawings, prints, photos, and maps from collections of museums and individuals within the state. The book is very similar to books in the American Heritage series, but with easier text. A revised edition to bring it up-to-date would greatly increase this book's usefulness—as it stands now, its value is strictly historical.

Nonfiction: intermediate–junior high

Sherman, Margaret R. **CALIFORNIA'S AMAZING AGRICUL-TURE.** Palo Alto, Calif.: Pacific Books, 1979. 273 p. B/w photos, indexes.

Content: The major portion of this book deals with types of agriculture and has information on dairy farming, desert farming, citrus and avocado farming, cattle ranching, fruit growing, rice and cotton farming, vegetable and berry growing, and poultry ranching. The appendixes list California's leading crops and sources where students can write for more information. There is a subject index and a short index on careers. There is some information on the history of farming from Spanish days through the mission period, the gold rush and on.

Comment: It is doubtful that an intermediate student would read the whole volume, but the first and last sections, plus a chapter or two of specific interest in the midsection, could help a young reader to learn a great deal about California agriculture. Chapters in the midsections have glossaries.

Nonfiction: intermediate

Shields, Rita. **NORAH AND THE CABLE CAR.** New York: Longmans, Green, 1960. 150 p. Illus. by Richard Bennett.

Content: It is St. Patrick's Day 1873 in San Francisco, and Norah O'Flaherty is looking forward to winning the step-dancing contest. Her grandpa's gold watch holds a lock of her mother's hair, and if she wins, a lock of her hair will be placed beside her mother's. Everyone is eager for her success, including her twin brothers, Hugh the lamplighter, and quiet James. Sadly, she doesn't win, but there is always next year. Norah's grandpa is against the cable car coming into existence. Family disagreements and changes bring sadness and pain, but the family is united before the next St. Patrick's Day. Norah's picture goes into grandpa's watch but not the way she expected.
Comment: The Association of Children's Librarians reviewed and recommended this book.
Fiction: intermediate

Shipman, Bret. **OLD CALIFORNIA: THE MISSIONS, RANCHOS, AND ROMANTIC ADOBES** Los Angeles: Camaro Publishing, 1983. 91 p. B/w illus. by Shirley Richards, bibliog.

Content: This touring guidebook contains pertinent information—history, productivity as a mission, restoration data, present-day phone number, road directions, nearby restaurants, dates of annual festivals, origin of name—of each of the twenty-one missions. There is a brief description of exterior and interior details of each mission and often, notes about what was going on in the thirteen colonies or the young United States at the same time as the events being chronicled about California. There are also fifty-five descriptive entries (38 from Santa Barbara on south) of chapels, asistencias (sub-missions), estancias (rancho chapels), and adobes. Finally, there are full page articles about each of the four Spanish presidios—at San Diego, Santa Barbara, Monterey, and San Francisco. Throughout the book are full-page line drawings of various sites.
Comment: A wonderful compendium of information not easily located. A great reference for California history. The missions are not the focal point and a great deal of the history is from mission days onward. Shipman is a staunch defender of the

mission system, and balances the negativism toward it found in many recent publications. Secularization, Governors Pio Pico and Echeandia, and earthquakes are the villains in this book.
Nonfiction: intermediate–adult

THE SHIRLEY LETTERS FROM THE CALIFORNIA MINES, 1851–1852. New York: Alfred A. Knopf, 1961. 216 p. B/w illus., maps.

Content: twenty-three letters written from Rich Bar mining settlement on the Feather River, over the course of one and a half years. The writer was a doctor's wife and one of four women in the mining settlement. She was writing to her sister in the East describing town buildings, miners and mining, food, clothing, entertainments, fights, foreigners, the countryside, and the weather.
Comment: The language is a bit flowery at times as typical of the period, but lively, and the observations are interesting to read. Individual letters could be selected to be read aloud to younger students.
Nonfiction: junior high–adult

Sibley, Gretchen. **LA BREA STORY.** Los Angeles: Los Angeles County Museum of Natural History, 1967. 44 p. Color and b/w illus. by Mary Butler, bibliog.

Content: Beginning with 40,000 years ago, the author takes us walking through the Los Angeles valley noting the animals, birds and vegetation of the area, to the Brea pits. There are two animals—a camel and a saber-tooth tiger—trapped in one of the pits. Then we visit the pits in 1492, 1769, several dates in the 1800's, and finally in the present-day, noting how the creatures change, the comments and uses man makes of the pits, and how they look today.
Comment: An easy book to read, and full of information. The variety of animal life thousands of years ago is an eye-opener. The illustrations are excellent.
Nonfiction: intermediate–junior high

Silverberg, Robert. **GHOST TOWNS OF THE AMERICAN WEST.**

New York: Thomas Y. Crowell, 1968. 309 p. Illus. by Lawrence Bjorklund, bibliog., index.

Content: The author gives a lively picture of mining camps-turned-towns in their heyday, with brief descriptions of the differences among placer, lode, and hydraulic mining. Thumb-nail sketches of people and some contemporary accounts are interspersed. Bodie and Columbia are the main towns described. The former is an example of the uninhabited, decaying ghost town; the latter an example of a continuously inhabited mining town where the old buildings have been restored, businesses reinstituted, and the atmosphere of the old days somewhat recaptured.

Comment: Some black and white drawings of miners are included.

Nonfiction: intermediate–adult

Silverberg, Robert. **JOHN MUIR: PROPHET AMONG THE GLACIERS.** New York: G. P. Putnam's Sons, 1972. 249 p. Bibliog., index.

Content: See Douglas, William O. *Muir of the Mountains.*

Nonfiction: intermediate

Smith, Fredrika Shumway. **FREMONT: SOLDIER, EXPLORER, STATESMAN.** Chicago: Rand McNally, 1966. 250 p. Photos, maps, index.

Content: The first five pages describe Fremont's background and childhood, mostly spent in Charleston, South Carolina. His career as an explorer and surveyor of the unknown West began with military surveys as an Army lieutenant assisting Jean Nicholas Nicollet in expeditions into the vast area between the Mississippi and Missouri Rivers.

Fremont then met the talented Jessie Benton, the daughter of the powerful Senator Thomas Hart Benton of Missouri. Their love affair surmounted family disapproval, and their marriage resulted in a loving partnership that lasted throughout Fremont's life.

Fremont's next expeditions led to Oregon and California, and to a mutually respectful partnership with Kit Carson. He became involved in the politics of the time—the growing rift between the United States and Mexico over California.

The last half of the books deals with Fremont's part in the Mexican War, his leadership in California and in national politics, and the financial and legal problems caused by his involvements.

Comment: This book is harder reading than Burt's *John Charles Fremont,* and it starts rather slowly. At times, a reader can get lost in the detail; however, the pace picks up as it goes along. The author does give a lot of information and background about Fremont and his times. She also uses many direct Fremont quotations and includes poems written about Fremont by John Greenleaf Whittier and others.

Nonfiction: upper intermediate–senior high

Smith, Gerald A. **THE MOJAVES.** Reprint. San Bernardino, Calif.: San Bernardino County Museum Association, 1977. 131 p. B/w illus., bibliog.

Content: "The purpose of this publication and a series of succeeding ones is the attempt to gather the known, fragmented histories of each of the five most-important Indian tribes of San Bernardino County into single publications." This is the first of the series, and covers dwellings, food, clothing, tools, games, government; the historic period—contacts with Spanish and Californios, mountain men, the United States Army, and the coming of the railroad; and the Mojaves today.

Comment: This is written like a research paper, and not many students will read it cover to cover. However, since there is difficulty in finding books on individual California Indian tribes, it fills a need. The table of contents makes it easy to locate specific information for research even without an index. Lots of photos, including bare-breasted females, and drawings of pottery designs.

Nonfiction: junior high–adult

Snedden, Genevra S. **DOCAS, INDIAN OF SANTA CLARA.** 1942. Reprint. Boston: Heath, 1958. (originally published, 1942)

185 p. Drawings by Jane Bateman, map, glossary of Indian and Spanish words.

Content: This is the story of Docas, an Indian boy growing into manhood and old age, in Santa Clara in early California. During his lifetime, change is almost-daily apparent, from the earliest missionaries and soldiers to the Spanish settlers and later, the Americans and John Sutter. It is an almost day-by-day, year-by-year account of how the Indians, and later the newer arrivals, lived.

Comment: This book is really dated, but it's still on library shelves. It is not really a historical novel and has poor characterization and plot development.

Nonfiction: intermediate

Snyder, Zilpha. **THE VELVET ROOM.** New York: Atheneum, 1967. 216 p. Drawings by Alton Raible.

Content: The old Model T broke down once again in June of 1937, stranding twelve-year-old Robin Williams and her migrant family north of their San Bernardino goal. But, while Mr. Williams was seeking auto parts, he found employment—it might even be permanent, and it *did* include housing! Robin has a chance to attend school, perhaps even for a full year in one place, makes friends with an old lady, and most important, finds her way to the enchanted velvet room.

Comment: The book effectively portrays the problems of the migrant worker's family, the effects of the depression, an unromanticized view of agricultural labor. The Association of Children's Librarians recommended this book.

Fiction: upper intermediate–junior high

Southworth, John. **DEATH VALLEY IN 1849: THE LUCK OF THE GOLD RUSH EMIGRANTS.** Burbank, Calif.: Pegleg Books, 1978. 85 p. B/w maps and photos, bibliog.

Content: This tale of the goldseekers who traveled through Death Valley in 1849 has many details of special interest to students: reasons other than goldseeking which led emigrants west; a brief history of the Indians of the area; separate chapters about the various groups of emigrants; the human interest and historic import of the Brierly family, in the chapter "The Preacher and his Lady". Excerpts from the logs of some of the groups are found in the appendix.

Comment: Though this soft-cover book is too detailed for use by younger students, upper-intermediate readers and up could benefit from reading, or hearing, portions of it, in order to get the flavor of the hardships endured by the wagon trains heading west in the 1800s. The maps included are a little hard to follow.
Nonfiction: upper intermediate–adult

Steffan, Jack. **MOUNTAIN OF FIRE.** New York: John Day, 1959. 191 p.

Content: "This is the story of a mountain . . ." begins the prologue. And so it is—the story of Lassen Peak, the Atsugewi Indians who lived there, and the disruption of Indian life by the white man. Paka, a young Indian who becomes chief, is the protagonist. Major Reading, a rancher of the upper Sacramento Valley, portrays the best of the white ways. Evil comes into the story through misunderstanding, distrust, and the thoroughly corrupt character of Jackson Pierce. The Atsugewis end up on a reservation, a sad departure from their earlier, freer life.
Comment: The story is an interesting fictional counterpart to the story of Ishi. Although it is out of print, it may be found in libraries.
Fiction: intermediate

Steffens, Lincoln. **A BOY ON HORSEBACK.** 1935. (Reprinted from **THE AUTOBIOGRAPHY OF LINCOLN STEFFENS**). New York: Harcourt, Brace, 1931. 258 p. Illus. by Sanford Tousey.

Content: This episodic tale of Steffen's boyhood in Sacramento represents an idealized version of life in the 1870s. Steffens lived from 1866 to 1936 and was a noted American author, editor, lecturer, and reformer. The book serves as an effective introduction to Steffens and his prominence in the muckraking movement.
Comment: Short on hard fact and long on mood-setting anecdote. This book would especially benefit the mature and sensi-

tive elementary-age reader. Students through sixth grade might want to end their reading at page 214, before Steffens starts reminiscing about college days and his own educational philosophy.
Nonfiction: upper intermediate–junior high

Stein, R. Conrad. **THE STORY OF THE GOLD AT SUTTER'S MILL.** Cornerstones of Freedom. Chicago: Children's Press, 1981. 31 p. Color illus.

J979.404
STE

Content: Touches the highlights of the gold rush including Sutter's history, the routes to California and their hazards, some immigrants who became rich by NOT mining such as Philip Armour and Levi Strauss, the growth of California within six years, and the origin of the phrase ". . . seeing the elephant." Contains interesting details, such as food prices, travel conditions, and miners' humor.

1 or
2 m

Comment: This is a fairly easy-to-read, uncomplicated, telling of the gold rush story. Younger readers could use this as an introduction to the gold rush; older, less-able readers could at least get a feel for it.
Nonfiction: upper primary–intermediate

Stein, R. Conrad. **THE STORY OF THE SAN FRANCISCO EARTHQUAKE.** Chicago: Children's Press, 1983. 31 p. Brown/white illus. by Nathan Greene.

979.4
STE

2 m

Content: Written in narrative form, this book basically describes the day of the great quake, April 18, 1906. An explanation of the fires and their damage follows the explanation of the quake and how it occurred. Quoted recollections from survivors are liberally used for human interest.

A brief history of the city concludes with discussion of its situation on the San Andreas Fault and near the Hayward Fault and the implications of that for the future.
Comment: In simple language and large print, the author paints a vivid picture and includes some wonderfully descriptive quotations which make the earthquake and fire easy to experience vicariously. There is no table of contents.
Nonfiction: primary–intermediate

Steinbeck, John. **THE RED PONY.** 1937. Reprint. New York: Viking, 1959. 120 p. Illus.

Content: This moving and beautiful story is of a boy, a sorrel colt, and sundrenched California. Jody, the young boy, dreams of a colt of his own, feels sorrow when his first colt dies, and remains unhappy until promised another. Waiting for the colt to be born, he helps on the farm, living with his family and their dreams.

Comment: In this book a young reader can be gently introduced to the idea of personal sorrow and to the realization that one cannot have every wish granted immediately, if at all.

Fiction: junior high–adult

Stewart, George R. **THE CALIFORNIA TRAIL: AN EPIC WITH MANY HEROES.** New York: McGraw-Hill, 1962. 339 p. B/w illus., bibliog., index.

Content: This is an account, year-by-year from 1841 to 1859 of the different attempts to establish the California Trail and of the emigrant parties and the individual trailblazers involved in this process. Hazards encountered, decisions made, supplies taken and not taken, and something of the emigrants themselves are recounted. Insights into the accomplishments of the emigrants and an appreciation of their courage is given, as well as good details of activities and life in an emigrant train.

Comment: This is a very readable account of a generally well known, but little-detailed, part of the westward movement.

Nonfiction: junior high–adult

Stewart, George R. **DONNER PASS: AND THOSE WHO CROSSED IT.** Menlo Park, Calif.: Lane Publishing, 1964. 96 p. Photos, drawings, maps.

Content: Stewart writes about early crossings of Donner Pass by wagon trains, gold miners, and railroad builders. He tells of the pass in winter, using many photographs taken from 1867 to 1960, gives place names of the area, and tells of geological development, and the plants and animals.

Comment: Though the book was not written for children, it

could be used as a resource to gather information on wagon trains, the building of the railroad, or facts about the Donner area itself. The many excellent, old photographs add greatly to the value.
Nonfiction: upper intermediate—adult

Stewart, George R. **ORDEAL BY HUNGER: THE STORY OF THE DONNER PARTY.** 1936 Reprint. New York: Pocket Books, 1971. 320 p. Maps, Bibliog., index of proper names.

Content: This is a chronological account of what is probably the most famous of California's emigrant parties. The author points out the critical moments, important events, miscalculations, bad judgments and decisions.

Two diaries of survivors are included in this edition, a personal account by twelve-year-old Virginia Reed and supplemental notes by the author, including a roster of the party and an itinerary.

Comment: This classic account was not written for children but could be source material for mature readers. Author Stewart not only had access to much source material relating to the tragic Donner crossing but also personally followed much of the trail used, even during the winter snows.
Nonfiction: junior high–adult

Stewart, George R. **TO CALIFORNIA BY COVERED WAGON.** New York: Random House, 1954. 182 p. Illus. by William Moyers, maps, index.

Content: This is the story of the Stevens Party's trek from Council Bluffs, Iowa to California in 1844. It tells of preparations for the journey, the daily life of the people, encounters with Indians, buffalo hunting, and the dangers experienced when the twenty-six members of this group left the Oregon Trail to go over the Sierra Nevada. The extremities of winter forced the party to separate into small groups. One seventeen-year-old, Moses Schallenberger, spent the winter alone in a rude cabin. (See Evansen's *Sierra Summit.*)

Comment: This older book is still on library shelves. Though the tone seems a bit condescending, it's an interesting, informa-

tive, easy-to-read story which handles the facts well. The index adds to its worth as a reference for young readers. The author used as his main source the diary kept by Schallenberger.
Nonfiction: intermediate

Stewart, John. **THE KEY TO THE KITCHEN.** New York: Lothrop, Lee & Shepard, 1970. 28 p. Color illus. by Robert Quackenbush.

Content: Mission San Gabriel's cook has just died, and which of the three women at the mission will inherit the key to the kitchen? A simple and amusing story that pokes fun at fancy cooking and self-important cooks.
Comment: Not much history is learned here, but the story has some flavor of the Spanish mission era which is emphasized in Quackenbush's lively and colorful illustrations. A good read-aloud.
Fiction: primary

Stirling, Betty. **REDWOOD PIONEER.** New York: Follett, 1955. 157 p. Illus. by Ursula Koering.

Content: Mikey O'Grady moves with his large Irish-American family from the "potato country" near Santa Cruz up into the redwood country in the Santa Cruz mountains. This 1870 tale records pioneer life, including a boy's wonder upon first viewing the ocean, seeing a train, helping his family build a new home, and establishing a new base. Simply having a friend his own age for one day was a marvel for Mikey.
Comment: The early tanning industry and the danger of grizzlies are examples of the real history woven into the story.
Fiction: intermediate

Stoutenburg, Adrien. **WILD ANIMALS OF THE FAR WEST.** Berkeley, Calif.: Parnassus Press, 1958. 150 p. Illus. by Ruth Robbins, index.

Content: The ten chapters cover a wide variety of mammals in categories such as those that eat meat, gnaw, leap and hop; those with hoofs and horns or with body pouches; those that

live in the sea. Each animal described is illustrated with informative sketches.
Comment: The index, together with the Latin names of the
animals, makes this a straightforward instructional book.
Nonfiction: intermediate

Stull, Edith. **THE STORY OF CALIFORNIA.** New York: Grosset
and Dunlap, 1968. 61 p. Brown tone illus. by H. B. Vestal,
index.

Content: This is a short history of California which includes the
discovery of San Diego and San Francisco bays, growth of
missions and pueblos, rule by the Mexican government, quests
for fur and gold, and building of the railroad.
Comment: This title indicates some of the problem areas—the
treatment of the Indians during mission days, the questionable
rationale for the Mexican War, the confusion over land ownership in the early American period.

The simplicity of language, generous use of subheadings in
the chapters, and the index make this a useful tool for young
researchers.
Nonfiction: intermediate

Suggs, Robert C. **THE ARCHAEOLOGY OF SAN FRANCISCO.**
New York: Thomas Y. Crowell, 1965. 132 p. Illus. by Leonard
Everett Fisher, glossary, bibliog., index.

Content: Starting at the Emeryville shell mound and telling of
the work of the archaeologist Uhle, the author goes on to
reconstruct the life of the California Paleo-Indians 10,000 to
15,000 years ago. Then he tells of Early Horizon Indian life
(4,000-2,000 B.C.), Middle Horizon Indian life (2,000-1,500
B.C. to 700-1000 A.D.), Late Horizon Indian life (300-1800
A.D.) which included interaction with white men, and, finally
modern life to 1900.
Comment: Although fascinating material is presented as simply
as the author could manage, the book would still be hard going
for most elementary students, but help older ones to separate
history and prehistory. The good glossary and index help, and
the author is conscientious about explaining terms as he intro-

duces them. The fine illustrations would have been of more value if captions had been included.
Nonfiction: upper intermediate– junior high

Sung, Betty. **THE CHINESE IN AMERICA.** New York: Macmillan, 1972. 120 p. B/w photos, bibliog., index.

J301.45|5

Im

> **Content:** After telling of the coming of the Chinese to California during the gold rush, the author describes various aspects of Chinese life and culture in America. Much attention is given to discrimination against the Chinese and its affect on their occupations, living conditions, and customs. Other subjects discussed include family life, festivals, and prominent Chinese-Americans.
> **Comment:** The thread of anti-Chinese discrimination that runs throughout the book is a bit repetitive, but otherwise, this is an overview that students will find easy and interesting to read.
> **Nonfiction: intermediate–junior high**

Surany, Anico. **MALACHY'S GOLD.** New York: Holiday House, 1968. 42 p. Color illus. by Leonard Everett Fisher.

JXX
SUR

Im

> **Content:** Malachy O'Toole is still looking for gold in the Sierra Nevada after the other prospectors have moved on to the Nevada mines. His mule, Miranda, is old and tired of wandering all over. Malachy decides to buy some land and help the Indian boy, Little Owl, after realizing his quest for gold was pointless.
> **Comment:** A simple little story with a satisfactory ending. Fisher's illustrations are strong, unsentimental scratch-board, done in magenta or olive and white. Good to read aloud. Gives a picture of the goldseeker hooked on prospecting even when the pickings are slim.
> **Fiction: primary**

Sutton, Margaret. **PALACE WAGON FAMILY: A TRUE STORY OF THE DONNER PARTY.** New York: Alfred A. Knopf, 1957. 210 p. B/w illus., bibliog.

> **Content:** The story of the Donner Party told from Virginia Reed's (a 12-year-old girl) point of view. A number of original

sources were used, as well as well known secondary ones to make this an authentic retelling for young readers.

Comment: Sullivan has written a realistic account of this tragic episode, including the dissensions, the pettinesses, and the cannibalism. This book is for a better or more mature reader than those who would read "Patty Reed's Doll" because of the length of the book and the greater detail included.

Fiction: intermediate–junior high

Swift, Hildegarde Hoyt. **FROM THE EAGLE'S WING, A BIOGRAPHY OF JOHN MUIR.** New York: William Morrow, 1962. 282 p. Illus. by Lynd Ward, Foreword by Eleanor Roosevelt, bibliog.

Content: See Douglas, William O. *Muir of the Mountains.*

Nonfiction: junior high–adult

Swinburne, Irene, and Lawrence Swinburne. **COWS AND COWBOYS: YESTERDAY AND TODAY.** New York: Parents' Magazine, 1976. 64 p. Illus. by Ray Burns, index.

Content: This is a fairly brief history of the cowboy from his Spanish beginnings to the present. "The first American cowboys did not speak English. Besides, they were slaves—not black, but Indian. They rode on ranges belonging to Spanish owners in California and Texas before there was a United States . . . They were called *vaqueros* (from *vaca,* Spanish for cow)." The authors include a chart of words used by the vaqueros, their English meanings, and the words cowboys came to use. For example, *chapperreras*—leather trousers, chaps.

Comment: This interesting book benefits from Ray Burns' illustrations of horses, Texas longhorns, saddles, boots, rifles, and more.

Nonfiction: primary–intermediate

Syme, Ronald. **JOHN CHARLES FREMONT: THE LAST AMERICAN EXPLORER.** New York: William Morrow, 1974. 190 p. Map, bibliog.

Content: A well-researched biography that traces Fremont's career from young boyhood to his death at age seventy-seven.

Fremont's surveying and mapping expeditions were important to the westward movement of American settlers, and this is brought out, along with his errors of judgment.

Comment: This is an interesting story, especially if preceded or followed by an equally well written biography of Fremont's wife, Jessie. Mr. Syme writes sympathetically of Fremont, but Fremont's faults are duly noted within the appropriate contexts, giving a rounded picture of a controversial figure in United States and California history.

Nonfiction: intermediate–junior high

Teal, Evelyn. **FLYING SNOWSHOES.** Caldwell, Idaho: Caxton Printers; 1957. Illus.

Content: This book is based on the true story of John "Snowshoe" Thompson who, for twenty years, carried mail across the Sierra Nevada between Placerville, California, and Genoa, Nevada.

Comment: The Association of Children's Libraries recommended this book with reservations. They felt Thompson was portrayed as ". . . larger than life" and that the illustrations were ". . . lacking in luster and feeling."

Fiction: intermediate

Terrell, John Upton. **THE DISCOVERY OF CALIFORNIA.** New York: Harcourt, Brace & World, 1970. 129 p. B/w drawings by W. K. Plummer, maps.

Content: This tells of the exploits of some little known and well known early explorers of the California area. Alarcon, exploring by land in 1540, was the first white man to see California. Diaz, also a land explorer, crossed the Colorado River later in 1540 to become the first white man to enter California. The better known 1542 ocean-based explorations of Cabrillo—and later his second in command, Ferrer (usually spelled Ferrelo)—are described with their discovery of San Diego Bay. A brief description of Francis Drake's landing at, or near, Drake's Bay, in 1578 or 1579 leads into the work of Unamuno who found Morro Bay and explored inland as far as present-day San Luis Obispo in 1587. The book ends with the reconnaissance of

Cermeno in 1595, the explorations of Vizcaino, and his discovery of Monterey Bay in 1602 or 1603.

Comment: The author gives detailed information about explorers little discussed in many accounts. Useful for many students. The maps are helpful additions. Some of the vocabulary seems difficult for young readers.

Nonfiction: intermediate–junior high

Terris, Susan. **TUCKER AND THE HORSE THIEF.** New York: Four Winds Press, 1979. 188 p.

Content: Abigail Tucker Delaney, known as Tucker and disguised as a boy, has come west to a gold mining town with her father to strike it rich with hydraulic mining. The rough life of California in the mid-1850s isn't as hard as life with her alcoholic, bigoted father who can't seem to regain his stability after a severe bout with fever on the trip west. Tucker makes friends with Sol Weil and his family, but, as they are Jews and her father objects to Jews, this friendship complicates her life. Also, Tucker fears Sol's discovering she's a girl.

A tragic conclusion to her father's efforts to get rich quickly and Sol's decision to go to San Francisco to be an actor leave a more mature Tucker with the determination to try to remain a California girl.

Comment: This is a more realistic story than those written for young readers up through the 1960s. The rough-and-tumble life in a gold mining town, the suspicion of Jews, the problems of living with an alcoholic—all are depicted believably. The pain of adolescence is compounded by Tucker's masquerade as a boy, and the worries of puberty are openly expressed.

Fiction: junior high

Tompkins, Walker A. **CALIFORNIA'S WONDERFUL CORNER: TRUE STORIES FOR CHILDREN FROM THE HISTORY OF THE SANTA BARBARA REGION.** Charlotte, N.C.: McNally & Loftin, 1962. 174 p. B/w illus. by Joseph Knowles, bibliog., index.

Content: The sixty-seven chapters deal with stories of the regional history of the Santa Barbara area from 1782 to the

1960s. Well known California persons—Father Serra, Father Lasuen, John Fremont—are featured, along with many whose contributions were mainly confined to the area. The origin of many of the Spanish place names is explained. The mission period and the rancho period are well documented, and the historical implications of the continuing need for water is emphasized.

Comment: The book was written as a supplementary reader to help in the study of California at the elementary level. Though the approach is rather pedantic, interesting information keeps the reader's attention.

Nonfiction: intermediate

Uchida, Yoshiko. **A JAR OF DREAMS.** New York: Atheneum, 1984. 131 p.

Content: Eleven-year-old Rinko, living with her family in Berkeley, in 1935, is a Japanese-American child trying to cope with a society she doubts will ever fully accept her. Influenced by her older brother, Ken, she tries to decide whether to follow her own dream or settle for a nonrisk future. The family is changed by the arrival of small, quiet Aunt Waka from Japan, who, somehow, infuses them all with the courage they need to pursue their own goals.

Comment: The dilemma of whether to risk or play it safe makes the story universal in appeal to young readers. The personalization of confronting racial prejudice would help white students to understand how it feels and strike a chord of recognition in other minority students.

Fiction: intermediate

Uchida, Yoshiko. **JOURNEY TO TOPAZ.** New York: Charles Scribner's Sons, 1971. 149 p. Illus. by Donald Carrick.

Content: This is a story of the Japanese-American evacuation from the West Coast after the 1941 Japanese attack on Pearl Harbor. Yuki, an eleven-year-old who lived in Berkeley, suddenly finds her entire life disrupted. Overnight, her parents become "enemy aliens," and her father taken by the FBI. Yuki, her mother, and older brother Ken, are moved to the Tanforan

Race Track Assembly Center where their home is a dark, small, horse stall.

Yuki makes a friend, Emi, and they are all shipped to Topaz, a barbed-wire enclosure in the barren desert of Utah. The harsh, bleak life with its terrifying dust storms brings illness and tragedy to Emi. Ken joins the American army to prove loyalty to the country. Father is released and gets a job in Salt Lake City, and the family finally leaves the camp for a better life.

Comment: This is one of the very few stories written for young people which shows the effect of Executive Order 9066 on the lives of Japanese-Americans during World War II.

The Association of Children's Librarians recommended this book.

Nonfiction: intermediate–junior high

Uchida, Yoshiko. **SAMURAI OF GOLD HILL.** New York: Charles Scribner's Sons, 1972. 118 p. Illus. by Ati Forberg.

Content: The year is 1869, and young Koichi becomes part of a great plan that takes him and his samurai father from their wartorn home in Wakamatsu, Japan to Gold Hill, California. They arrive right after the gold rush with tea leaves and silkworm eggs to start a new life. As aliens, they are objects of curiosity. Life on Gold Hill is full of disappointments. But in spite of all the tragedies that befall this small colony, Koichi learns that he can always be true to the spirit of Samurai.

Comment: This absorbing story was based on the historical founding of the Wakamatsu Tea Colony in northern California. The Association of Children's Librarians recommended this book.

Fiction: junior high

Underhill, Ruth. **INDIANS OF SOUTHERN CALIFORNIA.** 1941. Reprint. Washington, D. C.: U. S. Office of Indian Affairs, n.d. 73 p. B/w photos by Velino Herrera, bibliog.

Content: This book originally was one of a series describing the life and customs of southwestern American Indians, before being too changed by contact with Europeans. This edition was rewritten, illustrated with museum photographs and drawings, and intended for text use in junior and senior high schools. It deals with tribal life, language and customs of the Luiseno, Cahuillo, Serrano, Cupeno, and Diegueno tribes and covers dwellings, food, clothing, tools, crafts, government, family life, sacred stories and ceremonies. Also includes a brief history of Spanish days and American contacts.

Comment: Although this is a government document, the material is interestingly written; the print is large enough to read easily; the pictures are good and sufficient in number. A useful book for upper-elementary reference as well.

Nonfiction: junior high–adult

Vessel, Matthew F., Herbert H. Wong and Helen Mitchell. **CALIFORNIA EMBLEMS.** Palo Alto, Calif.: Fearon, 1965. 64 p. Color illus. by Ron King, bibliog.

Content: The first two chapters define and give history and description of U. S. national emblems. Succeeding chapters describe California's emblems—flag, seal, flower, bird, animal, trees, colors, fish, mineral and rock, and (unofficial) insect— and their history; the habitat and conservation tips are given for all but the flag, seal and colors. The last chapter titled "Things to Think About and Do" contains ideas for individual or class activities. Strongly conservationist, it includes name and address of the California Conservation Council.

Comment: Although this is written for upper-elementary students, teachers and other interested adults would find this book useful for basic information and for activities with student groups of varying ages.

Nonfiction: upper primary-intermediate

Wagoner, Jean Brown. **JESSIE FREMONT: GIRL OF CAPITOL HILL.** Indianapolis: Bobbs-Merrill, 1960. 200 p. B/w illus., glossary, bibliog.

Content: Most of the story tells of Jessie's childhood and how she was encouraged by her father, Senator Thomas Hart Benton, in her interest in the West. She apparently wasn't required to fit into the typical girl-child mold of the early nineteenth century. Her marriage to John Fremont and her role in his rise to prominence are briefly described. The story ends with their move from California to Washington, D.C. when Fremont became one of California's first senators. A time line in the back lists some of the important events that occurred in American history during Jessie's lifetime; also included are some research questions, projects to do, and questions about the story itself.

Comment: This book is not difficult to read and manages to show how Jessie developed her independent spirit.

Nonfiction: intermediate

Warburton, Austen D., and Joseph F. Endert. **INDIAN LORE OF THE NORTH CALIFORNIA COAST.** Santa Clara, Calif.: Pacific Pueblo Press, 1966. 174 p. Illus. and photos.

Content: In Part I, the authors describe Indian beliefs in "Myths and Stories." In Part II they tell of customs—including anecdotes and information about calendars, canoes, homes, doctors, gambling, money, tobacco, fish traps, food, baskets, sports, and burial artifacts. There are also anecdotes about particular Indians. The mood of the book ranges from the charming "Moon Takes a Wife" to the rough, frontier-type humor of "A Prank at 'Toot Toot Any' " and the gruesome "Schneider's Body".

Comment: The myths and stories of Part I are similar to others available to students, but Part II contains information less-commonly recorded about the California Indian way of life. The occasional use of dialect makes a few sections hard to decipher. An upper-grade student, however, could learn much by reading a few selections, especially about the customs. The pictures are clear and informative.

Nonfiction: upper intermediate

Warren, Dwight. **DEATH VALLEY NATIONAL MONUMENT: STORY IN PICTURES.** Rev. ed. Beatty, Nevada: Death Valley Natural History Association, 1981. 25 p. Color photos.

Content: This soft-cover booklet of twenty-five pages is published as an aid for those visiting Death Valley. In colorful photographs and simple text, it tells first of the history of people important in the area and then the natural history. William

Manly and the group of forty-niners who wandered into the valley are covered, the prospectors and their influence, the 1873 discovery of borax and its commercial development, the use of the twenty-mule teams, and, finally, Death Valley Scotty and the castle he and his financial backer, Albert Johnson, built. The remaining pages tell of the geological development and describe significant landmarks. Plant and animal life is included. **Comment:** Though too brief to be of much help with student research, the text and fine pictures give a good overview of Death Valley for readers seeking a little information. There is no table of contents.
Nonfiction: intermediate

Weaver, Harriett E. **THERE STAND THE GIANTS: THE STORY OF THE REDWOOD TREES.** A Sunset Junior Book. Menlo Park: Calif.: Lane Publishing. 1960. 70 p. Photos, prints, diagrams.

Content: The book includes information on the world's most famous trees, the largest- and oldest-living things. It also has information on the two kinds of redwood trees, why they live so long, harvesting them for lumber, and saving them for parks.
Comment: This book, now out-of-print, is still found on some library shelves. It is filled with the kind of comparative information fourth-graders love; the tallest redwood is 100 feet higher than the Capitol Building in Washington, D.C., higher than the Statue of Liberty, two-thirds the height of the Golden Gate Bridge tower. The text is written in a straightforward, easy-to-read style. Students looking for information for reports would find it invaluable. Some of the information is dated—a taller redwood has been found; the Wawona tree has fallen; the Dawn Redwood of China has been accepted as a legitimate part of the redwood family.
Nonfiction: intermediate

Wellman, Paul I. **GOLD IN CALIFORNIA.** Cambridge, Mass.: Riverside Press, 1958. 184 p. Illus. by Lorence Bjorklund, maps, bibliog., index.

Content: This story of California from the 1840s to 1870s emphasizes the discovery and mining of gold, mining methods, camps, people attracted to our state, the progress of mining, the value of gold in dollars, and the diversity of talents gold attracted. A section is devoted to bandits, especially Joaquin Murietta, and another to words introduced into our language from the mining camps. Emphasis is placed on the role gold played in moving our population westward as well as in helping to win the Civil War.

Comment: Interesting and fact filled, this can be read by young or old with satisfaction. Many anecdotes and legends reinforce the historical facts, and an index makes it a good reference book.

Nonfiction: intermediate–adult

Wells, William V. **HOW WE GET GOLD IN CALIFORNIA.** 1860. Reprint. Harper's Magazine. Golden, Colo.: Outbooks, 1981. 24 p. B/w illus.

Content: The author undertakes in a few pages to inform the public, mainly those in the Atlantic states who have little notion of the particulars of the gold rush, exactly how gold is mined. He explains panning, use of the cradle and long tom, diversion of rivers, dry mining, tunneling, quartz operations, ground sluicing, and finally, hydraulic mining. Intermixed with the explanations are anecdotes of miners and mining.

Comment: This authentic account, written by a true forty-niner miner, is reprinted in tiny type with illustrations from the original publication and some added from other contemporary publications. Both illustrations and text offer much interesting information. It would make a fine read-aloud, even to elementary students, when the gold rush is being studied.

Nonfiction: junior high–adult

Whipple, Mary Anne, and Nancy E. Heizer. **THE FIRST CALI-FORNIANS.** 2nd. rev. ed. Palo Alto, Calif.: Peek Publications, 1971. 83 p. B/w illus. by Virginia Seeger.

Content: Six separate stories describe activities and ceremonies of six California Indian tribes with a young person as the narrator. Food, housing and clothing are described as well. The six tribes are: Yurok, Miwok, Paiute, Chumash, Yokuts, and Mohave.

Comment: These stories flesh out aspects of tribal life peculiar to specific tribes. One can picture and put into context, a gathering of several neighboring tribelets for games and dances, the move to summer homes, or planning the pattern of a basket. The stories underscore the rather easygoing life-style that Californians had even then.
Nonfiction: intermediate–junior high

Wilder, Laura Ingalls. **WEST FROM HOME: LETTERS OF LAURA INGALLS WILDER TO ALMANZO WILDER, SAN FRANCISCO, 1915.** Edited by Roger Lea MacBride. New York: Harper & Row, 1974. 117 p.

Content: These letters from the woman who was to become America's noted children's author tell a great deal about 1915 life in general, and specifically about the great Panama Pacific International Exposition. Laura Ingalls Wilder came to San Francisco to visit her married daughter, Rose Wilder Lane. Rose was established as a poor, but noted, journalist. Laura's letters to her husband told about the exposition, trips to Mill Valley, Santa Clara Valley, and Berkeley. She also demonstrates, in her concern for her husband and the chores at home, the role of a wife, and the economy of the time.
Comment: This reveals life in 1915 San Francisco and a great deal about the exposition. Children who love Wilder's books about her earlier life could well enjoy a look into her life as an adult.
Nonfiction: upper intermediate–adult

Wilson, Neill C. **HERE IS THE GOLDEN GATE: ITS HISTORY, ITS ROMANCE, AND ITS DERRING DO.** New York: William Morrow, 1962. 243 p. Photos, drawings, maps, index.

Content: The author has treated every subject connected with the Golden Gate passage spanned by the famous bridge with its proper share of attention, from prediscovery days to 1962. The author gives a glimpse into the future, too.
Comment: The photographs are numerous and excellent, but a lot has happened to the Golden Gate since the early 1960s.
Nonfiction: intermediate

Wise, Winifred E. **FRAY JUNIPERO SERRA AND THE CALIFOR-NIA CONQUEST.** New York: Charles Scribner's Sons, 1967. 184 p. B/w illus. bibliog., index.

Content: The author uses many quotations from Serra's own writings and from Father Francisco Palou's biography of Serra, interspersed with her own narrative, to give an authentic picture of the settlement of California and establishment of the chain of missions. The appendix has some interesting information, including lists of goods needed to set up a mission—very practical as well as aesthetic; some Indian words with Spanish and English equivalents; Father Serra's account for 1774 of what had been accomplished at each of the five then-established Missions. There are also photos of the missions founded under Serra's leadership.

Comment: Biographies of a saint, or an almost–saint, as Serra is, can be tricky and often so pious as to be uninteresting. Wise has managed to portray a real person with the extensive use of contemporary writings. However, this is not an easy literary style to read; excerpts could be read aloud to bring home the incredible hardships and hazards that the original Californians faced with such courage and devotion.

Nonfiction: junior high–senior high

Worcester, Donald E. **KIT CARSON: MOUNTAIN SCOUT.** Boston: Houghton Mifflin, 1960. 192 p. B/w illus. by Jo Polseno.

Content: Most of Kit Carson's life was spent as a trapper, Indian fighter and scout. His instinctive skill with a gun and his tracking ability made him a valuable addition to wagon trains and trapping expeditions. He was with a party that crossed into California in 1828 and trapped up and down the Central Valley. He became one of John Fremont's guides on exploring and mapping trips throughout the West, and in 1847, when they entered California, Carson was involved in the action which resulted in California becoming a part of United States.

Comment: Only two chapters deal with California. One, in part, tells of Carson's first trip into California; the other tells of the American takeover of the area during the Mexican War, especially the Battle of San Pascual. As in other books about the

mountain men who trailblazed into California, the value of this one is in showing what kind of men were involved in opening up the West, and the life they led while doing so.
Nonfiction: intermediate

Worthylake, Mary M. **CHILDREN OF THE SEED GATHERERS.** Chicago: Melmont Publishers, 1964. 46 p. Color illus. by Henry Luhrs.

Content: The Indian boy and girl follow the Pomo Indian pattern, but the foreword states that this way of life was characteristic of most acorn gatherers who lived in the central valleys of California and Oregon. Included are: gathering acorns, making shell money, gathering food, trading, making baskets, curing a sickness, a boy's coming of age by seeking his power spirit, a boy's first hunt and kill with the celebratory feast where he receives his adult name.
Comment: The book gives, in simple language, many details of California Indian life.
Nonfiction: upper primary–lower intermediate

Wright, Ralph B., ed. **CALIFORNIA'S MISSIONS.** Arroyo Grande, Calif.: Hubert A. Lowman, 1978. (orig. pub. in 1950). 94 p. B/w illus., map.

Content: An introductory history gives background on the Spanish theory of the mission system—training and religious education of natives, communities established for Indians only—with some examples as achieved in South and Central America. It also tells of the establishment of missions in Baja California, the reasons for extending them to Alta California, and what the plan for secularization was to be. The histories of the missions are covered, in founding rather than geographical order, and include present-day (1950) descriptions. There are pencil drawings of each mission facade, as well as drawings of interiors, artifacts, and architectural details.
Comment: Although this book is used in fourth grade class-rooms, it is not a children's book in language or illustrations. It has good historical information and is well written. Since it hasn't been updated from the original publication date, its

present-day descriptions are not current. It can be purchased at mission bookstores.

Nonfiction: junior high–adult

Yep, Laurence. **DRAGONWINGS.** New York: Harper & Row, 1975. 245 p.

Content: In 1903 eight-year-old Moon Shadow leaves his mother and native China to join his father, Windrider, in San Francisco. Living with his father and other male relatives in Chinatown, he helps run the family laundry and starts to learn the English language and American ways.

When a violent quarrel with a distant relative makes it advisable, Moon Shadow and his father move into the white community. The 1906 earthquake destroys their quarters and clears the way for Father to pursue his great dream—to build an airplane as the Wright Brothers had recently done. With the test flight of the airplane, Dragonwings, imminent, they are robbed and feel they are beaten, but friends and family come to their rescue. Father flies and crashlands but emerges not too badly hurt. His dream now centered on bringing his wife to join them in America, he rejoins the family laundry business.

Comment: This exciting, well-written tale is based on some fact and a lot of history. In the afterword, Yep tells of his inspiration, a newspaper article about a young Chinese flier, Fung Joe Guey, who actually flew in the Oakland hills in 1909. Also, the story presents a view of Chinatown at the turn of the century and the problems Chinese immigrants faced in a hostile society. Accounts of San Francisco after the 1906 earthquake are based on facts, too—notably, the separation of Chinese from other homeless refugees camping out and the attempt to drive the Chinese from their location in the center of town during rebuilding. The Association of Children's Librarians reviewed it and recommended it, too.

Fiction: intermediate–junior high

Yep, Laurence. **THE MARK TWAIN MURDERS.** New York: Four Winds Press, 1982. 151 p.

Content: San Francisco, summer 1864, and fifteen-year-old

Dougherty, who calls himself the Duke of Baywater, finds himself in the company of Mark Twain. Twain, a new reporter in town at the time, is struggling to overcome the reputation of being a prankster. The two of them learn to respect and like each other while unraveling the mystery of the murder of Dougherty's stepfather and others. The complicated plot implicates confederate sympathizers; someone is out to embarrass President Lincoln. Because of Twain's past journalistic hoaxes in Nevada, he can't get the police and military to take him seriously. He and "the Duke" have to track down clues and risk their lives on their own. Eventually, the crusading pair catch the confederates robbing the U.S. Mint and foil their plans.

Comment: It's an interesting yarn with some slow spots. The plot helps link California to the rest of the "States" during the Civil War, a connection many California students don't make. The novel is based on actual events of the time.

Fiction: upper intermediate–junior high

Yep, Laurence. **THE TOM SAWYER FIRES.** New York: William Morrow, 1984, 134 p.

Content: This sequel to *The Mark Twain Murders* is again set in San Francisco in 1864. The teenage street urchin who calls himself the Duke of Baywater watches a suspicious fire in an old chemical factory, the dramatic fire fighting and the infighting of competing volunteer fire companies. The Duke joins up with his writer friend, Mark Twain, and the heroic fire foreman, Tom Sawyer, to investigate. The arrival of a glamourous actress captures the attention of the city as fire breaks out again. Now the three are sure arson is the cause, and soon they discover that the arsonist is the same crazed, confederate major they fought in *The Mark Twain Murders*. Though the Duke, Twain, and Tom Sawyer have several close calls, they track the major to a masked ball where he ends up burning himself instead of his intended victims.

Comment: This title has the same Confederate villain as *The Mark Twain Murders* but doesn't explain his drive as fully. Its main historical interest is its 1860s San Francisco setting. The first chapter gives a vivid, romantic look at the volunteer fire

companies that were a vital part of the city. There actually was a remarkable fireman of the time named Tom Sawyer who claimed to be the inspiration for the Twain character.
Fiction: upper intermediate–junior high

Young, Alida E. **LAND OF THE IRON DRAGON.** New York: Doubleday, 1978. 213 p.

Content: Lim Yan-Sung and his father migrated to California from their native China. Soon after they arrived in San Francisco, a fire in the store where they had been living kills Lim Yan-Sung's father, and the boy is left alone in a strange land. With the help of a lovely Chinese slave girl, Lim Yan-Sang makes his way to Sacramento to join the Chinese crews building the first transcontinental railroad. Struggling to grow up in this hectic world, he makes some friends and a few enemies as the story builds to its startling climax.
Comment: The novel is very readable. However, The Association of Children's Librarians does not recommend it, saying, ". . . emphasizes misunderstanding among races, but the constant name calling . . . and flat characterizations tend to reinforce stereotypes rather than dispel them."
Fiction: intermediate–junior high

Young, Bob, and Jan Young. **THE 49'ERS—THE STORY OF THE CALIFORNIA GOLD RUSH.** New York: Julian Messner, 1966. 190 p. Illus., maps, bibliog., index.

Content: Starting with the discovery of gold at Coloma, this book includes stories of the mining fields, of the people who came there and how they came, how California became a state, and San Francisco's growth, as well as several chapters on the Spanish and Mexican eras. It concludes with a postscript bringing the state's history up to the 1880s.
Comment: The authors present a great amount of detail, much of it interesting and lively. However, there is a sense of including more than the book demands. An example is the short but reasonably complete account of the Donner Party, which has nothing to do with the gold rush or the forty-niners. The authors

would have done better to limit the book to what the title indicates.

Nonfiction: junior high–senior high

Zauner, Phyllis, and Lou Zauner. **CALIFORNIA GOLD, STORY OF THE RUSH TO RICHES. A MINI-HISTORY.** Tahoe Paradise, Calif.: Zanel Publications, 1980. 50 p. Color sketches, photos.

Content: The authors first give a general look at the gold-rush period and then describe each gold-rush community historically and as it is today. The communities told about in some depth are: Coloma, Placerville, Auburn, Volcano, Murphys, Angels Camp, San Andreas, Mokelumne Hill, Jackson, Sutter Creek, Sonora, Columbia, Mariposa, Downieville, Nevada City, and Grass Valley. Thirteen smaller communities are given shorter descriptions.

Comment: This attractive, brown tone soft-back, like the others by Phyllis Zauner, is informal and chatty in style. It also resembles her other books in that the boxed inclusions of direct quotations add to the color and interest. Somehow this book seems like a travel guide, though there certainly is information about the gold rush here, too.

Nonfiction: intermediate–adult

Zauner, Phyllis. **LAKE TAHOE.** Tahoe Paradise, Calif.: Zanel Publications, 1982. 52 p. Color photos.

Content: In one- and two-page sections, the author presents information on Lake Tahoe, the way it was then and is now. Each area of the lake is described and its history given; many old photos and quotations from early visitors are included. Side boxes given anecdotes about notable people and events. According to the author, south Tahoe was initially explored because it lay in the path to riches, the silver in Nevada. After the gold and silver rushes, Tahoe drew lumbermen, and then by 1900, recreation seekers. Until the end of World War II, Lake Tahoe was strictly a summer resort but is now developed as an all-year vacation center.

Comment: This is a browsing book, fun to read for those interested in the Tahoe area. The lack of a table of contents and

an index makes it hard to use for research purposes. Several pages of advertisements follow the suggested side trips at the back of the book.
Nonfiction: intermediate–adult

Zauner, Phyllis. **SACRAMENTO, A MINI-HISTORY.** Tahoe Paradise, Calif.: Zanel Publications, 1979. 52 p. Color illus. by Neva Roberts, photos.

Content: "The way it was then and now" describes the contents of this soft-cover book. There are several short articles on Sutter and Sutter's Fort, a one-page biography of Sam Brannan, the gold rush and its effects on Sacramento, and the choice of Sacramento as the permanent capital. The floods of 1849 and 1862 are described—and one of the solutions, raising the entire downtown by twelve feet! Early schools and newspapers are noted as is the use of the Sacramento River as a major highway. The first railroad west of the Rockies—the line that ran from Sacramento to Folsom—is described as the work of Theodore Judah who envisioned and started the transcontinental railroad. The reader participates in the coming of electricity to the city in 1895, celebrated by a Great Electric Carnival. Moving toward the present, Zauner describes the farming of the region, what to see in the area now, and the restoration of the capitol building.
Comment: Though there is no table of contents, readers of almost all ages could get a lot of information from this informal history by browsing through. As in the other Zauner mini-histories, the historic photographs and the inclusion of direct quotations, diary entries, and old newspaper clippings add to the flavor. As in her other booklets, there are unexplained advertisements on the last pages.
Nonfiction: intermediate–adult

Zauner, Phyllis. **SAN FRANCISCO: A MINI-HISTORY.** Tahoe Paradise, Calif.: Zanel Publications, 50 p. Color photos.

Content: This soft-cover booklet is filled with short anecdotal biographies of San Francisco characters. Short sections also deal with the gold rush and earthquake, vigilantes, economic bust from 1855 to 1859, Chinese immigration, the "champagne days" of the 1870s to the 1890s, the cable car, 1915 Panama Pacific International Exposition, Fisherman's Wharf, bay bridges, depression and war years, frontier journalism, and sights to see now.

Comment: This is good browsing for those interested in area history. The vocabulary makes it more suitable for good upper-elementary readers. The lack of an index, table of contents, and significant dates makes it hard to use for reference. There are some unexplained, modern-day advertisements mixed with historical text and photos at the end.

Nonfiction: intermediate–adult

Ziebold, Edna B. **CALIFORNIA FROM EXPLORATION TO STATEHOOD.** Seaside, Calif.: Perc B. Sapsis, 1969. 64 p. Photos, maps, glossary, bibliog., index.

Content: This book relates the history of California from the coming of Cabrillo through the mission and rancho days and the discovery of gold. The flags flown over California from 1542 to 1846 are shown.

Comment: This very enjoyable book seemed easy to read with its double-spaced pages and bold print. Children will learn a great deal from the photographs which are of exhibits in the Los Angeles County Museum of Natural History.

Nonfiction: intermediate

Ziebold, Edna B. **INDIANS OF EARLY SOUTHERN CALIFOR-NIA.** Seaside, Calif.: Perc B. Sapsis, 1969. 48 p. Photos, bibliog., glossary, index. Maps.

Content: In simple text, alternating with full- or half-page photographs of dioramas, the author gives basic information about early Indian life—appearance of the people, their shelter, food, food gathering, clothing, recreation, and religious ceremonies.

Comment: This would be an excellent book to use for young researchers. The map at the beginning gives a graphic idea of the early Indian groups and their locations in California.

Nonfiction: primary–intermediate

2
Contemporary
Life

Aaron, Chester. **SPILL.** New York: Atheneum, 1977.

Content: This story is about a family living close to the Audubon Canyon Ranch near Bolinas, Marin County during the 1971 oil spill. A son, fourteen, and a daughter, thirteen, grow away from each other and from the family. Then, thanks to their work with the bird rescue, they find their way back to each other.

Comment: This title would supplement environmental studies about California, though the story isn't too plausible. The oil spill of 1971 is the event around which the story is built.
Fiction: junior high

Alexander, Anne. **TROUBLE ON TREAT STREET.** New York: Atheneum, 1974. 116 p. Illus. by John Jones.

Content: This story concerns two young boys—Manolo, a Chicano, and Clemuel, a black. They live in the same building; Clem is the newcomer. Manolo has long hoped for a real friend and Clem is his age, but they are "on-sight" enemies until the threats from a group of juvenile delinquents force them to get to know each other.
Comment: According to the author, *Trouble on Treat Street* is authentically San Francisco, with Treat Avenue being the actual setting.
Fiction: intermediate

Battles, Edith. **501 BALLOONS SAIL EAST.** Reading, Mass.: Addison Wesley/Young Scott, 1971.

Content: This classic book on balloon lifts tells of the movement of the wind currents, the offshore chill factor, and the effect of the intervening mountains.

Comment: This book is pointedly California in setting. It is fiction but has nonfiction teaching aids and has been used in classrooms.
Fiction: junior high–senior high

Bonham, Frank. **MYSTERY OF THE RED TIDE.** New York: E. P. Dutton, 1966. 127 p. Illus. by Brinton Turkle.

Content: Tommy is sent to his Uncle Mike's on the California Coast. His mother is dead, and his father is having a hard time taking care of the family. Uncle Mike is a marine biologist who collects sea creatures from the tide pools. Mysterious things happen. Lunches are opened, but sandwiches are missing. The puzzling Red Tide offers the solution.
Comment: Intermediate grade students love mysteries and this has a scientific element which is so much the better.
Fiction: intermediate

Clark, Ann Nolan. **BEAR CUB.** New York: Viking, 1965. 63 p. Illus. by Charles Frace.

Content: Written in poetic stanzas of free verse, this is the story of a bear cub from the time of its birth until it is ready to begin life on its own in its second year. From the winter of its birth, the hand-sized cub is protected, fed, entertained and taught by its mother. The escape from man and the forest fire add excitement to the simple story.
Comment: What a lovely story of bearhood and motherhood! The writing style offers vivid descriptions.
Fiction: intermediate

Couffer, Jack, and Mike Couffer. **SALT MARSH SUMMER.** New York: G. P. Putnam's, 1978. 91 p. Photos.

Content: Descriptions and stories of the wildlife in a marsh area near Newport Bay in southern California. The authors, father and son, are dedicated environmentalists, and in this book they tell how encroaching development changed the "critter" population, and the successful efforts to create an ecological reserve.
Comment: An amusing, factual, and interesting look at part of

California's environment, which has been changing since the arrival of the Europeans. This book gives insights into one aspect and shows that individuals who care about the environment, when united, can make a difference. This is important for California's young people to know.
Nonfiction: intermediate–senior high

Davis, Charlotte, and Lois Trainor. **PORTS OF CALIFORNIA.** Los Angeles: Elk Grove Press, 1979. 80 p. Photos. and illus. by Jim Gindraux, glossary, index.

Content: The book is divided into four parts. First, northern California is introduced and the ports of Crescent City and Humboldt Bay described. Next, the San Francisco Bay area is described, with Monterey included. The Great Central Valley with its ports at Sacramento, Stockton, and Hueneme constitute part three. And last, southern California with Los Angeles, Long Beach, and San Diego, is featured.
Comment: Though it provides a much-needed and very simply written source of information about California ports, the book is dated. It ignores the Port of Oakland, now the largest container port on the West Coast of the United States and much busier than San Francisco. The products of each area are noted because they pass through the ports. The special facilities, financing, and governance of each port are described. Unfortunately, the photographs are not captioned and the illustrations scantily labeled.
Nonfiction: intermediate

Eckert, Allan W. **IN SEARCH OF A WHALE.** Garden City, N. Y.: Doubleday, 1970. 158 p. Color illus. by Joseph Cellini, index.

Content: This is based on a story for the "Wild Kingdom" television series, wherein Marlin Perkins goes on a hunt for a pilot whale for Marineland of the Pacific. We learn how sea creatures are captured for Marineland, and about whales and their habits, as well as about others—sea elephants, sharks, porpoises—who live in these waters.
Comment: This is very informative; any young person interested in whales, as many are, will learn much about them. It's

interesting to read how tentative scientists were in 1970 regarding the sounds whales make, conjecturing that these might be ways of communicating. By the way, did you know whales have bad breath?

Nonfiction: intermediate–junior high

Ellis, Ella Thorp. **CELEBRATE THE MORNING.** New York: Atheneum, 1972. 177 p.

Content: Fourteen-year-old April has to deal as an adult with her schizophrenic mother, the welfare department, and the sheriff. Of course, she also has the everyday problems most adolescents face—doubts and insecurities about her relationships with her peers. April does enjoy the steadying friendship of Fermin, the neighboring Mexican-American, who loves both April and her mother. Also, her ripening friendship-love with Allan, a budding ornithologist, gladdens her life. The story is set in a California coastal, agricultural community.

Comment: It's a well-told story; the very slight instructional value would be in the presentation of the Mexican-American character, a brief look at the demands and risks of agriculture, and an introduction to the problems of the modern impoverished.

Fiction: upper intermediate–junior high

Evarts, Hal G. **JAY-JAY AND THE PEKING MONSTER.** New York: Charles Scribner's Sons, 1978. 185 p.

Content: Set in the 1970s, this book is a semifantasy. It explores the possibility that the remains of Peking Man, missing since Pearl Harbor, might be hidden on Camp Pendleton Marine Base (called Pennington in the book) in southern California.

Comment: There is very little historical justification for reading this fast-paced mystery. There is some look at life on and around a military base, some incidental references to a very early Indian tribe and a current Indian reservation, and a subplot which portrays a greedy developer.

Fiction: intermediate

Fitch, Bob, and Lynne Fitch. **SOY CHICANO: I AM A MEXICAN-**

AMERICAN. Mankato, Minn.: Creative Educational Society, 1970. 64 p. Photos by the authors.

Content: This is a contemporary story of Guadalupe Maria Saludo, a thirteen-year-old Mexican-American girl living in Earlimart. Through story and pictures, the first-person narrative stresses the United Farm Workers Union and the plight of uneducated laborers in California.
Comment: The first half of the story seemed didactic and slow moving, but eventually the reader really becomes involved with Guadalupe Maria Saludo, her dreams, and her concerns.
Fiction: intermediate

Franchere, Ruth. **CESAR CHAVEZ.** New York: Thomas Y. Crowell, 1970. 52 p. Color illus. by Earl Thollander.

Content: "A quietly forceful biography of the leader of the National Farm Workers Association [now known as United Farm Workers of America] which relates in simple language Chavez' life as a child on his parents' farm in Arizona, his years in California as a migrant worker . . . and his part in the continuing struggle to improve the working and living conditions of farm workers." (ALA, *The Booklist*)
Comment: A sympathetic view of the problems of migrant workers.
Nonfiction: intermediate

Gee, Maurine H. **CHICANO, AMIGO.** New York: William Morrow, 1972. 96 p. Illus. by Ted Lewin.

Content: Kiki is an eight-year-old Chicano who wants to become a good boy scout. His single-mindedness seems commendable, yet infuriating to Marc, chief of the den, and Kiki's adopted protector. However, when Kiki's life is endangered during an earthquake, Marc realizes his affection for Kiki and works desperately to save him.
Comment: The book gives some insight into the problems of children from ethnically different or economically depressed environments. And, of course, it deals with the ever-present California danger—an earthquake.
Fiction: intermediate

Gee, Maurine. **FIRESTORM.** New York: William Morrow, 1968. 94 p. Illus. by Charles Geer.

J GEE

Content: Ken, Merv, and Cubby all live in Rosario Canyon in southern California. Merv, the newcomer, learns about the dangers and peculiarities of area fires from the old-timers, Ken and Cubby, and brings some problems and questions into the boys' lives. Is it right for them to spring the coyote traps the government workers set? Ken and Merv both have beloved pet dogs, and when Merv's pedigreed, Abdul, wanders off in the midst of an endangering fire, the boys' adventures intensify.

Comment: The story touches lightly on environmentalist-governmental differences with more emphasis on the threat of fire

2m

in dry, urban, southern California and the planning and organization in fighting fires there.

Fiction: intermediate

Gee, Maurine H. **FLOOD HAZARD.** New York: William Morrow, 1966. 127 p. Illus. by Charles Geer.

J Gee

Content: Doug Markel is new in his southern California school and longs to be accepted by the Secret Six. But instead of making friends, he gets in wrong with the leader of the group. Doug agrees to help elderly Mrs. Snead take care of her dog, Buff, in order to earn money, but Mrs. Snead dies, and Doug ends up trying to save Buff from being put to sleep. During the heavy winter rains, Buff gets away; Doug, searching for him finds out that the reservoir is giving way. His alert saves lives

1m

and property.

Comment: The slight instructional value this book has is the picture it gives of flood hazards.

Fiction: intermediate

Gray, Anne. **THE WONDERFUL WORLD OF SAN DIEGO.** Gretna, La: Pelican Publishing, 1975. 78 p. Photos.

Content: This history of the San Diego area is told in story form. Young Debbie and Dan fly to San Diego to spend summer with their ninety-five-year-old Great Uncle Justin and his daughter, Anna. Justin has lived through much of the history of the area, and Dan wants to write about it. First, Dan learns about the Indians of the area and Cabrillo's 1542 discovery, then about the mission era and rancho life. The story moves on to the transfer of power from Mexico to America, the building of San Diego by William Heath Davis, then to Alonzo E. Horton, Father Horton.

The children learn about modern times—Dr. Harry Wegeforth and the San Diego Zoo, George Millay and Sea World, the Scripps family and Scripps Institute. They conclude their summer learning about the navy coming to San Diego and how the area figured in early aviation.

Comment: Though the story is obviously contrived, a student could learn a great deal about the San Diego area, including the facts that there is an annual September reenactment of the Cabrillo discovery, and that Camp Pendleton is on the site of a former large rancho, *Santa Margarita y Flores*.

Fiction: intermediate

Hoyt, Olga. **AMERICAN INDIANS TODAY.** New York: Abelard-Schuman, 1972. 181 p. Photos, bibliog., index.

Content: The book has chapters on Indian problems, Indians and the government, Indians from various areas, including cities, and the future of Indians.

The introductory and concluding chapters, plus the one on California Indians would be pertinent to California interests.

The chapter on California Indians has information about the current Indian population, a look at the effects on them of the missions and the gold rush, and Indian reservations and rancherias are noted and described. Bureau of Indian Affairs spokesmen are quoted, as well as Indian responses to the BIA.

Several paragraphs are devoted to a description of the Cabazon band of mission Indians of southern California, the Chukchansi tribe of Coarsegold, and the Agua Caliente band of mission Indians at Palm Springs.

Comment: Though only a small portion of this book pertains to California, the information is valuable.

Nonfiction: intermediate–junior high

Hurd, Edith. **THE BLUE HERON TREE.** New York: Viking, 1968. 66 p. Illus. by Clement Hurd.

Content: The book tells of the heron rookery and sanctuary at the Audubon Canyon Ranch, Bolinas Lagoon. Starting with the arrival of "Big Blue," the heron, against a background of information about the geological formation of the lagoon, the story moves on to the choosing of a nesting place and a mate, the hatching and rearing of the young, and the defense of the nest against natural enemies.

Comment: Read aloud, the book could be used to further an understanding of the natural history of California; the study could be enriched with pictures or slides of the extensive plant and animal life mentioned in the text. The afterword tells of the fight between environmentalists and developers over the use of land. Useful for generating discussions.

Nonfiction: intermediate

Hurd, Edith. **THE FAR AWAY CHRISTMAS: A STORY OF THE FARALLON ISLANDS.** New York: Viking, 1958. 30 p.

Content: The author based this novel on the true story of a Coast Guard family who lived on the Farrallon Islands just off the coast near San Francisco. One year all of their presents and the turkey almost did not arrive in time for Christmas because of a big storm.

Comment: This book offers young readers a glimpse of islands often heard about—and perhaps seen on a clear day—but about which little is written for their age level.

Fiction: intermediate

Johnson, Stancil. **FRISBEE.** New York: Workman Publications, 1975. 184 p. Illus. by the author.

Content: This is the history of the frisbee, the plastic flying disc, and it's a California story. San Luis Obispo was its birthplace, and Los Angeles was its motherland.

Comment: This book covers the sport fully. It might be a good way to show students that history is a record of what has

happened—it doesn't have to be concerned exclusively with what happened long ago.
Nonfiction: intermediate–adult

Luger, Harriet. **BIRD OF THE FARALLONS.** Reading, Mass.: Addison Wesley, 1971. 61 p. Color illus. by Michael Hampshire.

Content: This is a recounting of the life story of a California murre from the time it is hatched from the egg until it is caught in an oil slick, and the attempts of a family to restore it to health.
Comment: Though this book is fiction, it has important natural history elements. Because of the intermixture of fiction and fact, some libraries classify it as nonfiction.
Fiction: intermediate

Luger, Harriet. **CHASING TROUBLE.** New York: Viking, 1976. 119 p.

Content: To keep her out of trouble, a tough city kid is sent to live in the California countryside where she reluctantly finds herself caring about the land, ecology, and a pocket gopher.
Comment: There are important natural history elements included.
Fiction: intermediate

Madian, Jon. **BEAUTIFUL JUNK: A STORY OF THE WATTS TOWERS.** Boston: Little, Brown, 1968. 44 p. Photos by Barbara and Lou Jacobs, Jr.

Content: With much use of narrative photography, this book tells of a young black, Charlie, who becomes fascinated with the junk-collecting of an old man. Ridiculing him at first, Charlie is eventually drawn by the man's gentleness and dedication, and follows him to find out what motivates the gathering of useless items. Thus, Charlie discovers the Watts Towers, huge structures built from junk by the old man in order to bring some beauty into the area. Charlie responds to the beauty and becomes a helper instead of a scoffer.

Comment: The postscript gives the factual history of Simon Rodia who, like the old man in the story, devoted more than thirty years to building a structure out of junk, in order to contribute beauty.
Fiction: intermediate

Martin, Patricia Miles. **NO, NO, ROSINA.** New York: G.P. Putnam's Sons, 1964. 47 p. Color illus. by Earl Thollander.

Content: Young Rosina is always left at home when her older brothers and Papa go off in their fishing boat, the *Santa Rosa,* from Fisherman's Wharf in San Francisco. Time and again she tries to go along, especially from November to early spring when they go for crabs, but Papa says no. "A woman on board brings bad luck, and your place is at home."

One day Rosina hides on board and surprises Papa when they are already through the Golden Gate and ready to bring up the first crab pot. Papa is angry, and at first, luck seems to be bad, but the catch improves.

Then, Papa even asks her to go again.
Comment: The pleasant story gives some information about the Bay Area crab industry and an opportunity for the artist, Earl Thollander, to depict some real San Francisco scenes.
Fiction: primary

Martin, Patricia Miles. **THE PUMPKIN PATCH.** New York: G.P. Putnam's Sons, 1966. 47 p. Drawings by Tom Hamil.

Content: Kate and her kindergarten class go on field trip to the pumpkin patch. Everyone except Kate buys a pumpkin to take home; she buys one inhabited by a mouse to leave in the field. Wally, who usually gets in trouble on field trips, knows what she has done and makes his pumpkin into a jack-o-lantern for her.
Comment: This story was researched at Half Moon Bay's famous Pumpkin Patch where a fall festival is held each year. Families from San Francisco and the Bay Area go to the festival and choose their own pumpkins right in the field.
Nonfiction: primary–intermediate

Martin, Patricia Miles. **THE RICE BOWL PET.** New York: Thomas Y. Crowell, 1962. n.p. Illustrations.

Content: This simple story concerns Ah Jim's search for a pet small enough to fit in his rice bowl.
Comment: Some exciting sections of San Francisco are presented as well as a glimpse into the life of a Chinese-American boy. The illustrations are excellent. (Adapted from the National Association of Independent Schools, *Junior Booklist*.)
Fiction: primary

Masten, Warren. **HOW TO TAKE A WALKING FIELD TRIP ON THE MONTEREY PENINSULA AND LIVE TO TELL THE STORY.** Carmel, Calif.: Sunflower Ink, n.d. 83 p. Drawings by Jerri Hansen and Warren Masten, glossary.

Content: In light-hearted, narrative style, the author identifies some of the plants and animals common to the Monterey Peninsula, explains the tidal zones, and describes animals of the tide zones from snails to sculpins and blennies.

He also describes plants and animals of the Monterey wooded area, starting with Monterey pines and ending with black widow spiders. The book concludes with the history and information about the much-maligned North American hairy spider, tarantula.
Comment: This is as much a book of humor as a nature guide. It's breezy and fun—and includes a fair amount of information as well. The author makes a strong plea for protecting the plants and animals of the area. There is room between sections for the reader to jot personal notes and drawings.
Nonfiction: intermediate–adult

Moeri, Louise. **DOWNWIND.** New York: E.P. Dutton, 1984. 121 p.

Content: The Dearborn family includes overstrung Mother, stable Dad, three siblings and the narrator, twelve-year-old Ephraim. Residents of the California valley not far from Stockton, they are "downwind" from the nuclear power plant. A

1980 accident at the plant sends residents rushing in panic to the foothills where they hope to be above the danger zone.

Ephraim feels great responsibility as he realizes the extent of his mother's hysteria. Later, as they head for the freeway, Ephraim in the trailer, cut off from his parents in the pickup cab, is left in charge of his sister and brother who were both injured by the lurch of the vehicle.

Encounters with angry and fearful people, with drunks, and even with a sinister duo leave Mother practically paralyzed with fear. Ephraim, his father, and a kindly couple cope with the seriously injured sister. As the crisis ends, Ephraim has gained understanding and realizes all have been changed by this crisis.
Comment: This is heavy stuff! The central focus on the threat of nuclear disaster is dire; the portrayal of a totally ineffective Mother could well be threatening to young readers, and then there is a veiled rape attempt. Several mature fifth- and sixth-grade readers found the story powerful, but not unduly upsetting. It should be used with great care and judgement. The setting is California, but the plot deals with general problems of society today.
Fiction: intermediate–junior high

Montgomery, Rutherford G. **A KINKAJOU ON THE TOWN.** Cleveland: World Publishing, 1967. 159 p. Illus. by Lorence Bjorklund.

Content: When Timothy has to return to boarding school, he gives his pet kinkajou to the Santa Barbara Zoo. The kinkajou makes several escapes to try to find his master, and with him we learn about the mountain terrain and creatures in the Santa Barbara area.
Comment: A nice, boy-and-his-pet story with a happy ending. There are good descriptions of the mountains and critters. There is a factual error—Solvang is said to be a Dutch town where the inhabitants have tried to recreate their homeland, but it is actually of Danish origin.
Fiction: intermediate

Niemeyer, Marie. **THE MOON GUITAR.** New York: Franklin Watts, 1969. 151 p. Illus. by Gustave E. Nebel.

Content: The setting is Chinatown, San Francisco, and the time the 1960s. Su-Lin is in junior high school and wants to live an "American" life—slumber parties and school orchestra. Her grandfather, a Chinese traditionalist, opposes any deviation from the life-style he prescribes for the family. Su-Lin befriends Tracy, a new, Caucasian girl at school, and together they solve a mystery involving an old, Chinese musical instrument known as the moon guitar. Su-Lin eventually wins the respect of her grandfather and her father's backing in living a life which encompasses both Chinese and American traditions.
Comment: Su-Lin's and Tracy's adventures as they track down the moon guitar are fast-paced for good reading and give Su-Lin many chances to explain Chinese tradition to Tracy.
Fiction: intermediate

O'Dell, Scott. **CHILD OF FIRE.** New York: Houghton Mifflin, 1974. 213 p.

Content: Two teen Chicanos from a California-Mexican border town are gang leaders, on parole, pursuing the same girl, and guided by the same parole officer. The story is told in the first person by the middle-aged parole officer, who works doggedly trying to help these adolescents. Ernie Sierra, one of the boys, shows up with too much money and headed for more trouble, but Manuel Castillo just might make it. Manuel's respect for history, tradition, and his rapport with others give him a chance, but his flair for the dramatic eventually brings him to tragedy.
Comment: Though neither of the boys "makes it," the novel is not downbeat. Current problems of some poor Chicanos are well delineated.
Fiction: junior high

Place, Marian T., and Charles G. Preston. **JUAN'S EIGHTEEN-WHEELER SUMMER.** New York: Dodd, Mead, 1982. 158 p.

Content: Juan Berna, a fifth-grader living with his Mexican-American family in a barrio near the west outskirts of Stockton, relives his exciting summer as he relates the story to his classmates. Juan realizes that his newly widowed mother can't afford the bicycle he covets. Then he and his family become involved in the life of a trucker who lives next door. Juan earns money as the trucker's apprentice, and learns a lot about the trucking industry as well as California and its agriculture. He caps it all by saving the life of the trucker who has become his good friend, and the trucker buys that very bicycle he has so long wanted.

Comment: This interestingly told story captures many aspects of the contemporary values and problems of the Mexican-American working in California agriculture. Prejudice and cultural differences are acknowledged without being dwelled upon.

Fiction: intermediate

Politi, Leo. **THE BUTTERFLIES COME.** New York: Charles Scribner's Sons, 1957. n.p. Illus. by the author.

Content: Stephen and Lucia love the sea and woods around their home on the Monterey Peninsula. One October day the sky is filled with thousands of Monarch butterflies which have come from Canada to spend the winter. Maria learns how happy the butterflies made the Indians in the old days, and is delighted that she will be able to participate in Pacific Grove's butterfly festival and parade.

Comment: Told in the author-illustrator's inimitable style. The nature facts in this story are true, as in his other books. Many Politi books, though now out-of-print, are on library shelves and tell California stories, often featuring ethnic minorities. The stories and the illustrations appeal to primary readers.

Fiction: primary

Politi, Leo. **MIEKO.** San Carlos, Calif.: Golden Gate Junior Books, 1969. 28 p. Illus. by the author.

Content: Little Mieko, whose name means "beautiful, graceful girl" in Japanese, lives with her parents near Little Tokyo in Los Angeles. All year she tries to be the best in everything, and it is her secret wish to honor her parents by being queen of the Ondo Parade during the Japanese-American Nisei Week. Although she finds that she is too young even to be considered, her parents assure her that she is special to them every day.

Comment: The love and respect each member of the family holds for the other is nicely brought out in the story, and Politi's illustrations capture the essential gracefulness of the Japanese culture.

Fiction: primary

Politi, Leo. **MOY MOY.** New York: Charles Scribner's Sons, 1960. 22 p. Illus. by the author.

Content: Moy Moy, "Little Sister," is just old enough this year to enjoy and remember the Chinese New Year festivities. She can take part in the children's parade and then watch the grown-up version.

Comment: The setting is Chinatown in Los Angeles, and Politi's colorful illustrations enhance the simple text to bring into focus a vivid picture of the traditional Chinese celebration.

Fiction: primary

Politi, Leo. **THE NICEST GIFT.** New York: Charles Scribner's Sons, 1973. 26 p. Illus. by the author.

Content: Carlitos lives in the barrio of East Los Angeles. With his dog, Blanco, he enjoys the warm, colorful life of this Mexican-oriented area. When Blanco gets lost, Carlitos needs a Christmas miracle to mend his broken heart.

Comment: A Mexican market and some Mexican food are described in the story. The tone is warm and upbeat—typical Politi!

Fiction: primary

Politi, Leo. **THREE STALKS OF CORN.** New York: Charles Scribner's Sons, 1975. 44 p. Illus. by the author.

Content: The setting is the old district of Pico Rivera, called "Old Pico." Little Angelica and her grandmother, along with many of the other residents, are of Mexican descent. Angelica's grandmother tells her about the vegetables grown in her garden and the importance of corn. At a fiesta in Pico Viejo Park, Angelica's teacher and school principal taste some of grandmother's good food, and like it so much that they invite grandmother to come to the school to teach the children how to prepare Mexican dishes.

Comment: The story stresses the historical importance of corn in the lives of all Mexicans. An added bonus—recipes for tacos and enchiladas are included.

Fiction: primary

Reese, John. **DINKY.** New York: David McKay. 134 p.

Content: Jerry Demarest feels inferior because he is not good in math and is the son of a world-famous, prize-winning mathematician. Jerry is a history buff and is mechanically inclined. He, with his family and best friend, spends a long summer vacation in the Sierra Nevada at an abandoned lumber camp in the heart of forty-niner country, where they discover "Dinky." This perfect, miniature railroad locomotive, built to the specifications of a "steam man," provides the vehicle for Jerry to find his own sense of values. Jerry's greatest satisfaction comes after a moment of danger draws him and his father closer together.

Comment: The reconditioning and operating of Dinky gives the reader a great deal of information about steam engines, and there is much interesting history of the area.

Fiction: intermediate

Taylor, Theodore. **THE MALDONADO MIRACLE.** New York: Doubleday, 1973. 189 p.

Content: Twelve-year old Jose Maldonado is an illegal. After his mother died, his father crossed over into California to work in the fields, and Jose is supposed to meet him in Oxnard. The father isn't there; Jose ends up on a farm near Mission San Ramon in Salinas Valley and becomes involved in a so-called miracle.

Comment: This story has several interesting elements: the reader can empathize with a youngster alone in a foreign country, illegally to boot; get a glimpse of migrant-worker camps; see what progress, in the shape of the freeway, does to communities (San Ramon strongly resembles, physically, San Miguel); and see a boy come to decisions that are satisfying and right.

Fiction: intermediate–junior high

Uchida, Yoshiko. **JOURNEY HOME.** New York: Atheneum, 1978. 144 p. Illus. by Charles Robinson.

Content: This sequel to *Journey to Topaz* tells of Yuki and her Japanese-American family coming back to Berkeley after World War II. Trying to reestablish themselves, they experience friendship from some and hatred from others.

Comment: This is a moving story, providing a glimpse into a tragic moment in our country's history. The Association of Children's Librarians recommended it, too.

Nonfiction: intermediate–junior high

Van der Veer, Judy. **HIGHER THAN THE ARROW.** San Carlos, Calif.: Golden Gate Junior Books, 1969. 132 p. Woodcuts by F. Leslie Matthews.

Content: Francesco Clare Queri, known as Francie to her family and friends, lives on an Indian reservation in southern California, along the flanks of the mountain known to the Indians as Higher Than the Arrow. At twelve, Francie is already showing great artistic talent, and she dreams of making a statue of St. Francis of Assisi with a young coyote in his arms. Francie is so involved with her project that she cannot find time to become friends with a new girl at school, Lucy Olson. Later, she became jealous of Lucy's artistic ability—with results which are almost tragic. Francie finally learns some of the humility of St. Francis and how to work with others instead of against them.

Comment: This excellent story makes the reader aware of present-day Indian life on a reservation and its high degree of responsiveness to nature and traditions.

Fiction: intermediate

Walter, Mildred Pitts. **LILLIE OF WATTS: A BIRTHDAY DISCOV-
ERY.** Los Angeles: Ward Ritchie Press, 1969. 61 p. Illus. by
Leonora Prince.

Content: Lillie, a black girl from Watts, was eleven and excited
about her birthday. Because her teacher would play a special
tribute to her on his violin, Lillie overcame her mother's
objections and wore her only good outfit to school. Art period
brought disaster to her sweater, and letting the cat of her
mother's employer get away brought more grief at home.
Comment: The poverty of many people in Watts and the special
problems of minorities and one-parent families are gently illumi-
nated in this short novel.
Fiction: primary–intermediate

Walter, Mildred Pitts. **LILLIE OF WATTS TAKES A GIANT STEP.**
New York: Doubleday, 1971. 187 p. Illus. by Bonnie Helene
Johnson.

Content: Lillie is excited but frightened about starting junior
high. She and a more affluent friend, Gladys, begin to learn the
ropes. Lillie's financial inability to buy lunch in the cafeteria
troubles her greatly, leads to her skipping lunches entirely, with
a subsequent drop in her energy, attitude, and grades. She also
begins to lose touch with Gladys. Becoming interested in the
Afro-American Cultural Club, Lillie gains some knowledge and
pride in her own heritage.
Comment: The story portrays sensitively the differing points of
view of the older and younger blacks, the agonies of young
adolescents, the trauma of poverty. Though the vocabulary is
simple and the sentences almost clipped, the use of nonstandard
grammatical constructions and terms would make this book
hard for a young reader not familiar with dialect.
Fiction: intermediate

Weaver, Harriett E. **BELOVED WAS BAHAMAS, A STEER TO
REMEMBER.** New York: Vanguard, 1974. 179 p.

Content: The fiction element of this story deals with a teenage
boy who loved and raised a steer, the boy's loneliness and need

to communicate with his father, and the boy's growing affection for a vivacious girl.

Comment: The story is based on an almost unbelievable incident that occurred during the disastrous 1964 flood in northern California. Bahamas, a mature, black Angus steer, was washed out to sea in debris tossed down the Klamath River and later rescued when he drifted into Crescent City harbor—thirty-nine miles to the north—still on the pile of debris. That much of the story is factual, as is the description of the flood itself and the damage it caused.

Fiction: intermediate

White, Florence M. **CESAR CHAVEZ, MAN OF COURAGE.** New York: Garrard, 1973. 96 p. Illustrated by Victor Mays. Index.

Content: This very simple biography of Cesar Chavez emphasizes his family life and his humanity, as well as his desire to help his people without resorting to violence. It tells of his organization—the United Farm Workers—and of their early strikes and boycotts.

Comment: This book can be read by second-graders. Older students might want a more sophisticated reading level, but the book offers an interesting insight, even for adults, into the life and work of Cesar Chavez.

Nonfiction: primary

Yep, Laurence. **CHILD OF THE OWL.** New York: Harper & Row, 1977. 217 p.

Content: Set in 1964, this contemporary story tells of Casey, her gambling father, Barney, and her wise grandmother. When Barney is injured in a mugging, twelve-year-old Casey is forced to abandon the nomadic life the two of them have led. While Barney recuperates, Casey goes to San Francisco's Chinatown to live with Paw-Paw, the maternal grandmother she had never before met. Casey's awareness of her Chinese heritage and her emerging consciousness of her own character are major aspects of the story.

Comment: The wise-cracking Casey, the broken-spirited Barney, and the "diamond in the rough," Gilbert, portray Chinese-

Americans in a fashion far removed from stereotypes! The advantages and disadvantages of living in Chinatown are examined, as well. The Association of Children's Librarians liked it, too.

Fiction: intermediate

3
Nonbook
Media

THE BELLS OF EL CAMINO. El Cerrito, Calif.: Long Filmslide Service, 1977. Color filmstrip, 75 frames, cassette, 25 min, audible and inaudible signals. Accompanying script.

Content: The first ten slides give the historical background of California preceding the mission era. Then the pictures and narrative describe each mission from south to north. The principal padres of mission foundings are named as well.

Comment: The curiously flat and hesitant voice of the narrator intoning a stilted script diverts attention from the meaning and the pictures, though a guitar background adds a nice musical touch. There is occasional confusion concerning the relationship of the narration to the picture shown. Mrs. A. S. C. Forbes and her husband are named as the people who started putting up the mission bells in 1906, but the filmstrip didn't deal as much with the bells as the title would lead one to suppose.

Sound filmstrip: intermediate–junior high

CALIFORNIA. Huntington Beach, Calif.: Creative Teaching Press, 1982. Color poster, 20 by 26 inches.

Content: The poster shows a map of California with the twenty-one missions marked and pictures of the state flag, tree, flower, and bird.

Comment: An attractive addition to a California bulletin board.

Teaching Aid—Poster: intermediate–senior high

CALIFORNIA. Visual Publications, 1976. Color filmstrip, 40 frames, cassette, 18 min. Script.

Content: The first twelve frames and script give geographic information intermixed with early political history. The next series of pictures explains the development of water resources—Hoover Dam, Shasta Dam—for electric power, irrigation, and recreation. The final section gives information on such California industries as food processing, banking, iron and steel production, and aircraft assembly. The cities shown are Fresno, Los Angeles, Berkeley, Oakland, San Francisco. Throughout the background information in the script there is quite a bit of historical information.

Comment: This is more geography and economics than history. It would be a good idea to have this kind of information available for students studying the history of the state in order for them to see the whole picture of state development. There is an accompanying script with added background information to be used at the leader's discretion.

Sound filmstrip: upper intermediate–senior high

CALIFORNIA. Our 50 States series. No. 705. Jonesboro, Ark.: ESP Inc., n. d. Cassette, 13 min. side 1, 12 min. side 2.

Content: Side one gives all kinds of information including geographical, state motto and emblems, eight main land regions, descriptions of different land areas, climates of different areas, the water system, national parks and forests, agriculture and industry, and some history, including immigration into the state during and after World War II. Side two visits towns and life in them, the agricultural riches, the freeways, and specific cities or places such as San Diego, Los Angeles, Yosemite, and Disneyland.

Comment: This tape is loaded with facts—geographic, scenic, touristic—and cries for use with maps and pictures. Without these visual aids, the information would not in all cases be easy for students to retain. This tape has been used successfully, however, with children who have difficulty reading and who may replay the tape several times to get the information.

Cassette tape: intermediate–junior high

CALIFORNIA. No. 822. Stamford, Conn.: Educational Dimensions Group, 1976. Eight color and b/w filmstrips, 40 frames each, eight cassettes, 8-10 min. each. Manual and automatic sides.

Content: "The Shape of the State" explores the state's varied topography. "The First Californians" shows California Indians' houses, clothing, food, boats, sweathouses, and migration over the Asia-Alaska land bridge. "Westward with Sail and Sword" describes the Spanish conquest of Mexico, Manila galleons, Sir Francis Drake, and the Spanish missions in Baja California. "Missions and Ranchos" explains the establishment of the mission chain in Alta California, training of the Indians in numerous skills, ranchos started, missions secularized, and the arrival of more settlers. "Rush to the Golden State" tells of the U. S. annexation of territory from Mexico, gold discovery and ways to get to California, mining methods, law and order, statehood. "California Goes Boom" describes the influx of people, railroad construction, agriculture, John Muir and the Sierra Club, land boom, minorities, and the Modoc War. "The Power of Oil and Water" describes the 1906 Quake, water needs of people and agriculture, oil boom, movies, Dust Bowl migration, and World War II veterans. California is still changing—what can we do about it? "People of Tomorrow" identifies the kinds of problems that confront the state, careers available for young people, and asks students, "What will you do to make California better?"

Comment: This is a very good set of filmstrips and tapes. The narration is smooth and interesting; background music is unobtrusive and in keeping with topics and times. Part eight, with its specific observations and questions can be used to start discussion within the class.

Sound filmstrip: intermediate

CALIFORNIA. SP 803. New York: Great American Puzzle Factory, 1977. Color Puzzle, Over 500 pieces, 18 by 24 inches.

Content: A puzzle map of California with important cities, points of interest, mission & Spanish trails noted or pictured on the map itself and in the surrounding space.

Comment: A game approach to California geography.

Teaching Aid—Puzzle: intermediate–senior high

CALIFORNIA CONFLICT: MIGRANT FARM WORKERS. Focus

on America—The Pacific States series. Chicago: SVE, 1972. Color filmstrip, 93 frames, cassette, 18 min. Manual and automatic sides. Reading Script.

Content: The stated objectives are: to show why the Central Valley is the most productive farm region of the United States; to show different life-styles of two families who depend on the agricultural industry of the valley; to show how unionization of farm laborers has affected their lives. Included are: words and phrases to know, questions for review and discussion, and enrichment activities.

Comment: Shows how a man of modest beginnings was able to own the largest-producing farm in the world and the importance of educated, scientific management of farms. The section on unionization has an excellent introductory overview of migrant labor; why Caesar Chavez organized the United Farm Workers; and how the union has helped farm laborers to receive education, medical care, and a stable life.

Sound filmstrip: intermediate–junior high

CALIFORNIA CONTRAST: MT. WHITNEY TO DEATH VALLEY, by Eugene L. Podhurst. Warren, Rhode Island: Budek Films and Slides of California. 1969. Color filmstrip, 36 frames.

Content: The pictures and narrative script focus on the geological contrasts between Mt. Whitney and Death Valley. Mt. Whitney is described as to place, size, and topography. The Inyo Mountains, Owens Valley, Panamint Valley are briefly described and shown. Then information about Death Valley is featured, including its geology.

Comment: This natural history would be of interest to a limited audience.

Filmstrip: intermediate–junior high

CALIFORNIA DESERT COUNTRY, by Eugene L. Podhurst. Warren, Rhode Island: Budek Films and Slides of California. 1969. Color filmstrip, 38 frames.

Content: The filmstrip features the Mojave Desert and Colorado

Desert. The dry lake beds, sandy plains, sand dunes, and mountains of this region—and how they were formed—are described. The salt deposits, cinder cones, and Death Valley are examined. The Ubehebe Crater is described as an example of volcanic craters seen in the area. Changing the Colorado Desert into valuable agricultural lands through irrigation is explained, as is use of the Joshua tree and other plants as food and medicine in earlier times.

Comment: The natural history in this filmstrip would be of interest to a student studying the area.

Filmstrip: intermediate–junior high

CALIFORNIA FIELD TRIP. 1967. Reprint. American Geological Institute. Earth Science Curriculum Project. Northbrook, Ill.: Hubbard Scientific Co., 1972. Color filmstrip, 31 frames. Two small charts. Teaching Guide.

Content: This is "designed to give some insight into the characteristics of mountain ranges." Charts show the range of geological zones, and elevations. The teaching guide explains what is shown, and rock characteristics. Additional information on the various areas is given, with supplemental photos.

Comment: Theoretically, this is for a fourth–grade California history unit, but it is hard for this grade level. It isn't easy for teachers to use either.

Kit: junior high

CALIFORNIA FUN, by Pat & Tony Stefano. The Learning Center, 1976. 25 p. B/w illus.

Content: ". . . a book of worksheets and activities to be used to make the study of California more fun . . ." includes fill-in maps, crossword and other puzzles, word hunts, match-ups, picture time lines. A teacher's guide at the back explains and gives suggestions how to use several of the activity sheets. Answer page in back.

Comment: A very good resource book that is used and enjoyed by teachers and students.

Teaching Aid—Activity Worksheets: intermediate

CALIFORNIA HERITAGE. Rancho Palos Verdes, Calif.: Frank Schaffer Publications, 1980. 20 p. Spirit masters. Bibliog.

Content: Each page has information with questions based on the reading. Covers the time span from Indians to today. The pages have illustrations or maps. There is a page of ideas and activities to supplement the ditto pages.

Comment: The book provides basic historical information and can be used as a short complete unit or as supplemental material.

Teaching Aid—Spirit Masters: intermediate

CALIFORNIA HISTORY. Troy, Alabama: Associated Educators, n.d. Eighteen color filmstrips, 48-54 frames each; nine cassettes, 45 min. each side. Audible signal.

Content: There are three sets of six captioned filmstrips and three cassettes each. Sets I and III were not personally reviewed, but publisher's information indicates they are the same format as Set II which was reviewed. Set I covers the Indians, the original Californians; Spanish discovery and exploration; colonization of California; missions, pueblos and presidios; foreign inroads into Spanish California; rancho life in California. Set II describes Mexican California and Yankee infiltration; the eve of American rule; American conquest; discovery of gold; statehood and its problems; and life and culture after the gold rush. Set III presents the Civil War and California; growth of cities, agriculture and minorities; politics and culture at the turn of the century; progress in the early 1900s; the depression and cultural growth; and a glimpse of California history through 100 years.

Comment: The narration quotes the captions plus additional information; one could almost use these materials instead of a textbook. The length of the tapes might be difficult for younger students to sit through, as there is no natural break, but with captions only and some teacher fill-in they would be good. The pictures are excellent. Individual filmstrips have been used with fourth-graders as a springboard for further research. These materials can all be ordered on approval. The filmstrips can be ordered separately from the cassette tapes.

Sound filmstrip: intermediate with captions only; junior high-senior high with cassettes.

CALIFORNIA INDIAN ACTIVITIES, by James McCarthy and Frances McCarthy. Jackson, Calif.: Conceptual Productions, 1980. 40 p. B/w illus., answer key.

Content: Reproducible pages with puzzles, map activities, creative writing starters, coloring pages, dot-to-dots, word searches and scrambles.
Comment: These materials could be used for a complete California Indian unit, or selectively in a more comprehensive California history unit. Lots of good things here.
Teaching Aid—Activity sheets: upper primary–lower intermediate

CALIFORNIA MISSIONS. Covina, Calif.: Hubert A. Lowman, 1950, 1972. Eighty color slides, two cassettes, 25 min. each. Manual. Twenty-two color study prints. Book, ed. Ralph B. Wright. Illus. by Herbert C. Hahn. Complete cassette text, by Hubert Lowman.

Content: The book covers the past history and present condition of each of the missions. The drawings show architectural details, artifacts and present facades of the missions. The tapes provide narration to go with the slides. The slides show scenes of the various missions.
Comment: This is used successfully with fourth graders, but would be interesting for older students as well. Narration, by the photographer Lowman, is well-paced and interesting.
Kit: intermediate–high school

CALIFORNIA NATURE SERIES. Ogden, Utah: Great Basin Film Co., 1972. Six color filmstrips, 47-50 frames each, six cassettes, 13-16 min. each. Audible and inaudible signals. Teacher's filmstrip guide with each.

Content: Titles of series: Mammals, Birds, Reptiles, Insects, Wildflowers, Deserts, Seashore.
In Mammals, forty-seven types are shown and described,

ranging from the common deer mouse found statewide to the bison, introduced by private interests into the state. In each case, the habitat is given—grassy lowlands, forest, Western California.

In Reptiles, again forty-seven types are shown and described, the majority of them lizards.

Wildflowers are grouped by habitat—desert, coastal, mountain. Several sentences about each flower give detailed information.

For Deserts, the locations of the Mojave and Colorado Deserts are shown; then the plants, animals, and geographic features are identified.

Seashore gives locale and types of seacoasts: protected or unprotected, salt marshes, mud flats, driftwood beaches. The tide zones and marine life in them are shown.

Birds shows and describes briefly the fifty varieties found in the state. It notes effects of pesticides and hunting.

Insects gives an overview of forty-seven of the most common insects. The destructive aspects of insects are stressed.

Comment: Deserts and Seashore seemed to us most useful. The other titles were too fast and too detailed for most elementary users.

Sound filmstrip: intermediate–junior high

CALIFORNIA REDWOODS by Eugene L. Podhurst. Warren, Rhode Island. Budek Films and Slides of California. 1969. Color filmstrip, 34 frames.

Content: The Sequoia *sempervirens* (everlasting redwood) in its habitat along the northern coast as well as the Sierra Nevada, and Sequoia *gigantea* (giant redwood) are described as to size, age, color, and growing habits. Their leaf and root structure, cones and bark, and methods of reproduction are contrasted. The need to preserve these trees and the conservation methods being used is noted.

Comment: This natural history would be of interest to a student studying northern California or the redwoods themselves.

Filmstrip: intermediate–junior high

CALIFORNIA: REGIONAL GEOGRAPHY. Bothell, Wash. BCS

Educational Aids, 1981. Six color filmstrips, 110-130 frames each, six cassettes, 17 to 23 min. each. Audible and inaudible signals. Teacher's Handbook (scripts). Activity sheets.

Content: Explains the major regions of California—Central Valley, coast ranges, Sierra Nevada and Cascade Ranges, desert regions, transverse and peninsular ranges—and has sections on water resources and earthquakes as well.

The other five filmstrips study the major regions in turn. In each, the present geography and how it evolved is explained; the cities of the region and their industries are examined.

Comment: There's a great deal of information in the "Overview" section which would help students understand historical data—why it was hard to enter California from the east, why agriculture has developed in the Central Valley, why water allocation is a problem. There's a particularly good graphic representation of the differing areas of water resources and water use. Many intermediate students might need help sorting out the locations of the mountains noted.

Each section of each filmstrip is self-contained. The teacher could easily build a lesson, or lessons, around each one. The five filmstrips on particular regions are very detailed—probably with more information than an intermediate student wants or needs. However, it could be useful to study the one filmstrip which describes the area students live in or are studying in detail.

Sound filmstrip: intermediate–junior high

CALIFORNIA SEEDGATHERERS. Indians of the Western Hemisphere series. Educational Services Inc., 1968. Color filmstrip, 38 frames, cassette, 9 min. Manual and automatic.

Content: This discusses homes, clothing, food, crafts, general areas where various tribes live, medicine men, coming-of-age rites, and tribal customs. Concludes with summary statements, discussion and activity suggestions.

Comment: Each frame is captioned, so this could be shown to younger students or used as a short review. The cassette repeats the captions but expands the information. Some words used in the narration would possibly need prior definition.

Sound filmstrip: intermediate

CALIFORNIA STATE HISTORICAL COLORING BOOK. Los Angeles, Calif.: Mussatti-Wyatt Productions, 1978. 32 p. B/w illus.

Content: There are captioned coloring pages of historical people and places, state emblems, flag and capitol, and contemporary places of interest. Inside front and back covers list geographical and historical facts, famous people, and places to visit.
Comment: This would be useful for additional activities.
Teaching Aid—Activity Sheets: upper primary–intermediate

CALIFORNIA STATE RAILROAD MUSEUM TOUR. El Cerrito, Calif. Long Filmslide Service, 1982. Color filmstrip, 64 frames, plus 9 review frames, cassette, 13 minutes. Audible and inaudible signals. Accompanying script.

Content: First showing some early steam locomotives with only train sounds as background, the filmstrip moves on to the important role played by Sacramento in railroad history and to show the facade of the California State Railroad Museum as its purpose is explained. Youthful guides are introduced, and their voices explain the significance of the interior exhibits pictured. Narrow gauge rails, standard gauge rails, wheel arrangements on engines, steam domes, sand domes, are noted and some explained. The fine handwork and decorative touches in the old railroad cars are shown. The use of railroads to carry mail and produce as well as passengers, is made clear. Museum rules are reviewed at the closing.
Comment: Designed as a previsit activity, this filmstrip would really help students learn what to look for and learn about. Some good discussion questions are imbedded in the script, and most are shown again at the end when the narration is over.
Sound filmstrip: intermediate

THE CALIFORNIA STORY: A COLORING BOOK, by Edward W. Ludwig. Los Gatos, Calif.: Polaris Press, 1978. 35 p. B/w illus.

Content: Contains spreads of pages to color along with corresponding pages of text on such topics as the Indians, missionaries, Russians and Fort Ross, gold rush, ethnic population, modes of transport, oil discovery, the 1906 earthquake, and the movie industry.

Comment: The text provides good capsule historical information, but the coloring pages are a bit simple for the age normally using the text. Otherwise, the book provides good supplemental activity.

Teaching Aid-Coloring Book: intermediate

CALIFORNIA STUDIES. Chicago: Eye Gate Media, 1985. Three color filmstrips, 76 frames, 101 frames, 91 frames, three cassettes, 9 min., 17 min., 13 min. Audible and inaudible signals. Teacher's guide.

Content: "The Land" zeroes in on California from outer space, showing its place in the world and defining its boundaries. Then, using maps and pictures, the sound filmstrip defines and explains bays, valleys, canyons, mountain ranges, islands, deltas, earthquakes and faults, deserts, and reclaimed land. Some major cities are named and shown; the Central Valley is shown and explained. The information is summarized at the end.

"A Cultural History" deals with the Indian inhabitants, the Spanish discovery by Cabrillo, the landing of Francis Drake, and the eventual Spanish settlement. Discussion of Father Serra, Portola, and the mission era is followed by information on the decline of the missions and the large land grants. Quickly, the filmstrip moves on to the Mexican War, the gold rush, and statehood. The racial tensions of those days are acknowledged. The building of the transcontinental railroad and the 1906 earthquake are portrayed, and then information on the water disputes, the growth in importance of the auto and the oil industries, and, finally the depression of the 1930s. Hollywood and the movies, World War II and its affect on California population leads to the conclusion.

"People and Resources" describes the history of the state's economy. Stating at the outset that California is the richest and most populous state in the union, the sound filmstrip explains the bases of the economy from Indian times to the present. The use of the natural resources by each group is stressed from the reliance on nuts, berries, hunting, and trade by the Indians through the land-based economy of the rancho period and the gold-based economy of the mid-1800s. As the more recent economy is explained, the narrator names, and amplifies on, the important industries of recent times and today—agriculture, manufacturing, oil and natural gas, the auto and film industries, aerospace and high technology, lumbering, foreign trade, export-import, service and financial businesses, and tourism.

Comment: "The Land" offers a good geographic introduction to any study of California. It would help students understand the history of the state.

The scope of "A Cultural History" is breathtaking. There is so much information and the commentary so rapid. It would have to be used—for upper intermediate and above—as a follow up, a review, or reinforcement of material already studied.

"People and Resources" would be interesting to use during a study of California history because it explains well the economic factors which influence history and does so in a straightforward, easily understood way.

The comprehension questions in the teacher's guide would require many viewings and note-takings to be answered by students, and there is an activity sheet for each filmstrip.

Sound filmstrips: intermediate–senior high

CALIFORNIA: THE NATURAL REGIONS. Bothell, Wash.: BCS Educational Aids, 1976. Six color filmstrips, 111-130 frames each, three cassettes, 20-25 min. each side. Audible and Inaudible. Teachers' Handbook. Instructional aids, research topics.

Content: 1—gives an overview of the natural regions; 2—The coast ranges; 3—The tranverse and peninsular ranges; 4—The Central Valley; 5—The Sierra Nevada and Cascade Ranges; 6—The desert regions. Each of the sound filmstrips gives information on geological and geographical features of the regions, as well as climate, weather, economy, and natural resources. The handbook has the script for each filmstrip and there are sets of questions for each, along with vocabulary terms, and forty-seven varied topics for student research.

Comment: These are interesting, and show how geography influences the economy of an area and the way people live there, as well as showing the great diversity of California's natural features. Although these filmstrips are long, there are natural breaks that can be utilized for discussion or to enable viewing in several short periods.

Sound filmstrip: intermediate–senior high

CALIFORNIA TODAY, by Richard Quantamatteo, Nancy Quantametteo and James McCarthy. Jackson, Calif.: Conceptual Productions, 1979. 45 p. B/w illus., maps.

Content: Reproducible activities worksheets that include map skills, time lines, word searches, puzzles, research starters on California natural resources, weather, environment, parks, place names, problems, emblems, government, to name some.
Comment: Many of the activities in this book seem to require prior information given by the teacher or textbook, and there are more that are geared to sparking student research than the book *California's Past,* by the same authors. Good for new or different ideas.

Teaching Aid-Activity Sheets: intermediate–junior high

CALIFORNIA TREASURES. Edited by Gail Evenari. San Francisco School Volunteers. Presented by Museums Affiliated with Public Schools, n.d. 193 p. B/w illus. Contributing artists, Betty Silverman and Jeannette Young.

Content: This curriculum workbook contains specific information and worksheets to enrich field trips in the San Francisco area. The content pertinent to California history includes pre- and postvisit activities for Alcatraz Island, Cable Car Barn and Museum, Fort Point National Historic Site, Mission Dolores, Oakland Museum, and Presidio Army Museum.
Comment: This will be useful if you can find it in your curriculum office or school library, as it is no longer available. The specific activities and suggestions for previsit work would help prepare a student with the vocabulary and necessary knowledge to enrich a field trip.

Teaching Aid-Workbook: primary–intermediate

CALIFORNIA'S NORTHERN NATIONAL AND STATE PARKS

AND MONUMENTS. California Odyssey. Orange, Calif.: Academy Films, 1977. Color filmstrip, 71 frames, cassette, 17 min. Audible and inaudible signals.

Content: Following an introduction, information is given on Point Reyes National Seashore, Golden Gate Recreation Area, Point Lobos State Reserve, and Lassen National Park. Of more specific historical interest is the information on San Juan Bautista State Historic Park, Fort Point National Historical Site and Muir Woods National Monument; there is detailed information on John Muir and his home and on Vallejo's Petaluma Adobe State Historic Park. Lava Beds National Monument is included, with a brief mention of the Indian war there.

Comment: This filmstrip is of natural and political historic interest. It states that San Juan Bautista State Historic Park is perhaps the finest place in California to see evidences of the mission, Mexican, and American influences of the 1770's-1850's period. It cites Lassen volcanic rock as the "youngest volcanic rock in the United States." It would be interesting to see how many students realize that that statement shows the narration was written before the Mount St. Helens' eruption.

Sound filmstrip: intermediate–senior high

CALIFORNIA'S OFFICIAL STATE SYMBOLS. California Odyssey. Orange, Calif.: Academy Films, 1977. Color filmstrip, 73 frames, cassette, 18 min. Audible and inaudible signals.

Content: Information is given on the capitol building, the Bear Flag, the seal of California, and the governor's flag and seal. Also shown and described are the officially designated state animals and plants—the tree, flower, rock, mineral, gemstone, fossil, insect, reptile, bird, fish, and marine mammal.

Comment: This is the kind of "nickel knowledge" elementary students love! It's also of some interest to others who like to learn about their state.

Sound filmstrip: intermediate–senior high

CALIFORNIA'S PAST, by Nancy Quantamatteo, Richard Quantamateo, and James McCarthy. Jackson, Calif.: Conceptual Productions, 1979. 45 p. B/w illus., maps, answer pages.

Content: Reproducible activities worksheets that include maps, puzzles, time lines, research ideas, match-ups, flags, covering California history from Indian days up to statehood.

Comment: This is more sophisticated than "California Fun," and not necessarily intended to be as much fun. Many of the activity sheets are research starters. Has good new and different ideas.

Teaching Aid-Activity Worksheets: intermediate–junior high

CALIFORNIA'S SOUTHERN NATIONAL AND STATE PARKS AND MONUMENTS. California Odyssey. Orange, Calif.: Academy Films, 1977. Color filmstrip, 77 frames, cassette, 18 min. Audible and inaudible signals.

Content: Following an introduction, there is information about Cabrillo National Monument, Anza Borrego State Park, Picacho State Recreation Area, Joshua Tree National Monument, Hearst San Simeon State Historical Monument, Sequoia, Kings Canyon and Yosemite National Parks, Devil's Postpile National Monument, and Pinnacles National Monument. There is more detailed information about Death Valley National Monument and Channel Islands National Monument.

Comment: The emphasis is on natural history. However, some political history is necessarily interwoven.

Sound filmstrip: intermediate–senior high

CANNERY ROW: ECOLOGY AND HISTORY. Stanford, Calif.: Multi-Media Productions, 1975. Two color filmstrips, 57 frames, 51 frames, cassette, 11+ min. each side. Audible signals. Teacher's manual.

Content: Beginning with scenes of the Chinese fishing village on the Cannery Row site in the 1850s, the filmstrip gives the history of the area and describes Cannery Row today. First telling of the anti-Oriental feeling for the early residents, the story goes on to the beginning of the fishing industry—catching, then canning salmon and pilchard (sardines). The first cannery built in 1907 and the contributions of Knut Hovden, a Norwegian National Fisheries graduate, are noted. Later, the manufacturing and marketing of fish meal grew, and purse seiners (a type of net) were used for fishing. Memories of the fishing heyday are described, as is the whole canning process. The second filmstrip tells of the desperate need for cannery workers at the beginning of World War II. Following the sharp decline in the sardine supply, the canneries were closed and dismantled, and John Steinbeck made the area famous with his novels. Both Steinbeck, and the hero of several of his novels, "Doc" Ricketts, are quoted and featured. A current canning factory at nearby Moss Landing is shown and predictions made about what would happen if the sardines returned.

Comment: Lots of information! Students could use this filmstrip (which can be used on an automatic machine) to find out about historical minority problems, the growth and decline of a California industry, ecology, and the Monterey Bay area.

Sound filmstrip: upper intermediate–high school

THE CENTRAL VALLEY OF CALIFORNIA by R. S. Funderburk. Warren, Rhode Island: Herbert E. Budek Films and Slides. n.d. Color filmstrip, 31 frames.

Content: The 400-mile-long Central Valley is described from Mt. Shasta in the north to Bakersfield in the south. The Sacramento, American, and Kings River in the upper valley are noted, and the use of rangeland to feed sheep and cattle. Shasta Dam, Friant Dam, Millerton Lake, and Madera Canal are the parts of the water program described. Olive growing, rice and fruit production, clay products, cotton, citrus, and oil are the industries mentioned.

Comment: The Sacramento Valley seemed to get a disproportionate amount of the coverage. The San Joaquin Valley didn't even get its rivers mentioned. We would use this only for those looking for information on the northern Central Valley.

Filmstrip: intermediate–junior high

THE CHINESE 49'ERS. Stanford, Calif.: Multi-Media Productions, 1973. Color filmstrip, 49 frames, cassette, 9 min. 30 sec. Audible and inaudible signals. Teacher's manual.

Content: Information is given on the reasons for Chinese immigration to California. Initially, the Chinese were a welcome addition to the work force, but a change occurred in the 1850s when one-tenth of the California population was Chinese. By this time, unemployment had become a problem for Chinese and also for white laborers. The growth and character of prejudice is detailed.

Comment: Intermediate and junior-high students can get from this a clear picture of the prejudice faced by Asians in the 1800s. The information is geared to a younger audience than the more sophisticated version by Multi-Media Productions, *The other Fortyniners.*

Sound filmstrip: intermediate–junior high

CLEMENTINE. Weston, Conn.: Weston Woods, 1975. Color filmstrip, 36 frames, cassette, 9 min. Audible and inaudible signals. Script.

Content: With musical background, singers, and a narrator, a melodramatic version of the song "Clementine" is shown. The narrator intersperses comments before and after the familiar refrain as the story—the traditional villain wanting his money or the daughter—unfolds. The hero arrives in the nick of time to save Clementine from the "foamy brine," marry her, and share in the happiness of finding a large, gold nugget. The villain comforts himself by wooing Clementine's sister.

Comment: The filmstrip was developed to accompany a book of the same name by Robert Quackenbush published by Lippincott, but could effectively be used alone. The filmstrip is done in attractive pastels, each frame ornately framed. The melodrama, and the repetition of the familiar refrain, makes it hard to resist joining in on the song.

Sound filmstrip: intermediate–junior high

COLUMBIA, CALIFORNIA—A GOLD RUSH TOWN. El Cerrito, Calif.: Long Filmslide Service, 1969. Color filmstrip, 37 frames, cassette, 8 min. Audible signal. Accompanying script.

Content: Columbia is identified and located on a map. Its historic significance is noted (87 million dollars in gold taken from area) and an aerial view of Columbia today shown. Then the slides and narration take the viewer down main street and the important side streets, explaining the significant restored buildings along the way—Fallon Theater, Masonic Hall, Wells Fargo Office, old bank building, court room, Chinese drug store, American drug store, photographer's studio, jail, school, museum, barber shop, fire department. Several slides are devoted to the yearly parade of old-fashioned fire equipment. The opportunity to take a stagecoach ride—and perhaps be heldup—is mentioned.

Comment: This colorful, clear, and simple sound filmstrip would be a fine pre- or postvisit activity for a class or group. As it emphasizes the old fire engines, it would be a good idea to arrange in advance with the ranger to have your group take part in a mock fire fighting re-creation, with the "bucket brigade," which was a real part of life in Columbia during gold-rush days. If a visit isn't possible, this filmstrip could show young people what a gold-rush town looked like.

Sound filmstrip: primary–junior high

COLUMBIA STUDY GUIDE, by John J. Lesjack. Fresno, Calif.: Valley Publishers, 1979.

Content: This study guide leads students on a walking tour of Columbia State Historic Park and restored gold-rush town. It invites participation in a museum tour, bucket brigade, stagecoach ride, gold panning, and visits to fire departments and a Chinese joss house. The entire town is covered, from the old schoolhouse at one end to the old church at the other.

The study guide provides discussion questions, behavior guidelines, and activities. Students keep the book as a souvenir of their time spent reliving the gold-rush days.

Comment: The guide was written by a fifth-grader teacher who visited Columbia with his class every spring for ten years.

Teaching Aid-Study Guide: intermediate

THE DELTA—AMERICA'S HOLLAND. El Cerrito, Calif.: Long Filmslide Service, 1977. Color filmstrip, 83 frames, plus 10 review frames, cassette, 17 min. Audible/inaudible signals. Accompanying script and suggestions for use of review frames.

Content: After setting the scene with the use of maps, ground

level and aerial photographs, the filmstrip goes on to describe
the geological development of the area. Frames twenty-six to
thirty-seven deal specifically with the history of the man-made
development of highly productive land. Agricultural problems
with the delta are addressed—erosion, flooding, encroaching
salinity, drainage—and the building of dams to help meet some
of those problems. Types of irrigation are shown, and the types
of crops grown in the area—mainly potatoes, beans, onions in
gold-rush days; mainly tomatoes, sugar beets, field corn now—
are identified. The filmstrip ends by posing questions: can the
delta accommodate increasing and diverse demands as a site for
agriculture and recreation, as a wildlife sanctuary, and as a
water carrier for southern California?
Comment: As the script says, "The history of its (the delta's)
growth and development is a fascinating story of man's struggle
to control his environment." Intermediate students might need
to learn some unfamiliar words before viewing.
Sound filmstrip: upper intermediate–senior high

THE DISCOVERY OF SAN FRANCISCO BAY. El Cerrito, Calif.:
Long Filmslide Service, 1975. Color filmstrip, 53 frames, cassette, 16 min. English and Spanish narrations.

Content: The filmstrip covers the last 100 miles of Portola's trek
from San Diego looking for Monterey Bay, starting from the
campsite at Salinas River, to the discovery site, and back down
to Palo Alto. Aerial photos are used to connect Portola's
campsites with the present-day terrain.
Comment: The use of aerial photos helps a great deal not only to
pinpoint Portola's trail, but also to show the difficulties involved in the passage. An interesting filmstrip.
Sound filmstrip: intermediate–senior high

DO YOU KNOW SAN JOSE?, by Susan Bergtholdt. San Jose,
Calif.: Rosicrucian Press, 1977. Coloring book.

Content: An attractive array of thirty-two sketches of interesting places in the San Jose area is accompanied by a simple text
describing each.
Comment: This could serve as good introductory material for

leaders to use with children's groups in preparation for field trips within the community. The sketches are a little too complicated for a youngster to color at this age level. Vocabulary also is difficult.
Teaching aid—workbook: primary

DO YOU KNOW SANTA CLARA VALLEY?, by Susan Bergtholdt. San Jose, Calif.: Rosicrucian Press, 1978. 16 p. B/w illus.

Content: A coloring book of buildings and places of historical interest in Santa Clara County. The pictures are captioned, additional places of historical interest are listed on the inside back cover, and a map with the sixteen coloring places marked is on the back cover.
Comment: This could be used for pre- or post-field trip activities or a local history unit.
Teaching Aid—workbook: upper primary–lower intermediate

DRAKE. Washington, D.C.: National Geographic Society, 1978. Color filmstrip, 41 frames, cassette, 10 min. Automatic and manual.

Content: Uses photographs, old engravings, and paintings to show that part of Drake's career spent in harassing and raiding Spanish ports in the New World. His stop at or near San Francisco Bay is shown briefly along with a map and pictures.
Comment: Since the account of Drake's landing at San Francisco is so brief, its main usefulness is in showing why the Spanish were angered by Drake's activities which were a factor in the Spanish settlement of California. Marvelous pictures.
Sound filmstrip: intermediate–junior high

AN EDUCATIONAL COLORING BOOK OF CALIFORNIA MISSIONS, by Linda Spizzirri, ed. Medinah, Ill.: Spizzirri Publishing Co., 1984. 31 p. Drawings, map.

Content: For each mission, a drawing as it appears today, and a brief historical explanation of construction, mission life, deterioration, and restoration. A short introduction gives the background for establishment of the missions, their physical aspects, and secularization. The map shows mission locations, with a list of missions in founding order and dates.

Comment: Useful as supplemental material for a missions unit of a California history course. The information given, while brief, is a good review for older students. The pictures for coloring show each mission's distinctive appearance.

Teaching Aid—Activity Book: upper primary–junior high

THE ENCHANTMENT OF CALIFORNIA. Children's Press and Current Affairs Films, 1979. Color filmstrip, 69 frames, cassette, 11 min. each side. Automatic and manual. Teacher's Guide.

Content: The filmstrip very briefly describes the history of discovery and settlement; natural resources; famous people such as Levi Strauss, Luther Burbank, Sarah Winchester, and Junipero Serra; and manufacturing and agricultural products. Pictures consist of photos and drawings. The teacher's guide includes the script, a discussion and activities section, a short student quiz, and a bibliography.

Comment: This can be used as an introduction to a unit on California history. The kit can also be packaged with Allen Carpenter's book *California,* from the New Enchantment of America series, to provide additional information for younger students.

Sound filmstrip: intermediate–junior high

EXPLORING THE CALIFORNIA MISSIONS: ACTIVITY CARDS, by Carol O. Martin. San Ramon, Calif.: Bay Area Explorers, 1984. 84 p. Glossary.

Content: This booklet contains an activity card for each mission, plus twenty-eight others. Every mission card gives the founder, founding date, location and a one-paragraph history, points of interest, architectural notes, and a "Did You Know?" of names or events. On the back of each mission card is a math activity such as translating mission measurements to meters, plotting on graph paper or making to scale. Each activity card identifys materials needed, and objective, along with suggestions for further activities or resources. A curriculum code label of music, arts, crafts; math; social studies; environmental science; or language arts is also included.

Comment: These cards, geared for fourth-grade Social Studies, grew out of the author's graduate work in curriculum development. Some of the "action" activities (as opposed to strictly paper and pencil activities) are rather interesting, such as designing and planting a mission garden; making a sundial or adobe bricks; constructing a working model of mission irrigation. Every activity won't appeal to or be possible for every teacher, but everyone will probably find several to try.

Teaching Aid–Activity Book: intermediate

FATHER JUNIPERO SERRA: MISSION TO CALIFORNIA. Man Against Nature series: Biography, set 1. New York: McGraw Hill, 1968. Color filmstrip, 48 frames, cassette, 12 min. Audible and inaudible sides.

Content: First, there are maps to "set the stage." Brief background information on the Spanish conquests in the New World is given, then on Serra's career from ordination and assignment to the Baja California missions to the establishment of the mission chain in Alta California. Stress is laid on his missionary zeal and his kindness to the Indians.

Comment: This could be a good introduction to Father Serra and his career. In this short presentation, the disadvantages of the mission system for the Indians are not touched upon.

Sound filmstrip: lower intermediate

GOLD AND DREAMS OF GOLD. Chicago: Family Filmstrips, distributed by SVE, 1974. Four color and b/w filmstrips, 56-60 frames each, two cassettes, 9-11 min. each. Manual and automatic.

Content: This set of four filmstrips describes how gold towns of the old West developed, what happened to change them into ghost towns, how the land changed through hydraulic mining and lumbering, how gold is mined by different methods, and modern-day mining and uses. The set concludes by showing how a present-day prospector named George goes about looking for gold.

Comment: This interesting set shows what happened *after* the rush. Most accounts of the gold rush stress the social and political results; this shows the physical aftermath and updates to the present what happens when someone gets gold fever. The narrator has an easy western drawl which makes for pleasant listening and adds a touch of realism.
Sound filmstrip: intermediate–junior high

GOLD RUSH, by Jay Holmes. Rev. by San Mateo County Office of Education. San Mateo, Calif.: Softswap, n.d., Apple Computer compatible. Diskette.

Content: This decision-making game simulates the purchase of supplies and transportation for gold mining in 1849; digging for gold, and depending on skill and how much is found, spending it wisely.
Comment: This game is fun to play. However, the instructional point of it is to bring some prior knowledge about mining and its conditions to the game's goldfields for more informed decisions. This makes it realistic. The game brings out the fact that finding a lot of gold was often chancey. A game can last for five minutes or a much longer time, depending on the player's luck and skill.
Software: all ages

THE GOLD RUSH. Westward Migration series. Chicago: SVE, 1960. Color filmstrip, 52 frames, cassette, 16 min. Manual and automatic. Reading Script.

Content: This brief account of early days in California shows where gold was discovered; describes the differences between gold and pyrite, placer gold and gold veins, and explains several mining methods. It also tells what happened to John Sutter and James Marshall.
Comment: The filmstrip is helpful for an introduction or review of the gold rush. The narrator gives a stiff and dull reading, so by–passing the cassette and doing one's own narration by reading the script would be better.
Sound filmstrip: intermediate–senior high

THE GOLD RUSH ERA, by Nancy Quantamatteo, Nancy Urban, Richard Quantamatteo and James McCarthy. Jackson, Calif.: Conceptual Productions, 1981. 45 p. B/w illus., answer key.

Content: Reproducible pages of stories with questions, puzzles, map activities, vocabulary, on gold-rush topics such as John Sutter, mining methods, bandits, routes to the goldfields, and the Nevada and Alaska gold rushes.

Comment: These materials could be used *in toto* or in part for a gold-rush unit, or to accent certain elements of the gold rush.

Teaching Aid—Activity workbook: intermediate–junior high

GOLD TO BUILD A NATION: THE UNITED STATES BEFORE THE CIVIL WAR. Stanford, Calif.: Multi-Media Productions, 1977. Three color filmstrips, 75-82 frames each, three cassettes, 14-15 min. each. Audible and inaudible signals. Teacher's manual (including 3 worksheets.) Program script.

Content: Part One describes conditions in the United States following the Mexican War, the discovery of gold and the rush it started, and early mining techniques. Part Two looks at life in the California mining camps, partly as seen through the eyes of Louise Amelia Clappe (who is Dame Shirley of *The Shirley Letters*). The narrator discusses problems of the miners, new mining methods, the lack of women, and injustices to minorities in the mining camps. Part Three shows California in the 1850s when the independent miner was squeezed out by organized mining and though the first flush of gold fever had passed, the find left its effect on California and on the United States.

Comment: The strength of this three-part series is its comprehensive look at California and the United States as a whole before, during, and after the gold rush. It could easily be used one part at a time.

Sound filmstrip: junior high–senior high

THE GREAT SAN FRANCISCO EARTHQUAKE. Stanford, Calif.: Multi-Media Productions, 1983. Mostly b/w filmstrip, 72 frames, cassette, 15 min. 45 sec. Audible and inaudible signals. Teacher's manual. Script.

Content: Using many actual photographs from the period, this filmstrip and narration depicts San Francisco before the quake on April 18, 1906 and after. It shows clearly the damage done and explains the helplessness of the firemen to stop the fires which followed because the water main had ruptured. It's all here: the response of the outside world to the emergency; the wild rumors which surfaced and spread; the human interest stories; and the rapid rebuilding of the city.

Comment: This informative filmstrip could supplement, reinforce, or introduce students to a well-rounded picture of the earthquake and its effects.

Sound filmstrip: intermediate–senior high

THE HISTORY OF CALIFORNIA. Englewood Cliffs, New Jersey: Prentice-Hall Media, n.d. three color filmstrips, three records, 33 ⅓ rpm. Automatic and manual sides.

Content: Part #1 (17:57 min.): Indians to rancheros—traces California history from Indian migration from Asia through the beginnings of other immigration (includes mission and ranchero life). Part #2 (14:32 min.): Golden ore to golden grain—covers the Gold Rush, routes to California, growth & decline of mining towns, growth of agriculture, lumber industry, and statehood. Pony Express, telegraph and railroads; the Chinese, and other immigration from the U.S. and foreign countries, and the industries it brought. Part #3 (approx. 15 min.): Farms to factories—covers the history of agricultural and industrial products. All three parts feature "stop action" for discussion questions.

Comment: The pace is a little slow, but gives a good overview of history and growth of California including some ethnic makeup. These three filmstrips with accompanying records can be used in separate sessions as the information is needed. There is no teacher's guide or script of the narration.

Sound filmstrip: intermediate–junior high

HISTORY OF CALIFORNIA. No 1039. Stamford Conn.: Educational Dimensions, 1974. Four color filmstrips, 71-81 frames each, four cassettes, 15-18 min. each. Manual and automatic sides.

Content: These four filmstrips cover wilderness to statehood; the gold rush to super state; minorities and majorities; and cultural history.

Comment: These are good filmstrips which are better suited to older than to younger students. Concepts and language are a bit above intermediate students. The last two explore elements of California life that could promote interesting discussion and research.

Sound filmstrip: junior high–senior high

HOW TO STAGE A GOLD RUSH CARNIVAL: SUGGESTIONS FOR PRODUCING A COLORFUL AND PROFITABLE SPECIAL EVENT WITH A "THEME", by John J. Lesjack, Sacramento: Creative Book Co., 1978, 35 p. Illus.

Content: The author gives detailed information on the goals, organization, best days, donations and donors needed, costume and booth suggestions, advertising and publicity, ticket sales and prizes, celebrity appearances, preserving the event on film, a final checklist, and addresses to write to for gold rush information.

Comment: This even includes sample letters to solicit parent help and merchant cooperation, as well as menus and recipes for a Spanish-Mexican meal or a gold miner meal.

Teaching Aid—Program Planner: intermediate

IS THERE AN ACTOR IN THE HOUSE?: DRAMATIC MATERIAL FROM PANTOMIME TO PLAY, by Virginia Bradley. New York: Dodd, Mead, 1974. 320 p.

Content: This is a collection of original dramatic material—pantomime, puppet plays, variety programs, sketches, full-length plays—along with suggestions for putting on the show and stressing improvisations.

Comment: The subject matter ranges from holidays to history, sports to space, gardening to ghosts. The author is a teacher of creative writing in the Los Angeles schools.

Teaching Aid—Program Planner: intermediate–senior high

THE JAPANESE AMERICANS: AN INSIDE LOOK. Stanford, Calif.: Multi-Media Productions, Inc., 1973. Color and b/w, two filmstrips, 41 frames each, cassette, parts 1 and 2, 15+ min. each. Manual and automatic. Script. Teacher's Manual.

Content: The story is narrated by a second generation Japanese-American, a Nisei, who experienced the removal of her family from the West Coast during World War II. She tells of how relations between America and Japan started, recounting the forced opening of Japan's ports by Commodore Matthew Perry in 1853. The first colony of Japanese in America was the Wakamatsu Colony of northern California, and Japanese were encouraged to immigrate when laborers were needed on the West Coast for building railroads, fishing, and farming. When the Japanese arrived, they were able to obtain only the lowest-paying jobs, but through hard work, some families were able to buy land—as her family did in Livingston, California. Prejudice against them grew as they achieved success; she cites several ways in which that prejudice was shown.

When Japan attacked Pearl Harbor and World War II started, in 1941, the narrator's family, along with other Japanese-Americans, were forcibly relocated to concentration camps inland. She tells of life in the concentration camp in Colorado and recounts that released by the courts, they returned to Livingston to find their house demolished, their land sold to others, and hostility from the white community. They worked to reestablish themselves, but have never regained their prewar prosperity. Part II concludes with the Japanese-American effort since the war to gain first-class citizenship, names some of those who have been elected to office, and summarizes "(This) is a story of how sometimes even a government as good as ours can make mistakes . . . It is a story about citizenship . . ."

Comment: Although this is about Japanese-Americans and the United States, it centers a great deal in California. The story is clearly and fairly told, but it's not an easy one to hear. At the elementary level, a leader would have to help children accept the facts and then look at the situation now, assess it, and discuss the future.

Sound filmstrip: intermediate–junior high

JOHN C. FREMONT: PATHFINDER OF THE WEST. Stanford,

Calif.: Multi-Media Productions, 1975. Mostly b/w filmstrip, 75 frames, cassette, 20 min., 35 sec. Audible and inaudible signals. Teacher's Manual.

Content: This concentrates on the four Fremont-led expeditions between 1842 and 1849 which provided accurate information on the way west just in time for the pioneers and then gold rushers. Fremont's wife, Jessie, helped him in writing up reports on the expeditions which made them much more informative and readable than his earlier reports. Many names Fremont gave to geographic features still are used such as the Golden Gate, Pyramid Lake, the Great Basin. Also, many areas in theWest have been named after him.

Fremont played a part in the Mexican War, trying to hold California for the United States. Later he made, and lost, a fortune in the gold rush, was a senator from California, ran for president in 1856, and served as a general in the Civil War. But the narrator makes it clear that Fremont's greatest contribution was giving accurate information on the routes west.

Comment: This material is aimed at the secondary student, but selected younger students could also use it successfully. The narration starts without giving the title, and the operator has to be careful to make sure the filmstrip and narration are coordinated.

Sound filmstrip: upper intermediate–senior high

LET'S TOUR CALIFORNIA. St. Louis, Missouri: Millikin Publishing Co., 1970. Twelve Color transparancies, six duplicating masters. Teachers Guide.

Content: The transparancies show maps, pictures of economic activities, natural wonders, tourist attractions, and the missions. The duplicating masters have maps of the state and agriculture. Diagrams and questions are included for industry in California, the missions and agriculture, along with a crossword puzzle, a test and review. A teachers' guide suggests activities. Each transparancy is supplemented by a narration and background information which includes ". . . facts which would be learned by actually visiting the places presented."

Comment: Because this was published in 1970 it doesn't include

information on the important "Silicon Valley" computer industry. However, as a cursory review of some aspects of California, it has value and provides another mode of transmitting this information.
Teaching Aid–Activity Book: intermediate

LIFE AND TIMES OF JOHN SUTTER. El Cerrito, Calif.: Long Filmslide, 1976. B/w filmstrip, 55 frames, cassette, 15 minutes. Audible and inaudible signals.

Content: The filmstrip depicts California in the 1830s at the time John Sutter arrived—the large ranchos, the geographic barriers that insulated it from the rest of the world, and the neglect the area experienced following the transfer from Spanish to Mexican rule. Into this arena burst the flamboyant Sutter, amassing land and fortune and earning his titles as the Wheat and Cattle King of California. His hospitality encouraged cross-country pioneers to come to California instead of the Oregon Territory, and his belief that Americans would benefit California led him to support their desire for annexation. The unforeseen gold rush was his financial undoing. His fort abandoned and sold, he died in 1880.
Comment: This is an informative and balanced presentation which culminates in aptly calling Sutter the "Great Catalyst" in California development.
Sound filmstrip: intermediate–senior high

LIVE AGAIN OUR MISSION PAST, by George Kuska and Barbara Linse. Larkspur, Calif.: Art's Books, 1983. Distributed by Education Book Distributors. 165 p. Illus.

Content: Contains a brief general history of Spanish settlement, short histories of individual missions, ideas for plays, writing and craft activities, maps, glossaries, bibliographies, recipes, and lots of interesting bits of information. Permission is given to photocopy anything in the book for classroom distribution. The illustrations are line-drawings, with several pages of color photos. The bibliography includes cookbooks, arts and crafts books, and films on different aspects of mission life and activities. There is a detailed table of contents.

Comment: An excellent resource book for teachers, not only for activity ideas, but also for the information section and mission drawings that can be copied for student handouts.
Teaching Aid—Activity Book: primary–intermediate

THE LOS ANGELES BASIN. by R.S. Funderburk. Warren, Rhode Island: Herbert E. Budek Company, Inc. 1962. Color filmstrip, 50 frames.

Content: The filmstrip starts with three frames of script giving information on the geography of the basin, its industry, and its importance to the state. Then there are subsections on the basin's physical features, agriculture and industries, the invasion of people, the need for water, and its tourist attractions.
Comment: This is a text on film; it suffers from a lack of maps. The viewer gets lots of location names but never a way to place the parts to the whole.
Filmstrip: upper intermediate–senior high

LOS ANGELES: CITY OF AUTOMOBILES. Focus on America— The Pacific States series. Chicago: SVE, 1972. Color filmstrip, 83 frames, cassette, 16 min. Manual and automatic. Reading Script.

Content: This filmstrip attempts to show the seemingly unplanned, uncontrolled growth of Los Angeles; how the city is linked by the freeways; how the livelihoods of three residents— a freeway engineer, a used-car salesman, and a used auto-parts buyer—revolve around the auto. At the conclusion there are: a list of words and phrases, questions for review and discussion, and enrichment activities.
Comment: Very good photos illustrate how the auto has affected the Los Angeles area; the narration moves well and is uncomplicated.
Sound filmstrip: intermediate–junior high

LUMBERING IN THE PACIFIC NORTHWEST by Eugene L. Podhurst. Warren, Rhode Island: Budek Films and Slides of California. 1969. Color filmstrip, 30 frames.

Content: The filmstrip identifies the trees—the Douglas fir, pine, redwood—the tools, and the specialized jobs commonly associated with lumbering in the Pacific Northwest. It shows and tells exactly how trees are cut and readied for market.

Comment: This simple overview of lumbering could add to information being gathered by a student in a beginning research project.

Filmstrip: primary–intermediate

MAK-A-MAP PUZZLE: A COUNTY MAP OF CALIFORNIA/NEVADA. Placentia, Calif.: Mak-A-Map Co., 1975. 14 by 16 inches.

Content: The puzzle pieces are cut on the lines of the counties of California and Nevada. Also shown, along with the county names, are the county seats, national parks, main rivers and bodies of water, the San Andreas Fault line, and the names of bordering states and country. The counties with their land area, county seats and 1970 populations are also listed inside the puzzle-box cover.

Comment: An entertaining way to learn county names and place relationships; especially useful when the textbook used includes information on the counties.

Teaching Aid–Puzzle: intermediate

THE MAN FROM DEER CREEK: THE STORY OF ISHI. Stanford, Calif.: Multi-Media Productions, Inc., 1982. Color filmstrip, 92 frames, cassette, 19 min. Audible and inaudible signals. Teacher's manual, Program Script.

Content: First, the old world of the Yahi Indian is shown and described, followed by the encroachment of the white man and the effect it had on that world. Ishi is introduced, the last wild Indian to be found in California. In 1911 he wandered into Oroville and went from there to San Francisco with anthropologists who came to see if known-Indian languages would correspond with his. Ishi's life at the San Francisco Museum, his teaching of the Indian way, and his impressions of white men's ways are all included.

Comment: This sensitive portrayal of the last native Califor-

nian—one who shared the wisdom and culture of his people—is informative and beautiful. Our students should know of Ishi, and this filmstrip used with Kroeber's or Meyer's books about him would do it. Includes two worksheets.
Sound filmstrip: intermediate–adult

A **MEXICAN-AMERICAN COLORING BOOK,** by Edward W. Ludwig. English text by Edward Ludwig and James Santibanez; Spanish text by Angie Rocha. Los Gatos, Calif.: Polaris Press, 1977. n.p. Illus. by Vincent P. Rascon.

Content: There are seventeen full-page illustrations of people and places important to Mexican-American history with descriptive text in English and Spanish. Suggestions for coloring are offered in the story—"The Aztecs loved color both in their clothing and buildings—bright reds, yellows, oranges, blues and greens." The illustrations include "Tenochtitlan," "The Arrival of Cortes," "The Aztecs and the Horses," "Cortes and Malinche," "Moctezuma and Cortes," "Under Spanish Rule," "A New Race: the Mestizos," "Contributions of the Spanish," "Father Hidalgo," "General Santa Ana," "The Vaqueros," "Joaquin Murietta and Tiburcio Vasquez," "The Revolution," "The Warriors," "The Paratroopers," "The Braceros," and "La Huelga."
Comment: This unusual and interesting coloring book includes "The Warriors" showing Mexican-American soldiers in World War I and "The Paratroopers" depicting Mexican-American soldiers in World War II. The epilogue comments on the Chicano voices heard in the 1970s and concludes, "This is not the end of Chicano history. This is the beginning."
Teaching Aid–Coloring Book: primary–intermediate

MINING IN THE SOUTHWEST, by Eugene L. Podhurst. Warren, Rhode Island: Budek Films and Slides of California. 1970. Color filmstrip, 36 frames.

Content: The filmstrip emphasizes the importance of mining in luring settlers to the West, starting with the gold rush to California. The use of early, primitive mining equipment is shown as well as the ghost towns miners left when they moved on. It then records the change in mining as modern equipment became available, and copper and uranium replaced gold and silver as the most-commonly mined minerals. Open-pit and tunnel mining are described.

Comment: This information could be useful and interesting to students studying the gold rush period. It would help them learn about the mining industry from the mid 1800s to the present.

Filmstrip: intermediate–junior high

MISSIONS OF ALTA CALIFORNIA. El Cerrito, Calif.: Long Film-slide Service, 1976. Color filmstrip, 97 frames, cassette, 36 min. Audible and inaudible signal. Accompanying script.

Content: After showing a sampling of missions and aerial views of the cities of today which grew up around them, the filmstrip gives a brief background of the California in which the missions were built. We learn that missions had already been built in the American Southwest and in Baja California, and are given reasons why missions were needed on the Alta California coast. Each is described in detail, in the order of founding. Serra and Lasuen are the principal padres discussed. Jose de Galves, the administrator from New Spain who named Portola and Serra to found the missions, and Bucareli, the Viceroy of New Spain who carried on the mission plans, are named, along with the better known priests, as the heroes of the mission era.

Comment: Some of the pictures and narrative of this filmstrip also appear in "The Bells of El Camino." The information given in ninety-seven frames makes this material too long and too detailed for most intermediate students.

Sound filmstrip: junior high–senior high

THE MISSIONS OF CALIFORNIA: SPANISH IMPERIALISM AND THE WESTERN INDIANS. Stanford, Calif.: Multi-Media Pro-ductions, 1975. Color filmstrip, 77 frames, cassette, 19 min. Audible and inaudible signals. Teacher's manual.

Content: This filmstrip and narration tell of the conflict between the Indian way of life and the Spanish culture which mission-aries imposed on the Indian. Beginning with native life before the missions were established, the narration shows that Indians were first drawn to the missions through interest in the art brought to decorate the churches, as well as the music.

The Padres taught the Indians many skills—how to build and farm and irrigate. Their children were schooled, and the brighter ones even sent on to Mexico for higher learning.

However, the enforced close living, the rules and regulations, and their loss of freedom caused many Indians to try to return to their old life, only to be brought back forcibly to the mission. Now, the once-deserted missions have been restored and are visited by tourists, but the Indians they were built to "help" are gone.

Comment: These pictures are the same as those in *The Spanish Missions: Yesterday's Dream,* and the script is much the same but more detailed and comprehensive. This presentation strips the romanticism from the mission period and makes the viewer consider the Indian point of view. This is not a chronicle of the establishment of missions. No mission is even named.

Sound filmstrip: intermediate–senior high

MONTEREY: CALIFORNIA'S PAST RESTORED. Stanford, Calif.: Multi-Media Productions, 1974. Two color filmstrips, 62 frames, 51 frames, cassette, 13 + min. per side. Manual and automatic. Teacher's manual.

Content: The first part gives information on Cabrillo, Cermenho, Vizcaino, Portola, Serra, the pirate de Bouchard, Larkin, Isaac Graham, and Commodore Thomas C. Jones. Included is some information on the Costanoan Indian culture and on the rancho activities and economy. In the second part Fremont, Commodore Sloat, William Sherman, Vallejo, Robert Louis Stevenson, and others are discussed in the light of how they influenced California history in or about the Monterey area. The constitutional convention is well described, and attention is paid to the whaling and sardine industries.

Comment: The story of early Monterey involves almost everyone important in early California history, and this material presents them effectively. It's informative without being pedantic. The teachers' manual includes a glossary of Spanish terms,

an outline of the presentations, discussion topics, and references.
Sound filmstrip: upper intermediate–senior high

THE MOUNTAIN MEN. Chicago: Pathfinders Westward series.
SVE, 1981. Color filmstrip, 52 frames, cassette, 16 min. Manual
and automatic. Script.

Content: The life of the Mountain Man is described, using
Ashley and Henry Trapping Company as an example. The
topics discussed are the dangers from bears and Indians, the
Rendezvous, Jed Smith's journey to California, and the roles of
James Ohio Pattie and Ewing Young in the furtrapping trade of
the Southwest and their entry into California.
Comment: Shows the locations of the various places mentioned
in accounts of mountain men (see biographies of Jed Smith, and
Kit Carson, for example), and maps of various westward trails.
An interesting filmstrip on a type of man unique to the times and
the setting.
Sound filmstrip: intermediate–senior high

NATIONAL PARK SERVICE AREAS OF THE PACIFIC COAST
AND NORTHWEST. National Park Service Areas of the United
States series. Chicago: SVE, 1966. Color filmstrip, 31 frames—
California section. 60 frames.

Content: Shows scenes of different national parks in California
with their variety of terrain, climate, and sights. The photos are
captioned.
Comment: This filmstrip can be used to show how the National
Park Service has preserved areas of California in an original—
or nearly so—state of natural beauty.
Filmstrip: upper primary–intermediate

NEW TOWN: VALENCIA, CALIFORNIA. Focus on America—The
Pacific States series. Chicago: SVE, 1972. Color filmstrip, 87
frames, cassette, 15 min. 45 sec. Manual and automatic. Reading script.

Content: The filmstrip shows the concept of new towns as self-contained cities by highlighting Valencia, a preplanned new town. The lifestyles of two families who live and work in this new town are shown along with the advantages and disadvantages of such a community. It concludes with a list of words and phrases, questions for review and discussion and enrichment activities.

Comment: Briefly explores a new concept for urban planning, and the implication that it could also be used for planning with existing urban areas.

Sound filmstrip: intermediate–junior high

THE OTHER 49'ERS. (The Basis for our Beliefs). Stanford, Calif.: Multi-Media Productions, Inc., 1972. Two color fimstrips, 38 frames, 39 frames, cassette, Part one on side one, 10 min. 30 sec., Part two on side two, 11 min. 55 sec. Manual and automatic. Teacher's Manual.

Content: This is about the Chinese in the early days of California. The filmstrips show pictures, political cartoons, and posters copied from *Wasp,* a San Francisco magazine of the late nineteenth century and from other anti-Chinese pamphlets distributed in San Francisco from 1852 on.

The cassette narrative is a talk on the reasons for Chinese immigration, the initial welcome and then growing prejudice, and the unreasonable fears and beliefs held by many whites about the Chinese population.

Comment: The sophisticated level of the narrative and the visuals make this interesting historical information appropriate for use at seventh grade or higher. There is no direct correspondence between the filmstrip pictures and the specific information being given on the cassette. *The Chinese 49'ers,* another filmstrip by Multi-Media Productions, uses much of the same material and gears it to the intermediate student.

Sound filmstrip: junior high–adult

OVER A CENTURY AGO–DAILY LIFE IN THE SANTA CLARA VALLEY 1870-1900. San Jose, Calif.: San Jose Historical Museum, 1981. B/w and color filmstrip, 78 frames, cassette, 13 min. Manual and automatic.

Content: With old photographs, young people are shown what houses looked like and how they were furnished, schools, women's work, transportation, recreational activities, and orchards.

Comment: This gives a good picture of how people lived and worked at the end of the nineteenth century. The outhouse, chamberpot, and Saturday bath routine will undoubtedly bring a laugh. Except for the parts dealing with the orchards and canning industry, most of it gives a picture of almost anywhere in California during this era.

Sound filmstrip: intermediate–senior high

THE PERALTA ADOBE. San Jose, Calif.: The Junior League of San Jose, 1976. Color and b/w filmstrip, 53 frames, cassette, 13 min. Audible and inaudible sides.

Content: The filmstrip starts with a history of Santa Clara Valley–Costanoan Indians, and continues with the Spanish missions, the founding of San Jose (the first California pueblo), and Luis Peralta's career.

Comment: An excellent presentation that gives statewide appeal to information about Peralta and San Jose.

Sound filmstrip: intermediate–junior high

PRELUDE TO CENTURY THREE. San Jose, Calif.: Bicentennial Commission/Public Information Office of San Jose, 1977. Color and b/w filmstrip, 108 frames, cassette, 21 min. Manual.

Content: This is a brief history of the first 200 years of San Jose's establishment as a Spanish pueblo and growth through rancho days, as California's first capital, establishment of fruit-growing, -packing, and -canning industry; and finally as a center of the electronics industry.

Comment: Although this is a "booster" presentation, it does capsulize San Jose's history adequately.

Sound filmstrip: intermediate–junior high

RACE TO PROMONTORY POINT: THE FIRST TRANSCONTINENTAL RAILROAD. CENTRAL PACIFIC—EASTWARD. Stanford, Calif.: Multi-Media Productions, 1977. Color and b/w filmstrip, 55 frames, cassette, 17 min. Audible and inaudible signals. Teacher's manual.

Content: Theodore Judah had a dream for a railroad to the East, and the program tells of his collaboration with Dr. Strong, a druggist from Dutch Flat. They explored the route which the first transcontinental railroad would eventually take. Because Judah was seen as a visionary ("Crazy Judah") and needed capital, he enlisted some successful Sacramento merchants as backers—Hopkins, Huntington, Crocker, and Stanford. Judah and his wife, Anna, went to Washington, D.C. to secure more funding, returned triumphant, and work began. Huntington, realizing that much more money would be needed, forced out Dr. Strong—who didn't have money to contribute—and pressured Judah. In Washington to raise more money, Judah became ill and died.

The rest of the filmstrip tells the familiar story of building the railroad, the use of Chinese workers, and the tremendous challenge of penetrating the Sierra Nevada in winter and summer. James Strobridge, who suggested and then built the snowsheds, which helped solve the winter problem, is cited as the unsung hero of the railroad.

Comment: This tells effectively, and interestingly, the story of the leaders involved in the building of the Central Pacific Railroad.

Sound filmstrip: intermediate–junior high

THE RAILROAD BARONS OF CALIFORNIA. Stanford, Calif.: Multi-Media Productions, 1981. Color filmstrip, 58 frames, cassette, 15 min. Audible and inaudible signals. Teacher's Manual (includes 1 worksheet). Program Script.

Content: This filmstrip and narration gives a detailed look at the Big Four who built the Central Pacific Railroad—Collis Huntington, Charles Crocker, Leland Stanford, Mark Hopkins,—during the period after the transcontinental railroad was completed.

Collis Huntington, operating from New York, was the one most committed to running the railroad. All of them realized that they had to expand their line in order to make it profitable.

Crocker's involvement ebbed and flowed; Stanford and Huntington feuded and ended up enemies. Hopkins was treasurer of the company until his death. The building of the railroad monopoly and the eventual response to it by the public raises many interesting questions.

Comment: The filmstrip is informative and stimulating. What if the Big Four had sold out at the completion of the transcontinental railroad, as they wanted to do? What if their scheme to monopolize California transportation had become known earlier? Some good discussions could be generated!

Sound filmstrip: junior high–senior high

ROSIE AND THE BEAR FLAG, by Harry Knill. B/w illus. by Nick Taylor and Donna Neary. Santa Barbara, Calif.: Bellerophon Books, 1979. 64 p.

Content: The text covers California history from 1822 to 1846, concentrating on the Mexican and American people who were central to California historical events and the flags that were raised, even briefly, during these years. Rosie, of the title, was the daughter of Rosalia Vallejo and Jacob Leese; she played a part in the confused dramatics surrounding the capture of Mariano Vallejo in the Bear Flag Revolt.

Comment: This attractive soft-back coloring booklet includes some interesting historical detail, such as the importance of music in the California outposts and the failure of the strong Hudson's Bay Company to flourish here. The book also includes simple, dramatic, and appealing illustrations. However, the text is very difficult to follow and jumps from one subject to another. Lack of a table of contents and an index work against it, too, as a possibility for use by student or teacher.

Teaching Aid—Activity Book: intermediate–adult

SAN FRANCISCO, by Eileen M. Teclaff. Warren, Rhode Island: Herbert E. Budek Company, n.d. Color filmstrip, 45 frames.

Content: Captioned, contemporary photographs, interspersed with historical information frames, show what the city looks like in modern times, while touching on historical highlights—

the post-gold rush growth, 1906 'quake, and the 1915 and 1939 expositions.

Comment: Though this isn't dated, I think it's too old to use effectively. It shows the skyline without the Transamerica building, identifies Alcatraz as a federal prison, and spells Coit Tower as coyt. Those drawbacks, and no sound, make me feel one of the marvelous picture books on San Francisco would be more useful.

Filmstrip: intermediate–junior high

SONGS OF THE YOKUTS AND PAIUTES, by Alfred Pietroforte. Happy Camp, Calif.: Naturegraph, n.d. Photos and drawings.

Content: Indian folk singing adapted for grade school use by an instructor at the College of Sequoias. There are many pages of actual songs accurately transcribed.

Comment: As this is no longer listed in the Naturegraph catalogue, you'll have to find it in a school or public library.

Teaching Aid—Songs: intermediate–adult

THE SPANISH MISSIONS: YESTERDAY'S DREAM. Stanford, Calif.: Multi-Media Productions, 1975. Color filmstrip, 75 frames, cassette, 12 min. Audible and inaudible signals. Teacher's Manual.

Content: The filmstrip and narrative focus on the effect of the Spanish missions on the Indians. It shows the conflict between the organized, regulated mission regimen and the freer Indian culture. Mission fathers taught the Indians to make adobe bricks, clay tiles, tallow candles, to care for sheep and cattle and use their decorative art in the chapels, to use metal and care for stock, to build dams for irrigation. Yet, the Indians sickened, lost spirit, died or ran away. It was this clash of cultures which contributed to the decline of the missions.

Comment: This is not a chronicling of the establishment of missions. No particular mission is even called by name. Actually, the filmstrip would be more accurately named "The Spanish Mission vs. the Indian Culture." The narration shows that each culture had strengths; it was the attempt to have the Spanish culture displace the other that led to tragedy. It would

make a good discussion starter. For a more mature narrative using the same pictures, see *The Missions of California* by Multi-Media.
Sound filmstrip: intermediate–junior high

STORIES FROM THE OLD WEST. Chicago, Illinois: SVE, 1975. Four color filmstrips, 60-61 frames each, three cassettes, 17-20 min. each. Manual and automatic. Teacher's Guide and Scripts.

Content: There are six filmstrips in this set, but these four are the only ones that deal with California in whole or part. "El Camino Real" explains why the Spaniards came to Alta California, how the missions were built and their place in California history, and Portola's march north, but no mention of San Francisco Bay discovery. "Vaquero! Vaquero!" tells how the vaquero way of life developed in the southwest, including California, how he worked, and his sports and games. "The Pony Express Rider," using first-person narration by "an old pony express rider," tells how the service was started, how it helped development of the West, and what a rider faced in hazards and hardships. "Iron Horse, Golden Spike" presents the building of the first transcontinental railroad, and its effects. Each concludes with a list of words and phrases to know, review and discussion questions, enrichment activities, and a bibliography.
Comment: Interesting filmstrips and tapes illustrating facets of life in early California and the Old West that are often quite intriguing to youngsters. The music and sound effects are good.
Sound filmstrip: intermediate–junior high

THE STORY OF THE CALIFORNIA MISSION. San Francisco: Chevron, 1982. Chevron School Broadcast. Color filmstrip, 104 frames, cassette, 18 min. Teacher's Guide with 21 b/w studyprints of the missions.

Content: Tells of the native Indians, the coming of the Spaniards, Father Serra's founding of the missions; and mission life, secularization, deterioration, and restoration. Direct quotes from the padres, soldiers, and an early American visitor are briefly used. The guide includes review questions, follow-up activities, some discussion questions, a glossary, preteaching and history review.

Comment: This kit was produced especially for fourth graders in California schools, and is available to schools without charge. Use of contemporary Indian prints and photos of the deterioration of missions is particularly good, as is the background music.

Sound filmstrip and kit: lower intermediate

SUTTER'S FORT, by Horace Spencer. El Cerrito, Calif.: Long Filmslide Service, 1975. Color and b/w. filmstrip, 52 frames, cassette, 11 min. Audible and inaudible.

Content: A history of the building of the fort, its abandonment and restoration. It gives hours open, then proceeds with the self-guided tour of workshops (gun, carpenter, smith). Also shows trading goods; kitchen and food preparation; the main, and only original, building and what Sutter's jobs were under the Mexicans.

Comment: This gives an introduction to the fort, and shows the displays, so students can see good examples of tools and furnishings used in early nineteenth century California.

Sound filmstrip: intermediate–junior high

TEACHER'S GUIDE TO COLUMBIA STATE HISTORIC PARK. Sacramento, Calif.: Dept. of Parks & Recreation, 1978. 34 p. B/w illus., map.

Content: From the Introduction: ". . . suggestions on how to prepare . . . students for the visit; guidelines to follow while at the park . . .." There are sections on historical background, class activities, an annotated bibliography, and a town map with a key to the buildings.

Comment: Some information, such as that on mining methods, could be used for general reference. The introduction suggests that the guide should be adaptable for any age group—the activities and information could be as brief or as expanded as is suitable.

Teaching Aid–Activity Book: intermediate–senior high

THREE ROUTES TO EL DORADO. Westward Migration series. Chicago: SVE, 1960. Color filmstrip, 55 frames, cassette, 17 min. Manual and automatic. Reading Script.

Content: Describes the three routes to California—around the Horn, sail to Panama and cross the Isthmus, or the Overland Trail. Also includes information on life in San Francisco and in mining areas; shows several mother lode sites and equipment; shows the settlers who followed the miners.
Comment: This has excellent pictures, drawings, and maps. The narrator is dull, which problem could be solved by doing one's own narration with the reading script.
Sound filmstrip: intermediate–senior high

VOLCANO COUNTRY IN NORTHERN CALIFORNIA. Warren, Rhode Island: Creative Learning, n.d. Color filmstrip, 31 frames.

Content: This is mainly about Mt. Lassen. It explains volcanic rocks, cinder cones, fumaroles, mudpots, and hot springs.
Comment: The textbook-like captions make this filmstrip unnecessarily dry. It also seems misnamed as it is primarily about Mt. Lassen in isolation, not as one of a string of Cascade Range volcanoes.
Filmstrip: intermediate–junior high

THE WORLD OF FORT ROSS, A PICTURE BOOK, by David W. Rickman. Cupertino, Calif.: California History Center, 1984. Distributed by Western Tanager Press. n.p.

Content: The text of this soft-cover publication in coloring book format tells of the historic development of Fort Ross. After giving some background on the "Kashaya," the family of Pomo Indians living in the area, the author tells of the seventeenth and eighteenth century Russian frontiersmen, the *promyshlenniks* who kept pushing the frontiers eastward. The search for sea otters and seals brought the Russians to Alaska and then to Spanish California. Helped by the Aleuts—whom they treated more fairly than the Spanish, Mexicans, or Americans treated the Indians—they began establishing Fort Ross in early 1812. Nikolai Rezanov (the Russian-American Company's leader), Governor Baranov of Alaska, and Ivan Kuskov (Baranov's assistant) were all instrumental in the development of this California colony.

The fort itself is carefully described and shown. The difference between Russian and Spanish attitudes toward proselytizing the native popluation is explained; life at the fort is detailed, and, finally, the reasons for the failure and abandonment of the project in 1841 are noted.

Comment: Though the format makes one think of younger children, the intricacy of the pictures and level of the reading is definitely aimed at the intermediate and older student. The text would help a student understand more fully, and appreciate, the Russian foray into California; the author suggests that ". . . the Russian influence is growing with a new understanding of the role they played in California's history."

Teaching Aid-Activity Book: intermediate–junior high

YOSEMITE: NATURAL ART IN THE HIGH SIERRA. Warren, Rhode Island: Creative Learning. Color filmstrip, 31 frames.

Content: It shows and names the famous waterfalls, mountains, and rocks. Geological history is given, and the glacial beginnings explained as are the effect of ice movement and force.

Comment: This won't capture a child's imagination, but it does explain how Yosemite was formed. The emphasis is on the formation, not on the art in nature.

Filmstrip: intermediate–junior high

Appendix A

Selected Media Distributors and Suppliers

Academy Films Distribution
PO Box 3414
Orange, CA 92666

Associated Educators
Box 492
Troy, AL 36081

BCS Educational Aids, Inc.
PO Box 100
Bothell, WA 98011

Bear Films and AV Associates Inc.
805 Smith St.
Baldwin, NY 11510

Blackhawk Films and Eastin-Phelan Corp.
1235 W. Fifth St.
Davenport, IA 52805

Bowmar Co.
See Stanley Bowmar Co.

Budek Films & Slides
See Creative Learning, Inc.

Chevron School Broadcast
595 Market St.
San Francisco, CA 94105

The Children's Music Center
5373 W. Pico Blvd.
Los Angeles, CA 90019

Classroom Film Distributors, Inc.
5610 Hollywood Blvd.
Los Angeles, CA 90028

Classroom World Productions
PO Box 2090
22 Glenwood Ave.
Raleigh, NC 27602

Clearvue, Inc.
5711 N. Milwaukee Ave.
Chicago, IL 60646

Conceptual Productions
PO Box 1146
Jackson, CA 95642
(teaching aids)

Creative Book Co.
PO Box 21-4998
Sacramento, CA 95821

Creative Learning
PO Box 5331
Baltimore, MD 21209

Creative Learning
PO Box 324
Warren, RI 02885

Creative Teaching Press, Inc.
Huntington Beach, CA 92649
(teaching aids)

Creative Visuals, Inc.
PO Box 1911
Big Spring, TX 79720

Disney Productions
See Walt Disney Productions

Doubleday Multi-media
1371 Reynolds Ave.
Santa Ana, CA 92705

Educational Development Corp.
Learning Resources Division
Lakeland, FL 33803

Educational Dimensions
Box 126
Stamford, CT 06904

Educational Enrichment Materials, Inc.
110 S. Bedford Rd.
Mt. Kisco, NY 10549

Educational Media, Inc.
809 Industrial Way
PO Box 39
Ellensburg, WA 98926

Encyclopedia Britannica Educational Corp.
425 N. Michigan Ave.
Chicago, IL 60611

ESP, Inc.
1201 E. Johnson
PO Box 5037
Jonesboro, AR 72403-5037

Eye Gate Media
3333 Elston Ave.
Chicago, IL 60618

Films, Inc.
733 Green Bay Rd.
Wilmette, IL 60091

Folkways/Scholastic Records
50 W. 44th St.
New York, NY 10036

Great Basin Film Productions
PO Box 3006
Ogden, UT 84403

Hubbard Scientific Co.
2855 Shermer Rd.
Northbook, IL 60062

Imperial Educational Resources
19 Marble Ave.
Pleasantville, NY 10570

Junior League of San Jose
1615 Dry Creek Rd.
San Jose, CA 95125

Long Filmslide Service
7505 Fairmont Avenue
El Cerrito, CA 94530

McIntyre Visual Publications
716 Center St.
Lewiston, NY 14092

Modern Learning Aids
PO Box 1712
Rochester, NY 14603

Multi-Media Productions, Inc.
PO Box 5097
Stanford, CA 94305

National Geographic Society
Educational Services
Washington, DC 20036

National Public Radio
2025 M Street, NW
Washington, DC 20036

National Tape Repository
University of Colorado
Boulder, CO 80302

Perfection Form Co.
1000 N. Second Ave.
Logan, IA 51546

Pied Piper Productions
PO Box 320
Verdugo City, CA 91406

Pilot Rock, Inc.
PO Box 270
Arcata, CA 95521

Prentice-Hall Media, Inc.
Educational Book Division
Englewood Cliffs, NJ 07632

Presidio Press
PO Box 1764
Novato, CA 94948-1764LA

San Jose Historical Museum
635 Phelan Ave.
San Jose, CA 95112

Stanley Bowmar Co.
4 Broadway
Valhalla, NY 10595

Tapes Unlimited
Educational Corporation of America
984 Livornois
Troy, MI 48084

James L. Ruhle Associates
PO Box 4301
Fullerton, CA 92631

Warren Schloat Productions
See Clearvue, Inc.

Society for Visual Education, Inc.
1345 Diversey Pkwy.
Chicago, IL 60614

Time-Life Films, Inc.
43 W. 16th St.
New York, NY 10011

Troll Associates
320 Route 17
Mahwah, NJ 07430

UC Extension Media Center
2223 Fulton St.
Berkeley, CA 94720

Universal Color Slide Co.
136 W. 32nd St.
New York, NY 10001

Universal Educational and Visual Arts
100 Universal City Plaza
Universal City, CA 91608

Walt Disney Productions
Educational Films Division
500 S. Buena Vista Ave.
Burbank, CA 91503

J. Weston Walch
321 Valley St.
Portland, ME 04104

Weston Woods Studios
Weston, CT 06897-0501

Wible Language Institute
24 South Eighth St.
Allentown, PA 18105

Appendix B
Selected Publishers and Book Suppliers

Many cities, parks, and historic sites put out booklets that include color photos of important landmarks and buildings, with informational captions. These booklets can be a good addition to a classroom collection of California history materials, and can be secured on personal visits or by writing to Visitors' Information Bureaus and Chambers of Commerce.

Some missions have informational booklets or brochures (some more elaborate than others), that can be obtained by writing to individual missions. Experience has shown that if student or teacher includes a small sum with the request letter, there is more likelihood of receiving better or more materials (other than just a simple flyer).

Book suppliers and publishers listed here are for the most part small, local and hard to find in such bibliographic tools as *Literary Market Place,* which gives names and addresses of all major trade and textbook publishers.

Beautiful America Publishing Co.
9725 S.W. Commerce Circle
Wilsonville, OR 97070

Bellerophon Books
36 Anacapa St.
Santa Barbara, CA 93101

Reservation Office
State of California
Dept. of Parks and Recreation
PO Box 2390
Sacramento, CA 95811
(for information about state parks and historical landmarks)

Camaro Publishing Co.
90430 World Way Center
Los Angeles, CA 90009

Capra Press
Box 2068
Santa Barbara, CA 93120

Children's Press
1224 W. Van Buren St.
Chicago, IL 60607

Chinatown Adventures
622 Washington St.
San Francisco, CA 94111

Comstock Bonanza Press
18919 William Quirk Memorial Dr.
Grass Valley, CA 95945

Cougar Books
PO Box 22246
Sacramento, CA 95822

Creative Editions
See Cougar Books

Ghost Town Publications
PO Drawer 5998
Carmel, CA 93921

Heyday Books
Box 9145
Berkeley, CA 94709

Hubert Lowman
11015 Bobcat Lane
Arroyo Grande, CA 93420

Langtry Publications
7838 Burnet Av.
Van Nuys, CA 91405-1051

Lassen Volcanic National Park
Mineral, CA 96063

Marion Fisher Murphy
762 Juniper Ct.
Sonoma, CA 95476

Naturegraph
PO Box 1075
Happy Camp, CA 96039

Outbooks
217 Kimball Ave.
Golden, CO 80401

Pelican Publishing
Gretna, LA 70053

Polaris Press
16540 Camellia Terrace
Los Gatos, CA 95030

Rosicrucian Press Ltd.
PO Box 908
San Jose, CA 95016
(local history publications)

Sunflower Ink
Palo Colorado Canyon
Carmel, CA 93923

Valley Publishers
See Western Tanager

Western Tanager
1111 Pacific Ave.
Santa Cruz, CA 95060

Zanel Publications
PO Box 11316
Tahoe Paradise, CA 95708

Author Index

The following are page citations for the works of each author represented here. See Title Index for all titles as well as nonprint materials and other teaching aids.

Title Index

Subject Index

Autobiography/biography (continued)

McGlashan, C. F.
GIVE ME A MOUNTAIN
MEADOW (McGlashan)

Muir, John
FROM THE EAGLE'S WING, A
BIOGRAPHY OF JOHN MUIR
(Swift)
JOHN MUIR (Graves)
JOHN MUIR (Norman)
JOHN MUIR (Silverberg)
THE LIFE AND ADVENTURES
OF JOHN MUIR (Clark)
MUIR OF THE MOUNTAINS
(Douglas)

Multiple Biographies
BLACK PEOPLE WHO MADE
THE OLD WEST (Katz)
EXPLORING HISTORICAL CAL-
IFORNIA (Adler)
GREAT INDIANS OF CALIFOR-
NIA (Knill)
CALIFORNIA ORIGINALS

Pasquala
PASQUALA OF SANTA YNEZ
MISSION (Rowland)

Powers, Jack
DEVIL ON HORSEBACK (Ross)

Rose, Edward
EDWARD ROSE (Felton)

Serra, Junipero
CALIFORNIA'S FATHER SERRA
(Duque)
FATHER JUNIPERO SERRA (Bol-
ton)
FATHER JUNIPERO SERRA
(sound filmstrip)
THE FIRST CALIFORNIAN (De-
marest)
FRAY JUNIPERO SERRA (Wise)
JUNIPERO SERRA, PIONEER OF
THE CROSS (Scott)

Smith, Jedediah
JED SMITH, TRAILBLAZER
AND TRAPPER (Latham)
JEDEDIAH SMITH (Burt)
JEDEDIAH SMITH (Evarts)

Smith, Thomas
THE PEGLEG MYSTERY (Evarts)

Stanford, Leland
LELAND STANFORD (Hoyt)

Steffens, Lincoln
A BOY ON HORSEBACK (Stef-
fens)

Sutter, John
JOHN SUTTER (Booth)
LIFE AND TIMES OF JOHN SUT-
TER (filmstrip)
SUTTER'S FORT (Luce & Luce)

Thompson, John
FLYING SNOWSHOES (Teal)

Vallejo, Mariano
VALLEJO AND THE FOUR
FLAGS (Comstock)

Early Explorers

CALIFORNIA BEFORE 1776 (Prit-
chard)
THE DISCOVERY OF CALIFOR-
NIA (Terrell)
DRAKE (sound filmstrip)
GOLDEN CITIES, GOLDEN
SHIPS (Dines)
PASSAGE TO DRAKE'S BAY
(Montgomery)

Earthquake of 1906

DIASTER 1906 (Dolan)
DRAGONWINGS (Yep)
THE EARTH SHOOK, THE SKY
BURNED (Bronson)
FIRE DRAGON (Benezra)
THE GREAT SAN FRANCISCO
EARTHQUAKE (sound filmstrip)